VISIONS OF THE VIRGIN MARY

ABOUT THE AUTHOR

Courtney Roberts has been involved in astrology and tarot—studying, consulting, teaching, and writing—for over twenty years. She has lectured and published worldwide on the topic of Marian apparitions and other astrological subjects.

TO WRITE TO THE AUTHOR

If you wish to contact the author or would like more information about this book, please write to the author in care of Llewellyn Worldwide and we will forward your request. Both the author and publisher appreciate hearing from you and learning of your enjoyment of this book and how it has helped you. Llewellyn Worldwide cannot guarantee that every letter written to the author can be answered, but all will be forwarded. Please write to:

Courtney Roberts
℅ Llewellyn Worldwide
P.O. Box 64383, Dept. 0-7387-0503-9
St. Paul, MN 55164-0383, U.S.A.
Please enclose a self-addressed stamped envelope for reply,
or $1.00 to cover costs. If outside U.S.A., enclose
international postal reply coupon.

Many of Llewellyn's authors have websites with additional information and resources. For more information, please visit our website at http://www.llewellyn.com.

VISIONS OF THE VIRGIN MARY

AN ASTROLOGICAL ANALYSIS OF DIVINE INTERCESSION

COURTNEY ROBERTS

2004
Llewellyn Publications
St. Paul, Minnesota 55164-0383, U.S.A.

First Edition
First Printing, 2004

Book design and editing by Karin Simoneau
Cover illustration © 2003 Neal Armstrong / Koralik & Associates
Cover design by Lisa Novak

Chart wheels were produced by the Kepler program by permission of Cosmic Patterns Software, Inc. (www.AstroSoftware.com)

Library of Congress Cataloging-in-Publication Data
Roberts, Courtney, 1957–
    Visions of the Virgin Mary: an astrological analysis of divine intercession/
    Courtney Roberts.
        p.   cm.
    Includes bibliographical references.
    ISBN 0-7387-0503-9
        1. Astrology. 2. Mary, Blessed Virgin, Saint—Apparitions and miracles—
        History—Miscellanea. I. Title.

    BF1729.R4R63 2004
    133.5'8230917—dc22   2003069520

Llewellyn Publications
A Division of Llewellyn Worldwide, Ltd.
P.O. Box 64383, Dept. 0-7387-0503-9
St. Paul, MN 55164-0383, U.S.A.
www.llewellyn.com

Printed in the United States of America

To Liam McGinley of Glencolmcille,
a true *Anam Cara*.

CONTENTS

Acknowledgments   *ix*

Introduction   *xi*

One
La Salette: The Sad Lady of the Harvest   1

Two
Echoes of Babylon   23

Three
St. Catherine Laboure and the Miraculous Medal   39

Four
Lourdes: Our Lady, the Water Bearer   57

Five
Fatima and the Miracle of the Sun   101

Six
Beauraing and Banneux: The Virgin of the Poor   151

Seven
Apparitions: Then and Now   189

Eight
Drawing the Veil   231

Glossary of Astrological Terms   *239*

Bibliography   *255*

ACKNOWLEDGMENTS

There are a number of friends and colleagues I wish to thank who have either helped, inspired, or supported this work in some way, especially:

Tem and Kate at *The Mountain Astrologer,* for publishing my initial version of this project; the late, lamented Ed Steinbrecher, who so generously supplied me with data; the late, lamented Lois Rodden, who also supplied birth data; the late, lamented T. Pat Davis, who was a wonderful neighbor. May they all Rest In Peace.

Thanks also to Michael Conrad, for the drawings and for his continued help with just about everything; Tim Laffey, for his assistance with the data, and Paris; Nick Kollerstrom, for his encouragement and help with the data; Patricia Sharkey and family, for the warm hospitality, the kind use of their computer, and for the tea and tuna sandwiches; Fr. Lorcan Sharkey, for his generosity with his time and insights, the kind use of his computer in emergencies, and any number of good deeds; Fr. Joe Young, for the pilgrimage to Lourdes; Ann and Conal Curran and family of Stone Park, for their openhearted hospitality, the kind use of their computer, and the tea and tuna sandwiches.

And a special thanks to Sean and Irene Tighe, Jan Carr of Firbreaga, Hugh McGuinness and family, the Murrins, Noel Cunningham, and all my neighbors in Roshine and Firbreaga, Maeve and Georgie Murray of Fintragh Rd., Marinie and Mary Toman of Ardara, Mary at the Hostel in Glencolmcille, Attie and Anne Meehan of Stone Park, and to all who made me so very welcome in the homes of Donegal. I will never forget your kindness.

Eternal gratitude to St. Catherine of Alexandria, patroness of Killybegs, The Three Holy Women of Teelin, St. Mary of the Visitation, Killybegs, St. Conal Cael, and to my Lord, the source of all inspiration and love.

INTRODUCTION

The stories of the Virgin Mary's appearances to humble seers in remote places like Lourdes, Fatima, and Medjugorje fascinate both believers and doubters alike. While there is plenty of excellent material available on the subject, to my knowledge, no one has ever undertaken a serious astrological analysis. These compelling stories, and their intriguing characters, surely beg the astrological question, "What do the underlying planetary alignments reveal about these events, and just what sort of people are these visionaries?"

In pursuing this line of questioning, I've come to believe that astrology provides some distinct advantages when examining the complex and confusing subject of mystical experiences. Astrology lifts us above cultural and religious boundaries, elevating the mind to contemplate human behavior within a more cosmic framework. Astrology alone charts those fundamental forces within our being that have animated human consciousness from the beginning, revealing the dominant themes, both natural and supernatural, in any given moment. At a time when we are so tragically divided by the clash of religions and cultures, perhaps some common ground can be gained in the patient study of the cosmos, and in the recognition of our own timeless and universal archetypes in action—a very catholic goal, indeed.

Ironically, the very word "catholic," which means universal, broad, and all-inclusive, originated as an astrological term. According to Franz Cumont, it was introduced to distinguish between local, tribal gods, and celestial, planetary gods.[1] A catholic planetary deity was not limited in influence to any particular place or people, but ruled over activities or experiences that affected the entire Earth and the whole human race. Used in that sense, the introduction of this term represented a philosophical step forward from the pettiness of warring tribal gods to a more all-encompassing concept of divinity and order.

Even more ironic is the realization that the term "catholic" has through the ages, in the pursuit of orthodoxy and the persecution of heresy, come to signify its own opposite. I would like to use this potent word, but in that older, expanded sense. In examining the astrological forces underlying these Marian apparitions, we encounter truly catholic influences, not limited by place or local beliefs, but reflecting a larger, universal order that links us all together in time within the vast beauty of the cosmos.

I want to reassure any readers who fear they lack the necessary astrological background that I have made this material as accessible as possible. By introducing and defining technical terms as they arise, my hope is that, after reading this book, even a complete beginner would have gained some facility with the subject. A glossary of astrological terms is provided at the end, which should serve as a handy reference tool, and if at any point you start to feel overwhelmed or confused by the details, I encourage you to jump ahead to the apparition stories and experience the astrology in context. You can always go back and reread the parts you skipped once you have a better understanding of how the astrology is applied.

THE MOON AND THE HORIZON

Writers throughout the ages have recounted and analyzed the apparitions of the Virgin Mary from a variety of perspectives. These range from the reverent presentations of the faithful to more rationalized accounts, which tend to reclassify the visions and vision states within the terminology of the writer's field of expertise.

Some days, I wonder if that's not exactly what I'm doing. In this, as in all things, you see in it what you bring to it. Marian apparitions have been reworked as political plots, evidence of mental illness and hysteria, mass hypnosis, social-climbing, profiteering, adolescent hormones gone wild, demonic possession, and just about anything and everything in between. There is a more than a little truth in all of this.

The visions take place within a social matrix that gives rise to demands and expectations that can quickly distort the original impetus. The dismaying breadth of human nature, from the saintly to the pathological, is on full display in these stories. But before the crowds arrive and the sideshow descends, there is this one simple moment; a moment in which seemingly ordinary people, in the process of going about their ordinary day, are suddenly and overwhelmingly confronted with the appearance of a feminine deity. A heavenly goddess descends and reaches out to the seer. Whatever good or bad follows from it, it is that moment, at the beginning of things, that I am most interested in as an astrologer.

If we break down these initial visions into their most basic elements, a typical Marian apparition consists of a visit, a meeting, and perhaps the beginning of a relationship between the seer(s) and an otherworldly being, usually described as a luminous Lady in white. Sometimes it is only after extensive questioning that the visionaries recognize her specifically as the Virgin Mary, for instance, at La Salette and Lourdes.[2]

Modern astrology provides us with certain formulas, or equations, of planetary positions that describe these kinds of people and events. The idea of a meeting or relationship is generally described by links between the horizon indicators known as the Ascendant and Descendant, or the astrological 1st and 7th houses, and these terms will be fully explained shortly. Meanwhile, the shining, white Lady reflects the attributes of the Moon.

To an astrologer, the Moon is the ultimate heavenly Mother. She is intimately associated with the home, the family, nourishment, and the security of childhood. The Moon rules, or influences, the unconscious night side of life—our instinctive, emotional nature, where our earliest experiences leave the sort of indelible imprints that can consistently overrule our rational minds throughout our adult lives. Socially, the Moon also acts as a link or a common bond, uniting us intuitively in public opinion and public sentiment.

In the history of human devotion, the Moon has often been worshipped or imaged as a luminous goddess, resulting in a worldwide pantheon of lunar goddesses, including Luna, Isis, Artemis/Diana, Selene, and so many more. The most primitive fundamentalism, the dualistic worship of the masculine father Sun and the feminine mother Moon, is well-represented throughout the development of Western religion, and as the body of human religious experience evolves, these two have been cast and recast in increasingly sophisticated roles.

The Christian church has been particularly adept in channeling the people's instinctive devotion to a lunar mother goddess into the cult of the Virgin Mary. The love and loyalty she inspires are unparalleled worldwide. According to Marina Warner, "the moon has been the most constant attribute of female divinities in the Western world, and was taken over by the Virgin Mary because of ancient beliefs about its function and role that Christianity inherited."[3]

Many areas had some traditional cult to a mother goddess that was readily assimilated into Marian Christianity, and even continues to this day in the form of unique local customs or devotions. This is especially true of some of the apparition sites. Similarly, other female deities and spirits were often incorporated into the charming local saint cults. Recognizable attributes of the great goddesses of the pre-Christian world, such as Isis and the Magna Mater, were regularly cut-and-pasted onto the burgeoning image of the Christian Mother of

God,[4] drawing their followers and spiritual heirs into her train, for a rose, by any other name, still smells as sweet.

In light of all this, when examining the astrological underpinnings of Marian apparitions, it isn't entirely surprising that we find a frequent emphasis on the Moon in the astrological charts of both the seers and the initial apparitions. There is very often a New Moon or a Full Moon, or the Moon is highlighted in conjunction, or close alignment, with several other planets.

Cancer, the sign ruled by the Moon, is also well represented within these charts. As the astrological home base of the Moon, Cancer shares many feminine, lunar qualities with its ruler, including devotion to the home and mother, and a sentimental, dreamy type of mysticism. Planets passing through the sign of Cancer tend to impart these lunar qualities to the personalities or events formed under their influence. Astrological signs come in pairs, so the emphasis on the sign Cancer is often reflected or repeated by planets in the opposite sign of Capricorn.

The Nodes of the Moon also tend to be emphasized. These two seemingly abstract points are considered so influential that they have been regularly included in astrological charts around the world for thousands of years. The Arabs conceived of them as the head and tail of a great dragon who devours the Moon and Sun, while to Vedic astrologers, they represent the shadow planets, Rahu and Ketu, who routinely conspire to darken the lights.

In a strictly astronomical sense, the Moon's nodes mark the two points where the Moon crosses the ecliptic in her monthly orbit. The ecliptic is the apparent path of the Sun through the sky. We all know that it's really our own planet that is moving, but that's not how it looks. The Sun doesn't just wander all over the sky, but stays on its own straight track. The Moon's orbit is more complicated.

Because the Earth is tilted a bit on its axis, the same tilt that causes the seasons, the Moon, which orbits the Earth, has a tilted orbit that roams up and down across the Sun's path, the ecliptic. The ascending, or North Node, marks the point where the Moon in her monthly orbit crosses the ecliptic heading North, and the descending, or South Node, marks the point where the Moon crosses back over the ecliptic on her monthly journey into the southern hemisphere. The two Nodes always oppose each other across the zodiac, and it takes 18.6 years for the Nodes to make a complete circuit through the signs. More to our point, the Moon's Nodes define the eclipse cycle.

If only the Moon traveled along the ecliptic like the Sun, life would be simple and we would have two eclipses every month, at each New and Full Moon. As it is, a solar or lunar eclipse only occurs when the lunation (a New or Full Moon) takes place near one of the Moon's Nodes, because only then is the Moon close enough to the ecliptic to align with both the Sun and Earth and interfere with the path of the Sun's light.

So while they don't actually represent planetary bodies, the Moon's Nodes are indicative of the current condition and inclinations of the Moon itself, and they mark the points of strongest interaction or alignment between the Moon, Earth, and Sun. So it's not surprising that we often find the Nodes highlighted within the event charts for the visions, or the birth charts for the visionaries, indicating an intensified alignment between the Moon and Earth that manifests in these highly charged apparition events.

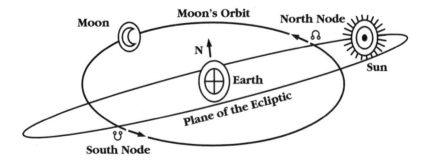

The Moon's orbit crosses the Plane of the Ecliptic (defined by the apparent orbit of the Sun around the Earth) at two points: the North and South Nodes.

THE FOUR CORNERS OF THE EARTH

In some of the charts we will be examining, the Moon's influence is strengthened by placement near one of the four points that astrologers call the *angles*. As we rotate along the Earth, all the planets and stars appear to circulate throughout our sky during the course of any day. However, a planet's influence is temporarily magnified within a particular location as that planet moves across any one of the following four specific sectors; whether culminating overhead at the Midheaven, rising

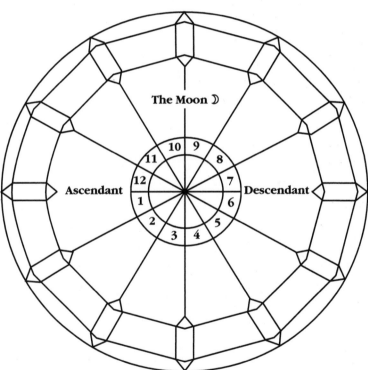

The four corners of the Earth: Midheaven (MC);
Ascendant; Descendant; Imum Coeli (IC).

in the east on the Ascendant, setting in the west on the Descendant, or arriving at the anticulmination point underneath, known as the IC, or *Imum Coeli* (from the Latin for the bottom of the sky). When the Moon is close to one of these angles, the lunar qualities of that specific time in that specific place tend to be enhanced.

They say a picture is worth a thousand words, and in astrology, we diagram these concepts in a chart, the primary tool of any working astrologer. An astrological chart is just a map showing the positions of the planets, the Sun, and the Moon, at a specific moment in time, relative to a specific place on Earth. The aforementioned angles, or pivot points, are depicted like a cross, or crosshairs, within the circle of the chart. The angles form a cross-shaped frame around the center of the circle, which represents the chosen location on Earth—the crucible wherein the celestial influences combine and manifest.

Pointing left, at nine o'clock, is the Ascendant, which, as the name implies, marks the point of rising in the east. The Ascendant also marks the cusp, or beginning of the 1st house, and the beginning of the chart itself. The houses, which look like the pieces of a pie, are simply twelve divisions, or areas, of the chart. Each house rules, or pertains to, certain types of experiences or activities.

Pointing straight up, at twelve o'clock, is the Midheaven, which, as the name implies, marks the highest point of culmination overhead. The Midheaven also marks the cusp, or beginning of the 10th house. The Descendant, the point of setting in the West, is directly opposite the Ascendant, and the IC is directly opposite the Midheaven.

The chart on the previous page shows the Moon culminating at the Midheaven, a vantage point from which it would dominate the landscape at that particular time, in that particular place. Most astrological charts will also include symbols and numbers (degrees) to indicate the exact positions of the Sun and the other planets, and we will be including those as we go along.

In classifying these apparition experiences as encounters, or meetings, between the seer(s) and this otherworldly being they recognize as the Virgin Mary, I am putting an astrological emphasis on the Ascendant/Descendant axis of the chart. This axis is depicted in the previous chart diagram by that horizontal line across the middle of the circle, with the Ascendant on the left (east) and the Descendant on the right (west).

The Ascendant and the first house, as the beginning of the chart, rules that which the chart describes. While in the course of this work we will be examining the birth charts for the Marian visionaries and the event charts for their initial visions, an astrologer can cast a chart for just about anything that has a beginning: a person, a business, a building, a marriage, a project, an event, or even a question in search of an answer. In each case, the Ascendant will describe or symbolize the subject of the chart.

The Descendant, directly opposite the Ascendant, symbolizes where that entity described by the Ascendant comes into contact with significant others. The Descendant marks the beginning of the 7th house, the area of the chart that describes important relationships: partnerships, marriage, contracts, open enemies. As we examine the charts of the apparition events and the visionaries, especially those for whom we have accurate birth times, we will be seeing some interesting and repeated emphases on the Ascendant/Descendant axis, and the 1st and 7th houses.

THE VIRGIN AND HER SON

Another pattern that regularly appears within the charts for the visions and the visionaries involves the sign Virgo and its opposite sign, Pisces. There is a long-standing connection between the Virgin Mary and the sign Virgo, one that is depicted in early Christian zodiacs.[5] However, the grain goddess of the sign Virgo, holding aloft her spike of wheat at the harvest, was venerated long before the coming of the Christian era.

Many of the attributes of the Earth and harvest goddesses associated with Virgo, such as Ceres/Demeter, were conflated into the early Christian presentations of the Virgin Mary, as well as the attributes and symbols of other local agricultural goddesses. In some of the older European traditions, the Virgin Mary is depicted as a type of corn goddess, with ripe grain embroidered on her vestments.[6] Lingering elements of agricultural and fertility rituals were elsewhere incorporated into the apocryphal stories of Mary's life, such as the popular grain miracles attributed to her during the Holy Family's flight into Egypt.[7] The good peasants of Europe never stopped praying to Mother Nature to grant them their harvest, but they did change her name.

Virgo's astrological counterpart, the long-suffering sign Pisces, was already associated with Christ through the symbol of the fish, which early Christians used to identify themselves. The symbol is usually explained as an acrostic derivation from the Greek word for fish, defining Christ as the Son of God and Savior. However, there was awareness in some quarters of the phenomenon of the precession of the equinoxes, and that the passing of the vernal equinox back into the constellation Pisces called for a new lord of the new age. While this type of sophisticated astronomical knowledge may not have been available to the average Christian,[8] it did play its part in uniting them under the symbol of the fish.

The signs Virgo and Pisces, like Cancer and Capricorn, are inseparable opposites, like two sides of the same coin, and wherever you find the suffering, sacrificial Christ, the dutiful Virgin is not far behind. Similarly, while the sign Virgo is well represented within the charts of the visionaries and their initial visions, its influence is often mirrored or reflected by planets in the sign Pisces.

OTHER INFLUENCES

The planet Neptune, which many astrologers have dubbed the planetary ruler of the sign Pisces, also puts in a strong showing. Since its discovery in 1846, just a few days after the famous vision at La Salette, Neptune has gained a reputation among astrologers for generating a highly mystical influence, one that dissolves the boundaries between the conscious and unconscious minds, allowing psychic and dreamlike experiences to filter through and illuminate our more rational reality. Neptune's otherworldly influence can be deceptive and delusional too, creating endless confusion when the rational mind attempts to assimilate the overwhelming imagery of the soul. The influence of Neptune in these apparition stories is unmistakable, both in their spiritual quality and the ever-present possibility of fraud, and we will see this planet highlighted again and again as we go through the charts.

There is a lesser, yet obvious pattern of emphasis on the planet Venus, the other planetary goddess. Many of the popular rites and attributes of Venus/Aphrodite were also cast upon the Virgin Mary during the development of her cults. Most notable among them is the role of Stella Maris, star of the sea and protector of sailors, a title originally claimed by Venus, the daughter of the waves, but charmingly appropriated and perpetuated worldwide by the devotees of the Christian Virgin Mary.[9] Accordingly, we often find a strong Venus, either by sign or position, or some emphasis on Venus's signs, Taurus and Libra, in either the birth charts of the visionaries or in the chart for the initial apparitions.

FINAL NOTES

These apparition events do not take place within a vacuum, but within an astrological environment where, above and beyond the cultural milieu and the prevailing religious mindset, the positions and alignments of the planets, the Sun, and the Moon combine to create a type of psychological and spiritual "weather." This psycho-spiritual "weather" can make particular types of events or experiences more likely at certain times than at others.

I do want to clarify that my emphasis here is not so much on causality as coincidence. I'm not sure that the planets are actually causing anything so much as serving as indicators of a greater and more universal order. Even when I refer to "planetary influences," I'm not at all certain how planets "influence" anything, as much as I am convinced there is a connection and am at a loss for a better word to describe it. Nevertheless, the charts that we will be examining in this work show not only a persistent emphasis on particular types of planetary patterns, but these patterns often reflect the unique differences among the various apparition stories.

My personal opinion is that the astrological perspective tends to lend some credence to the reports of the visionaries. In other words, if a group of children quite suddenly begin exhibiting synchronized trance behaviors and report that they are communicating with a glowing woman in white, as at Beauraing or Medjugorje, and the current planetary picture reveals an unusual astrological emphasis on the Moon, or the signs Virgo and Cancer, perhaps we shouldn't be too quick to dismiss their claims.

For those who do not believe in any kind of a higher power or higher mind, the apparition event might be perceived as an exclusively psychological phenomenon, arising as a result of random archetypal stimuli with little to no objective "reality." Those who do believe in some form of higher power or guiding hand, and I count myself among them, are going to see that possibility as well.

I find one of the most striking ironies of Christianity is that the Roman and Orthodox Churches, which seem so misogynistic in forbidding ordination and any real leadership roles to women, are also responsible for perpetuating the worship of the feminine attributes of God through the devotion to the Blessed Virgin Mary.

There is no parallel within the Protestant churches. While some have recently become more open to the idea of women in the clergy, their worship only extends to the masculine personification of God, sparing just a brief nod of remembrance to the role of Mary, if not actually scorning her idolatry altogether. This rejection of the Virgin Mary is a fairly recent development. In some of the areas now dominated by Protestantism, devotion to the Mother of God was historically quite strong—for instance, in England.

I don't want to appear to be taking sides in a religious war of the sexes. My personal opinion is that any balanced definition of God would admit that God is both male and female, containing and combining the attributes of both sexes while at the same time transcending them in a way that may be beyond our capacity to comprehend.

However, the fact remains that Protestant Christianity worships only a masculine God the Father, who incarnated in the form of Jesus Christ, His only Son. Orthodox and Roman Catholicism, while keeping with God the Father and the Son, have maintained a vital adjunct deity in the Mother of God, or God as Mother. In the parishes, in the daily life of the church, and in the hearts of the common people, she commands their love and devotion in a way that no masculine concept of God can inspire. The worship of the mother goddess is alive and well in any parish on the planet. The culture and creed may have changed dramatically, but the emotions and archetypes are the same.

I have tried to limit the scope of this work to the modern Marian visions that have been approved and accepted by the Catholic or Orthodox Churches. It not only helps to keep the workload manageable, but also offers some assurance against the possibility of fraud, hoax, or delusion. The Church and civil authorities do conduct their own extensive investigations and are usually in no hurry to condone this sort of activity.

People see things all the time, seemingly now more than ever, and I'm certainly not fit to judge the value of one vision over another. However, the primary prerequisite for Church approval is orthodoxy, so any visions or messages not in keeping with Church teachings on every point do not make the cut, which does leave some very interesting cases languishing by the wayside. I've included some of these, like Garabandel, San Damiano, and Medjugorje, in the last chapter.

I also need to add that in presenting the astrological side of the story, there is no intent on my part to detract from or diminish the meaning these visions hold within Roman Catholic and Orthodox Christianity. I have great love for both traditions. If anything, it is meant to expand the relevance and influence of the visions by placing them within a more universal context. I certainly hope that it is taken in that light, but I appreciate that many people may not feel the same way.

KEY

Over the years, astrologers have derived a system of symbols, a kind of astronomical shorthand, for the names of the planets, signs, and aspects. The following astronomical symbols will appear regularly throughout the text, particularly within the chart diagrams, and the reader is encouraged to refer to this key, as well as the glossary, whenever any question arises.

⊕ Earth	♅ Uranus	♌ Leo	☊ North Node
☽ Moon	♆ Neptune	♍ Virgo	☋ South Node
☉ Sun	♇ Pluto	♎ Libra	☌ Conjunction
☿ Mercury	⚷ Chiron	♏ Scorpio	☍ Opposition
♀ Venus	♈ Aries	♐ Sagittarius	□ Square
♂ Mars	♉ Taurus	♑ Capricorn	✶ Sextile
♃ Jupiter	♊ Gemini	♒ Aquarius	△ Trine
♄ Saturn	♋ Cancer	♓ Pisces	

Endnotes

1. Franz Cumont, *Astrology and Religion Among the Greeks and Romans* (New York: Dover Publications, 1960), 63.

2. This point is fully explored, with the appropriate references, in the following chapters on La Salette and Lourdes. At Lourdes, until the lady identified herself as the Immaculate Conception, some six weeks after the initial apparition, St. Bernadette stubbornly expressed no opinion on her identity. At La Salette, even years after the vision, Maxim Giraud could only say that he had seen a lady, and left it to the church authorities to determine who she was.

3. Marina Warner, *Alone of All Her Sex* (New York: Vintage Books, 1983), 256.

4. Anne Baring and Jules Cashford, *The Myth of the Goddess: Evolution of an Image* (London: Arkana, Penguin, 1993), 548–549. Also, Joseph Campbell, *The Masks of God: Occidental Mythology* (Harmondsworth: Penguin Books, 1976), 45.

5. Warner, *Alone of All Her Sex,* 264, and Baring and Cashford, *The Myth of the Goddess,* 578.

6. Warner, *Alone of All Her Sex,* 276.

7. Pamela Berger, *The Goddess Obscured: Transformation of the Grain Protectress from Goddess to Saint* (Boston: Beacon Press, 1985), 89–91.

8. The discovery of the precession of the equinoxes is usually attributed to Hipparchus during the second century BC. Precession and its measurement were hot topics among geometers and astronomers in the early Christian era.

9. Sally Cuneen, *In Search of Mary: The Woman and the Symbol* (New York: Ballantine Books, 1996), 195. The goddess Isis was also popularly worshipped as Stella Maris.

One

LA SALETTE: THE SAD LADY
OF THE HARVEST

On a fine September morning in the year 1846, two young shepherds drove their little flock of eight cows and a goat up to pasture in the remote mountains of the French Alps. Maximin Giraud, eleven, and Melanie Calvat, fourteen, had only met the day before when Maximin, new to shepherding, had approached Melanie, a more seasoned veteran, as she was heading up the slopes and suggested they herd together.

Melanie Calvat was something of a social outcast; extremely shy and reclusive, she longed for the solitude of the highlands and held off the chatty, impulsive lad as long as she could. But Maximin's considerable charm eventually wore her down, and by the end of the first day they were playing childish games together and had agreed to meet again in the morning.

Maximin was a rare friend indeed for this lonesome girl who had been driven from her own home and sent to work for strangers from the time she was seven. In her long hours of unlettered abandonment, Melanie had cultivated an intense spirituality in which the Christ Child and his Holy Mother took the place of the family that had so cruelly rejected her. Her deep and imaginative inner life was rarely counterbalanced by any meaningful human contact, and yet this lively boy had so quickly penetrated her defenses and drawn her out to play; this would indeed be a special day.[1]

Upon arriving at the pasturelands outside the village of Corps, surrounded by the imposing landscape of La Salette where the peaks average 11,000 feet, the herd was dispatched to its grazing and the children set about to play. Melanie introduced Maximin to one of her favorite pastimes, building what she called a "Paradise." Part playhouse, part pagan shrine, the Paradise was a two-tiered stone structure that Melanie had devised in her lonely hours on the hill-sides. The bottom story was the shepherd's house, while the top, open to the sky and decked with all the flowers of the mountain, represented Paradise, which Melanie said was "open to all who wished to enter it."

At noon, the Angelus bell rang out from the village below, and the children stopped for their lunch of bread and cheese. After watering their herd, they returned to the Paradise, where the warm afternoon sun lulled them to sleep. Melanie awoke first, sometime after 2:00 p.m., and immediately set off after her herd. Climbing to the top of a nearby hillock, she found them quickly enough, contentedly enjoying their own siesta. She came back down and awoke Maximin, who also climbed up the hillock to double-check on his charges.

As he was coming down again, Melanie spotted a luminous globe floating toward them from the ravine below. Egg-shaped and glowing like the sun, the object descended and hovered over their Paradise, then slowly opened to reveal a beautiful Lady inside. Resplendent in her silvery gown and headdress, and draped with a golden apron, she appeared to be sitting right over the top of the Paradise. But as the dazzling ball of light faded away to fully reveal her, the children saw that she was bent over, with her head in her hands, weeping bitterly.

In stunned silence, the children made a timid approach. The Lady turned to them and uttered her first words, "Come closer, my children." She said, "Do not be afraid. I am here to bring you great news."

The Lady then delivered a litany of complaints against the irreligious habits of the local folk, explaining that she could barely restrain her Son's anger nor keep him from raising his arm against them. Foremost on her mind was the neglect of the Sabbath.

"I gave you six days for work. I kept the seventh for myself, and no one wishes to grant it to me. This it is that causes the weight of my Son's arm to be so crushing."

Continuing, she bemoaned the foul oaths of the local cart drivers who regularly blasphemed her son's name. The Lady then linked these moral lapses to crop failure, saying that if the harvest was spoiled, it was the people's own fault. She spoke of the destruction of the previous potato crop, adding that when the people found the spoiled potatoes, they cursed them as well, rather than heeding the sign and mending their ways. She prophesied that the coming year's harvest wouldn't be any better.

About this point, there was some confusion because the Lady had been speaking to Melanie and Maximin in French, whereas they were only conversant in the local dialect. Maximin later said that he initially thought the Lady was crying because her son beat her. Sensing this, the Lady shifted to the familiar patois and then the children could understand her clearly.

Continuing in that dialect, she warned of widespread famine, implying that people would do their penance through hunger. She specifically mentioned failure of the wheat, walnut, and grape crops—the mainstays of the area. She then spoke to the children separately, delivering to each in turn a private message that the other couldn't hear.

Addressing them both again, she assured the two that if the people would heed the warning and mend their ways, even the rocks and stones could be changed into wheat and the potatoes would be found to have sown themselves. She then questioned Melanie and Maximin about their prayers, for both the children had been badly neglected, receiving little to no training at all, religious or otherwise. After instructing them to say at least an Our Father and a Hail Mary each morning and evening, she returned to her criticisms of the people's habits, specifically their lax attendance at Mass and failure to abstain from meat during Lent.

Changing the subject, she asked the children if they had ever seen spoiled wheat before. When Maximin replied that he hadn't, she corrected him, reminding him of an incident during the previous year when he and his father had visited a farmer who showed them his ruined crop. She related to him everything that had been done and said on that occasion, even reminding him that his father had given him a crust of bread on the way home. Maximin's father had worriedly instructed the boy to eat it now, for who could say what they would be eating next year if the crops continued like that? The Lady's words made a deep impression on young Maximin, for he was certain that he and his father had been alone on the road at the time.[2]

The Lady then turned to go, instructing the two to pass her words on to the people. The children stared in disbelief as their beautiful Lady glided over the top of the grasses and rose into the sky, disappearing back into the dazzling globe of light whence she came. As she left, a small stream began to bubble up in front of the Paradise where she had come to rest.

Melanie and Maximin hurried their flock down the mountain and back into the village. It didn't take long for the irrepressible Maximin to spill his story. He told his employer, the farmer Selme, everything. Selme went immediately to Melanie's employers, the Pra family, to discuss the matter. After questioning both children and hearing the identical story from each, Grandma Pra took the Lady's warnings

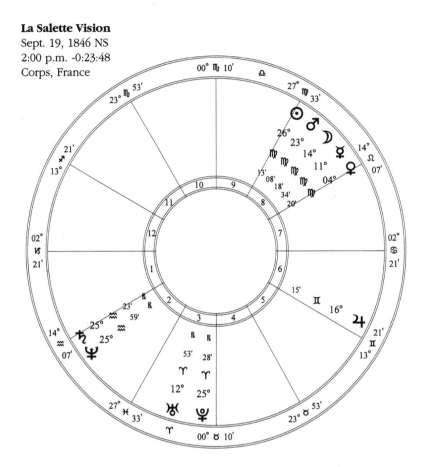

La Salette Vision
Sept. 19, 1846 NS
2:00 p.m. -0:23:48
Corps, France

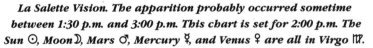

La Salette Vision. The apparition probably occurred sometime between 1:30 p.m. and 3:00 p.m. This chart is set for 2:00 p.m. The Sun ☉, Moon ☽, Mars ♂, Mercury ☿, and Venus ♀ are all in Virgo ♍.

directly to heart, and insisted the family abstain from working on the following day, the Sabbath. She was convinced the two had been speaking with the Blessed Virgin.

The next morning found the children knocking at the door of the parish priest, the Abbe Perrin. He immediately seized upon the Lady's warnings, and warned his congregation at Mass to start keeping the Sabbath and to stop cursing. Soon the mayor was knocking on

Melanie's door, and in no time at all, the press and official investigators had arrived. Life for young Melanie and Maximin would never be the same again, as the two were drawn into a whirlwind of controversy and devotion while the remote mountainside of La Salette was transformed by the crowds into the most popular pilgrimage site of the day.

It would be so easy to dismiss the entire story as childish babble, or some pastoral fantasy. There is no evidence other than the words of Melanie and Maximin, which, to their lasting credit, have withstood the most exhaustive scrutiny. However, take a look at the chart. It is nothing short of extraordinary! With a stellium of five planets, including the New Moon, in the sign Virgo, is it possible that these simple shepherd children were discussing wheat futures with the ancient goddess of the harvest?

THE HARVEST MAIDEN

Who is Virgo exactly, and how did she arrive at her place in the sky? Any Sun sign guide can tell you all about the perfectionist Virgo personality. Anyone who has ever lived with a Virgo should recognize that critical, nitpicking tone in the Lady's exhortations to moral purity, but there is so much more to this sign than those shrewd analysts among us who celebrate their birthdays in September.

One of the oldest and largest star groups in the zodiac, her mythological attributes show a fascinating consistency throughout the history of the constellation's development. The evidence indicates that the Babylonians originally called the constellation *Ab Sin,* meaning "the furrow," an agricultural reference to the virgin land about to bear fruit, but soon came to associate this constellation with their great goddess Ishtar (or later, Astarte) specifically, calling it "the errand or message of Ishtar." Ishtar's errand was to the proverbial underworld of the dead with her lover, the corn (grain) god, Tammuz. Tammuz was one of those archetypical dying gods of vegetation and plant life, the sort whose worship has never really died out. In the rites of Tammuz, he was annually cut down in his prime, only to be miraculously resurrected in the spring.

Ishtar's relationship with Tammuz was, even by modern standards, rather complicated. She was either his mother, grandmother, sister, and/or lover. The myths of this ancient goddess diverge on several points, reflecting a long history and a broad influence, in which different personalities and attributes were conflated onto her evolving image. The story of her descent into the underworld is found throughout ancient Mesopotamia; for instance, in the texts from the palace library at Ninevah, and in earlier Sumerian versions. In one Babylonian version of her story, Ishtar's errand was to travel the underworld during the winter months, as the constellation Virgo appeared to do, searching for Tammuz to bring him, and his life-giving qualities, back to earth. In less charitable renditions, Ishtar insists that Tammuz serve as the sacrifice that will free her from death and the underworld, but then mourns him dramatically afterward. Both versions embody the observational astronomy of the time, when the stars of Virgo stretched magnificently across the evening sky in the spring, as her dying god and consort was annually resurrected into new life.

The adventures of Ishtar and Tammuz spill over into the myths of Astarte and Dimuzzi, Adonis and Aphrodite, Attis and Cybele, and even share elements with the legends of Isis and Osiris. Common to all of these is the dying and resurrected young god, beloved of the goddess, whether she is his wife, mother, sister, lover, or some incestuous combination thereof. These same themes and characters all figure into the evolution of the stories of the life of Christ and his Mother, tracing a lineage for her worship that leads all the way back to the stars.

The ancient Persian astronomers called Virgo *Khosha,* meaning "an ear of wheat," but also knew her by another name, *Secdeidos de Darzama,* or "the Virgin in maiden neatness."[3] In India, the stars of

Virgo were called either *Kauni or Kanya,* meaning "the maiden," and associated with the virgin mother of the Hindu avatar Krishna, a pre-Christian example of "God-made-man." Krishna's legends parallel those of Christ in certain respects, including the manner in which his mother miraculously conceived her child from the Lord Vishnu.

Krishna, the little blue cowherd, is a much older deity than Christ, revealing in his sensual, pastoral pastimes the attributes of an earlier age. For those who accept the idea that the precession of the equinoxes spawns astrological ages (see chapter 2), Krishna was an avatar of the earthy age of Taurus, whereas the emergence of the suffering, sacrificial Christ and his fishers of men signalled the arrival of the age of Pisces.

According to the writers Eratosthenes and Avienus, the Egyptians associated Virgo with their great mother goddess Isis, although they generally depicted Virgo as a maiden clasping her spike of wheat.[4] In the elegant zodiac in the temple of Denderah, Virgo is pictured as a young woman holding her spike, while Isis sits beneath her, holding her divine son, Horus, blending the two traditions by proximity.

Isis was the faithful wife/sister of the murdered god/king Osiris. Isis was traditionally credited with bestowing the gifts of wheat and barley[5] while Osiris instructed mankind in agriculture. After his death at the hands of his enemies, Isis sought Osiris in a heroic odyssey throughout both the known world and the underworld, desperately trying to weave his life back together. She was eventually successful in miraculously conceiving his child Horus, in some versions from Osiris's dead and dismembered member. Horus, the divine sun-god king, lived to avenge his father's death and inherit his kingdom.

Of all the pre-Christian goddesses swept up into her train, Isis can claim some of the most distinct influences on the iconography of the Blessed Virgin. Whether depicted as a statuesque Madonna nursing the young Horus, or holding the dead and mutilated Osiris across her lap *a la Pieta,* or as the Black Virgin that still haunts her old precincts, her image has proven timeless and ineffaceable. From the apocryphal tales of the Virgin's grain miracles during the flight into Egypt, to the hymns extolling her ancient epithets as the Queen of Heaven and Universal Mother, this greatest of Egyptian goddesses lives on, gracing us still with an occasional glimpse through the veil of the Virgin.

Virgo's image as the virtuous, wheat-bearing Lady of the Harvest was well established among the classical Greeks. Virgo was commonly associated with Demeter, the Earth Mother and cereal goddess. However, the Greeks also recognized Virgo as Persephone, the maiden daughter of Demeter. The abduction of Persephone by dark Hades (Pluto), Lord of the Underworld, was offered as the explanation for the grief-stricken Earth Mother's annual abandonment of the plant life to the ravages of winter. In this story, which bears many parallels to the legends of Tammuz and Ishtar, and was ritualized in the Eleusinian mysteries, Demeter must leave Persephone in Hades for the winter months. As the Mother mourns, the earth grows cold and barren. Demeter then rejoices annually with her daughter's return in the spring, which coincides with the annual resurrection of Tammuz/Christ.

This identification with Demeter and Persephone carried over into Roman astrology, where Virgo was associated with their grain goddess Ceres and her daughter Proserpina. Later texts also refer to Virgo as Arista (harvest) or Aristae Puella (Maiden of the Harvest), and in other contexts associated her with Themis, the personification of innocence and virtue.

In yet another context, the Greeks identified Virgo with Astraea, the goddess of justice. This was partly due to her proximity to the constellation Libra, the scales, which she is pictured holding in one hand, while wielding a sword in the other. This image of the pure and idealistic Astraea lends some extra insight into the La Salette story. According to legend, Astraea administered justice in the Golden

Age, which was a more just age than any before or since. As
mankind declined, Astraea fled to the heavens in disgust, taking her
place among the stars as the constellation Virgo. However, she would
still condescend to visit the fallen race from time to time, to inform
them of their wrongdoings! When she did, she was very stern and
didn't mince words, so this idea of Virgo as a virtuous goddess
descending to earth to pronounce judgment has some roots in the
traditions of the Greek Golden Age.

With the advent of Christianity, the constellation Virgo became
increasingly identified with the Virgin Mary. St. Albertus Magnus, the
great Dominican astrologer and mage, even claimed that the Savior's
horoscope could be found in her sign.[6] In one of her more famous
renaissance apparitions, the Virgin Mary visited a merchant in Milan
in the fifteenth century, appearing in typical harvest goddess array.
The merchant commissioned a painting of his vision, in which the
Virgin's robes were decorated with ripe ears of grain. The painting
hung in the Duomo of Milan, where it was venerated and decked
with garlands by the faithful seeking its fructifying influence.[7] This
image, known as the Corn Maiden, enjoyed great popularity throughout Italy and Germany and surely struck some instinctive, ancestral
chord of devotion within the people.

So, whether in full consciousness or in a cloud of unknowing, it
seems we are the hereditary recipients of a longstanding tradition. An
ancient, archetypal lineage links the astrological idea of Virgo with
purity and the harvest, and also holds her as a time-honored partner
in an emotionally intense, familial relationship with the beautiful
dying god whose resurrection is still celebrated by adoring devotees
every spring.

CHRISTIAN ASTROLOGY?

The early Christian Church managed an ambivalent but accepting attitude toward astrology. While no lesser lights than St. Augustine and

St. Paul (Galatians 4:9–10) railed against astrologers, astrology itself still formed a standard part of the medieval educational curriculum and prospered in the intellectual environment of the early universities and monasteries. While opposing the abuses of fortunetelling in general, a position that still makes sense today, and declaring itself the guardian of free will in the face of the predestination and determinism implicit in the cruder forms of popular divination, Christianity still looked to astrology not only to reveal divine intentions, but also for self-validation. If the three astrologers known as the Wise Men hadn't come looking for Jesus, Matthew would have had to invent them.

Meanwhile, zodiacs and astrological figures were standard decorative motifs in cathedrals, psalters, calendars, and those delightful medieval "Daytimers," the Book of Hours, in which the propertied classes painstakingly scheduled their prayers. Popes, bishops, abbots, and even saints actively practiced and pursued astrology at every level.

In approximately AD 530, Dionysius Exiguus, a Scythian abbot and astronomer, was commissioned in Rome to determine the date and the year of Christ's birth. Now just what sort of astronomer could he have been, a full millennium before the Copernican revolution spun off astronomical gold from astrology's musty straw? We still accept the year and date that he chose, although December 25, which marks the "rebirth" or quickening of the Sun after its three days of deathlike standstill at the solstice, had been a popular birthday for solar deities (Mithras, Sol Invictus) since approximately 350 BC.

More germane to this idea of the identification of the constellation Virgo with the Virgin Mary is the astronomical connection found within the Roman Catholic calendar. The feast of the Assumption of the Virgin takes place on August 15, and the birth of the Virgin Mary is celebrated on September 8. While it is convenient that the Church has already determined for us that Mary was a Virgo, there is an even deeper astrological meaning contained within these dates, one that leads us back to the disciplines of the desert priests of Egypt and Mesopotamia.

Theirs was a purely observational astrology, and their priestly duties included ritual observations of the conditions surrounding each sunrise and sunset. Of particular interest in their auguries was the way planets and stars regularly disappeared, or were consumed within the Sun's rays, only to emerge, reborn, as it were, out of the other side of the Sun, each in its appointed time.

In the normal course of a year, the Sun does conjunct each planet and each star in its path along the ecliptic, at which point, it does appear to disappear into the Sun. We have long since lost that sense of magic and wonder in observing these cycles of planetary motion, but our astrological forebears took great care in pinpointing the heliacal rising and setting of their beloved stars. Those were potent days when a star went out in a blaze of glory, to be sadly mourned until reborn anew from the light of the Sun.

The constellation Virgo lies very close to the ecliptic, and the Sun appears to pass right through her. The celebration of the Assumption dates back to fourth-century Palestine, when August 15 marked the date that the stars of Virgo were assumed into the glorious light of the Sun. She then began to reemerge on September 8, reborn in her innocence. This purely astrological phenomenon is enshrined in the Church calendar, forever marking both the debt Christianity owes to the celestial art and the longstanding association of the astrological Virgin with the Christian Virgin.[8]

RETURNING TO THE MOUNTAINSIDE

Seen in this light, the details of the apparition of La Salette begin to take on a Virgo logic of their own. The specific issues developed in the Lady's conversation are different from the ones that will be raised, for instance, in St. Catherine Laboure's vision (see chapter 3) during the New Moon in Cancer. At La Salette, the influence of the Virgo New Moon puts the focus on "constructive" criticism and self-improvement, introducing a link between virtue and the bounty of the harvest, or lack thereof.

There were significant crop failures in the wake of the apparition at La Salette. Almost a million people died in Europe as a result of a wheat shortage, the French grape crops were destroyed by a pestilence, and the potato famine raged in Ireland. The bitter harvest loomed large in the public mind. There were plenty of conversions and good deeds too, and the local bishop soon found it necessary to establish an order of sisters to attend to the needs of the thousands of pilgrims flocking to La Salette. The Church had approved the apparition by 1851, an order of La Salette Fathers was established soon after, and a stately basilica was completed on the site in 1879.

The spring that welled up soon after the apparition became known as the "Miraculous Spring," and its water was much sought after for its curative powers. It wasn't exactly a new spring, for there had been an intermittent water source at the site that had dried up long before the apparition. However, since that fateful day, the spring has continued to pour forth the La Salette holy water. Many documented "miraculous" cures were attributed to its influence in the months immediately following, including several cases of blind pilgrims regaining their sight after bathing their eyes in the spring.

Among the country people of Europe, there lingers an ancient tradition of holy wells and springs, and the worship of feminine deities associated with water sources runs so deep that it was seamlessly assimilated into Christianity, where it continues to this day. We can spot the modern tributaries of these traditions flowing through apparition sites like Lourdes and Banneux where, as at La Salette, the Lady's blessings are believed to reside in the waters. In the entrance to any Catholic church, you will still find an oft-used font of holy water, and the origin of which is far from Biblical.

Meanwhile, the lives of our two little shepherds would never be the same. Public life and the demands of fame were hard on Melanie and Maximin. Their lives took a bit of a downhill turn after their sudden celebrity, but both, in their own way, remained faithful to the Lady and the vision until their dying day.

MAXIMIN

Maximin Giraud was born on August 27, 1835, although there are some sources that list the date as August 26.[9] There is no birth time available, so the chart here is set for noon on his birthday. When the birth time is unknown, it is common practice to use a solar chart like this one, placing the Sun on the Ascendant. Whatever the actual birth time, the planetary positions are not going to change much, except for the Moon. The Moon moves about 13 degrees a day, so in using the noon position of the Moon, we have to remember that the actual position of the Moon could be up to 6.5 degrees away, in either direction.

So young Maximin, seer of La Salette, was a Virgo himself. The planet Venus was on, or conjunct, his Virgo Sun at the time of the apparition. Maximin's mother had died when he was very young, and he had a difficult relationship with his stepmother, so this personal outreach from a heavenly mother must have been especially sweet for the boy. Maximin had that nervous, changeable temperament that can manifest under the Virgo influence. Chatty, charming, and maddeningly likable, he lived a short but eventful life.

A boy blessed with such spiritual favors would seem a good candidate for the priesthood, and Maximin did make a try at seminary. It was eventually decided by all concerned that he couldn't settle down sufficiently to study, so he had to move on. Constantly hounded by pilgrims and hangers-on, some of them more well-intentioned than others, he tried a number of different careers and schemes, but never stuck with any of them. He even served for a brief time as a papal guard.

Maximin Giraud
Aug. 27, 1835 NS
12:01 p.m. -0:23:48
Corps, France

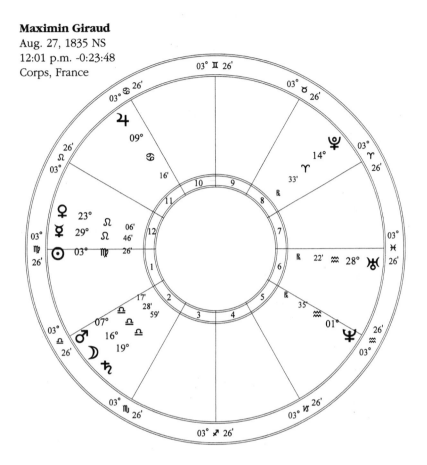

Maximin Giraud. The Sun ☉ in Virgo ℏ₽.

He proved something of an embarrassment to the Church, but the people always adored him. He never lost his boyish innocence and remained, until the end of his days, that lovable, mischievous lad who had seen the Blessed Virgin. He spent his last years living a relatively holy life, devoted to prayer, good works, and the sacraments, but his health had broken down. He died at the age of thirty-nine in 1875, and was buried at La Salette.

MELANIE

Melanie Calvat was a different character altogether, infinitely more complex and controversial. There are those who claim she should be sainted, and plenty more who see her as some kind of a crank. She certainly deserves the most sympathetic handling, for she was so unloved and mistreated in her early years, and then suddenly, so celebrated and sought after, that she probably never developed any sense of normalcy or trust during her long, restless life.

Even as a tiny baby, Melanie was hypersensitive, and contact with groups of people would send her into screaming fits. Noise was particularly stressful to her. Unfortunately, her mother was a light-hearted and sociable woman who never missed a party and resented having to leave every event early because of a screaming infant. According to Melanie's accounts, her frustrated mother cruelly disowned her and sent her to live in the woods when she was only four.

Melanie had a better relationship with her father, but he was usually far away, seeking work. He would take her part when he was home, but all too soon, he would be gone again and she would be left alone with her deeply unhappy mother. At the age of seven, her mother sold her into service and Melanie spent the next seven years, until the day of the apparition, moving from one farm to another as the most menial, and mistreated, of laborers. Surely no one was more deserving of the love of a heavenly mother than this poor child.

After such a chaotic childhood, it is no wonder her adult life proved even less stable than Maximin's. She tried two religious orders, but her temperament was so fundamentally critical and uncooperative that nothing would please her short of starting her own order. To make matters worse, when she published the contents of her "secret," the message the Lady had given to her privately, it was so critical of the clergy and church leaders that the inevitable result was undying enmity between Melanie and the French Church.

Melanie Calvat
Nov. 7, 1831
Local Mean Time
La Salette, France

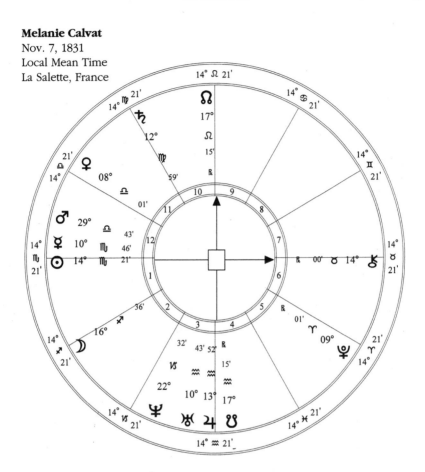

Melanie Calvat. Saturn ♄ in Virgo ♍; Sun ☉ and Mercury ☿
in Scorpio ♏; Jupiter ♃ and Uranus ♅ in Aquarius ♒.

Her "secret," published in 1879, opened with this pointed attack: "Some Priests and ministers of my Son, by their wicked lives, by their irreverence and their impiety in the celebration of the holy mysteries, by their love of money, their love of honors and pleasures, become cesspools of impurity." Regardless of the merits of her accusations, these "cesspools of impurity" did not take very kindly to Melanie or her further advice. The support she needed to found her own order was not forthcoming.

Constantly on the move, she sojourned all over Europe. Whatever antagonisms she left in her wake, there is no disputing the purity and holiness of her own habits. Devoted to prayer and the sacraments, chaste and abstinent to the extreme, there was never any question of Melanie's personal sanctity. She lived an exemplary life, but was perhaps permanently locked into disruptive behavior patterns by the emotional trauma of her early years.

Her birth chart[10] depicts her radical stance and detachment, featuring a tight square (90-degree angle) between her intense Sun and Mercury in Scorpio and the religious, but revolutionary, Uranus and Jupiter conjunction in Aquarius. These planets combine with the Moon's Nodes and the planetoid Chiron to make a Grand Cross in the fixed signs (Taurus, Leo, Scorpio, Aquarius). Melanie certainly had her cross to bear, and an endless impasse of challenges and obstacles to navigate throughout her life. Her extraordinarily strong character and stubborn will prevailed, but the struggle was sometimes terrible to behold.

Without exact birth times, or even an exact event time, we can't presume to do a complete analysis, but some things do stand out. Melanie does have a close Virgo contact with the apparition chart. She was born with Saturn in Virgo, and the current (or transiting) Mercury in Virgo was right on (conjunct) her Saturn during the apparition. Melanie passed away at the age of seventy-three on December 14, 1904, in Altamura, Italy. The Shepherdess of La Salette, as she liked to call herself, died in the tiny apartment where she spent the last six months of her life, living, as she had in the highland pastures of the Alps, in utter solitude.

CONCLUSIONS

The apparition at La Salette took place when the Sun, Moon, Mercury, Mars, and Venus were all in the sign of Virgo. That these uneducated children should report a spontaneous encounter with a Lady, who, while identified as the Virgin Mary, displays so many of the attributes historically associated with the astrological idea of "Virgo," does seem to indicate the compelling power of these truly "catholic" archetypes to consciously manifest.

The people of La Salette recognized and accepted this event as an apparition of the Blessed Virgin Mary, in keeping with the familiar framework of their local culture and beliefs. While the Lady never specifically identified herself as such, there are elements of her conversation (for instance, when she referred to being unable to restrain her son's arm) that do seem to confirm her identity. But which son is she referring to, Jesus Christ, the dying grain god, or the avenging Horus?

Four years following the apparition, in a controversial meeting with St. John Vianney, the venerable Cure of Ars, young Maximin gave an intriguing answer when asked by this famous confessor if he had truly seen the Virgin Mary at La Salette. Maximin replied, "I do not know if it was the Holy Virgin. I have seen something . . . a Lady . . . but if you know, yourself, that it is the Holy Virgin, it is necessary to tell all these people so that they believe in La Salette."

It was almost as if the boy, wise in his own ignorance, was asking the priest to put an interpretation on his vision that would best facilitate the people's belief and acceptance of the Lady's warnings. In fact, the influential curate angrily denounced Maximin as a fraud, although he later softened his stance.

So who was the Lady of La Salette? The Blessed Virgin Mary is as good an answer as any, especially if we consider her in a larger context, as the most recent, upgraded version in a long line of goddesses and divine mothers who have been identified with the constellation/sign Virgo. In that sense, there is something infinitely more timeless and universal going on in this apparition, revealing more of the innate, archetypal infrastructure of human consciousness, as it has evolved within, and in response to, it's greater environment within the cosmos.

Religions come and go, especially in the West. Every cult, priesthood, or sacred rite has had its true believers who were willing to
die, and even kill, to defend their select set of beliefs, but where are
they now? In comparison, the heavens seem relatively eternal. It
would seem that no matter what we call Virgo, or how we choose to
identify her, we still recognize her, and her influence still manifests.
In fact, her symbolism and attributes, while retaining a certain consistency, seem to evolve along with us. But who will be the next Virgo
in the next millennium? Who will be the dying god that she seeks? At
this point, I have better questions than answers.

Endnotes

1. Mary Alice Dennis, *Melanie and the Story of Our Lady of La Salette* (Rockford, IL: Tan Books and Publishers, 1995), 59–60; also, Melanie
   Calvat, "Apparition of the Blessed Virgin on the Mountain of La Salette"
   The Internet Modern History Sourcebook,www.fordham.edu/halasall/
   mod/1846salette.html, 1879.

2. The text of the Lady's comments is derived and compiled from several
   sources, all of which are fairly consistent, allowing for the usual vagaries
   of translation. In addition to the two works listed above, I have also
   relied on: Sandra Zimdars-Swartz, *Encountering Mary: Visions of Mary
   from La Salette to Medjugorje* (New York: Avon Books, 1991), 30;
   Catherine M. Odell, *Those Who Saw Her: The Apparitions of Mary* (Huntington, IN: Our Sunday Visitor Publishing Division, 1986), 62–75; Janice
   T. Connell, *Meetings with Mary: Visions of the Blessed Mother* (New York:
   Ballantine Books, 1995), 71–77.

3. Richard Hinkley Allen, *Star Names: Their Lore and Meaning* (Dover Publications, 1963), 460–464.

4. Ibid., 462.

5. Thomas Bullfinch, *Bullfinch's Mythology: The Age of Fable* (New York:
   New American Library, 1962), 333.

6. Allen, *Star Names,* 463.

7. Marina Warner, *Alone of All Her Sex* (New York: Vintage Books, 1983),
   276.

8. Edward Carpenter, *Pagan and Christian Creeds: Their Origin and Meaning* (New York: Harcourt, Brace, and Howe, 1920), 32–33.

9. Sandra Zimdars-Swartz, *Encountering Mary: Visions of Mary from La Salette to Medjugorje* (New York: Avon Books, 1991), 28.

10. Ibid., 27.

11. Ibid., 172–73.

Two

ECHOES OF BABYLON

The origins of Western astronomy and astrology lay hidden beneath the desert sands, buried with the astronomer-priests of Mesopotamia. Most ancient cultures had their stargazers, with their intricate geometries and elaborate oracles, and the evidence indicates there was plenty of interchange all around. However, it is the work of the priests of Babylon, blessed with a splendid view of the desert sky, that has remained with us to form the basis of our modern assessments of time and space. To see what I mean, just take a look at your watch.

In the twenty-four-hour day, the sixty-minute hour, and the sixty-second minute, we retain the remnants of the Sumero-Babylonian sexagesimal system, a means of calculating in base sixty. While the rest of Western culture reckons in base ten, we still mark time like the ancient Mesopotamians. We still map space like them too, locating planets in celestial longitude against the backdrop of a hypothetical 360-degree circle that outlines the path of the Sun and his planetary attendants through the sky. We call that circle the ecliptic, and it was first mapped out in the centuries long before Christ by those sleepless priests in their star-temples in the desert.

For convenience, the circle of the ecliptic is divided (sexagesi-mally) into twelve equal sections of 30 degrees each. Those twelve sections are more commonly called the *signs of the zodiac*. The zodiac is probably the simplest way to describe the positions of the planets in their orbits, and that may be why it has stayed in use for so long. Dividing each sign into 30 degrees of celestial longitude makes it easy to pinpoint planetary positions on the ecliptic by sign and degree. For instance, if Mercury is at 15 degrees Capricorn, then it is in the middle of, or halfway through, the sign Capricorn. At 10 degrees Taurus, Mercury is only one-third of the way through the sign of the Bull, whereas at 29 degrees Cancer, Mercury would be just about to leave Cancer and enter the next sign, Leo.

SIDEREAL OR TROPICAL?

This would be a good place to mention that there is an important dif-ference between signs and constellations. The constellations of the zodiac are mapped out according to the arrangement of their stars, while the signs of the zodiac are measured in 30-degree sections along the ecliptic. The zodiac of signs always begins on the ecliptic at the place where the Sun is on the first day of spring, or the vernal equinox. That point always signifies 0 degrees Aries; the first degree of the first sign. However, this starting point actually moves back-wards through the constellations of the zodiac, defining an important cycle known as the *precession of the equinoxes*.

A slight wobble in the earth's rotation causes the vernal equinox to precess backward through the constellations of the zodiac at a rate of about 1 degree of longitude every seventy-two years. The equinox makes a complete circuit of the ecliptic in about twenty-six thousand years. Right now, there is an approximately 24-degree gap between 0 degrees of the sign Aries and the beginning of the constellation Aries; although, to be fair, there is an acrimonious lack of consensus among the "experts" over exactly how big that gap is.

Celestial North

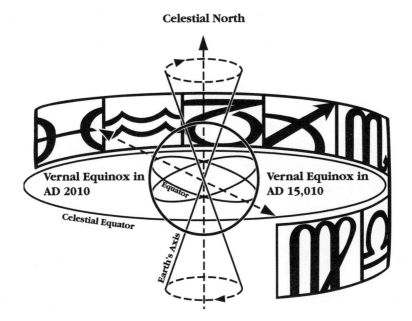

The tilt of the earth's axis traces a circular path in the sky. The Equinoxes follow a similar path, completing the circle every 26,000 years. So, while the Vernal Equinox points toward the cusp of Pisces in AD 2010, it will be pointing toward the cusp of Virgo (on the opposite side of the zodiac) halfway through the cycle, in the year AD 15,010.

The zodiac of the constellations is known as the sidereal zodiac, (from the Latin *sidus,* or star), and is generally used by astronomers. The zodiac of the signs is known as the tropical zodiac, and is generally used by Western astrologers. However, there are many astrologers who use the sidereal, or star-based zodiac. Indian, or Vedic, astrology is almost exclusively sidereal, and it is within Vedic astrology that you encounter many of the arguments over the ayanamsa, or "size of the gap." There is a strong contingent of Western sidereal astrologers, and even some astrologers who use both systems.

While this is hardly the place to explore the arguments for and against either system, it is worth pointing out that the ever-widening ayanamsa between the sidereal and tropical zodiacs is what gave rise to the whole "Age of Aquarius" ideology. Hipparchus of Nicea, a brilliant astrologer and philosopher who owed much to the Babylonians, is credited with discovering the precession of the equinoxes during the second century BC. In those days, the Sun did appear to enter the constellation Aries sometime around the first day of spring, although then, as now, there was considerable disagreement over exactly where that constellation began.

In the years following Hipparchus's discovery, the equinoctial point began to precess back into the constellation Pisces, roughly coinciding with the beginning of the Christian era. This marked the dawn of the "Age of Pisces," and since that time, the spring equinox has been moving backward through the constellation Pisces at a steady rate.

As philosophers and savants became aware of the phenomenon of precession, they naturally began to speculate about what it might mean. Various teachings arose regarding this change of the ages and how it would affect society. Among them was the idea that Hipparchus had only rediscovered precession, and that earlier astronomers, like the Egyptians, had not only known about precession all along, but had incorporated that knowledge into their sacred myths and architecture.[1] Again, there is tremendous disagreement on that issue and much work still needs to be done to sort out the facts.

The International Astronomical Union officially defined the dividing line between the constellations Aries and Pisces for their purposes back in 1928. Astronomers don't argue about this anymore because, unlike astrologers, they don't attach any particular meaning to it. Still, the IAU equinox is several degrees from the synetic vernal point, or SVP, which Western sidereal astrologers use to track the equinox through the constellations. According to the calculations of Cyril Fagan, the SVP is currently located in 5 degrees of the constellation Pisces.

So, if we can accept that the vernal equinox is now somewhere in the beginning of the constellation Pisces, and that it is precessing backward at a rate of 1 degree every seventy-two years, then it probably won't pass into the constellation Aquarius for at least another couple of hundred years. Consequently, some of our New Age celebrations may be a bit premature; but on the other hand, it does give us something to look forward to.

Having opened up that can of worms, I'd just as soon close it again, but not without stating that, as a Western astrologer, I will be giving planetary positions in the tropical, or sign-based, zodiac throughout this work—probably for the same reason that I will be writing in English. It's just the way I was raised. It may not be the best language in the world, but a lot of people speak it.

GEOCENTRIC OR HELIOCENTRIC?

For that matter, I will also be using the geocentric, or Earth-centered, planetary positions, rather than the heliocentric, or Sun-centered positions. This means that I will be using the planetary positions as they appear from our perspective here on planet Earth. It doesn't mean that I still believe that the Earth is the center of the universe, a charge that is frequently leveled at astrologers, but rather that I am writing from an earthling perspective about how planetary influences affect life here on Earth.

The Copernican revolution did not leave astrology behind, but it did change the art forever, sending the newborn heliocentric astronomy out to explore the stars while relegating astrology to the geocentric dust heap. Up to that time, astrology and astronomy were pretty much one and the same, and anyone who studied celestial motion also tended to interpret its meaning.

While most astrologers, both Western and Vedic, continue to work with the geocentric positions, many (myself included) also utilize the heliocentric, or Sun-centered, planetary positions. These can be at considerable variance with the geocentric positions, and that often makes the heliocentric influences glaringly obvious.

It doesn't pay to ignore the heliocentric perspective. Researchers are only just beginning to understand how the imbalances and tensions created by the constant movements of the planets affect the Sun and its equilibrium. Any influence affecting our Sun tends to be rebroadcast throughout the entire solar system, not only through the constant outpouring of light and heat, but also in the steady stream of ionized plasma known as the solar wind. Our home planet is in the direct path of these solar emissions, and their influence on everything from climate to communications is well documented.

Still, the geocentric, or Earth-centered, planetary positions represent our unique earthling perspective, describing how cosmic conditions impact our life here. That's exactly the kind of thing that most astrologers want to know. If I were researching the occurrence of Marian apparitions on the Sun, you can bet I would rely on the heliocentric planetary positions. Until such a time, the geocentric system will have to suffice.

OTHER ASPECTS

Having established all that, let's return to our friends, the astronomer-priests of the deserts and their sexagesimal system, which they put to good use in their efforts to describe the ever-changing relationships between the planetary gods. The tales of Greek and Roman mythology are packed with passionate stories of the soap-opera existence that was the life of the gods: forever loving, fighting, coming together, and falling apart. Sometimes Venus loves Mars, sometimes she dumps him and turns elsewhere, so Jupiter intervenes, and so forth. The world keeps turning and life goes on.

Our desert astronomers derived a set of relationships between the planets that we have come to call *aspects*. The Greeks picked up on them and further developed the concept of aspects within their philosophical and mathematical systems. Astrologers still use these aspects today to describe the relationships between the planets, which are constantly forming and dissolving in the course of their orbits. Because each planet rules, or influences, particular human attitudes and behaviors, tracking these ever-changing planetary relationships yields valuable insights into the prevailing trends.

The first type of relationship, or aspect, is called a *conjunction.* As the term implies, a conjunction brings planets together. It means that two planets are very close to each other in the zodiac, usually within a few degrees of longitude and usually within the same sign. Let's go back to our example of Venus and Mars. It is not by accident that Venus is represented by the female symbol, and Mars is represented by the male symbol, for these are indicative of their respective astrological influences. The symbol for a conjunction is ♂, so if I want to write that Venus is conjunct Mars, it looks like this: ♀♂♂.

The conjunction tends to blend the energies of the planets together, and it also creates a point of focus or emphasis. Sometimes, three or more planets come close together to form a special kind of conjunction, called a *stellium,* which means a bunch of stars. The New Moon, which occurs every month, is a case of the Sun conjunct the Moon, or ☉♂☽.

The next type of relationship, or aspect, is the *opposition.* An opposition is the opposite of a conjunction, because in this case, two planets are facing each other from opposite ends of the zodiac. Suppose that Jupiter is at 18 degrees of the sign Scorpio, and Saturn is at 18 degrees of the opposite sign, Taurus. Jupiter and Saturn would be opposing each other, pulling in opposite directions and desperately trying to meet in the middle. Oppositions tend to manifest in a set of conflicting demands that are difficult to balance. At the same time, they create an inseparable axis.

The symbol for an opposition is ☍, so if I want to write that Jupiter is opposing Saturn, it would look like this: ♃☍♄. The Full

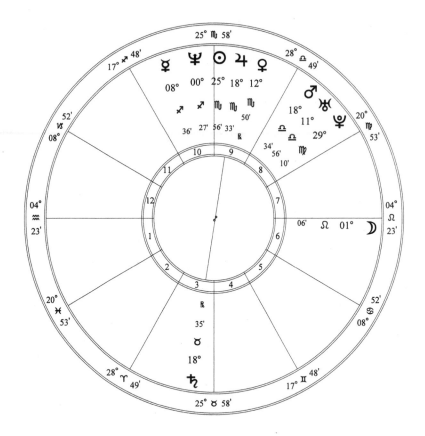

Opposition. Saturn ♄ in Taurus ♉; Jupiter ♃ in Scorpio ♏.

Moon, which also occurs every month, is a case of the Sun in opposition to the Moon, or ☉☍☽.

Now that we have divided our 360-degree circle in half with the opposition, the next step is to divide it by three. This yields our next aspect, the harmonious, lucky *trine*. The trine aspect describes a 120-degree angle, usually linking planets that are in signs of the same element, either fire, earth, air, or water. For instance, if the Moon is at 6 degrees Aries, a fire sign, and Uranus is at 8 degrees Leo, the next fire sign, Uranus and the Moon would be linked by the 120-degree trine aspect into a flowing, easy relationship. The symbol for the trine is △, so we would write Moon trine Uranus as ☽△♅.

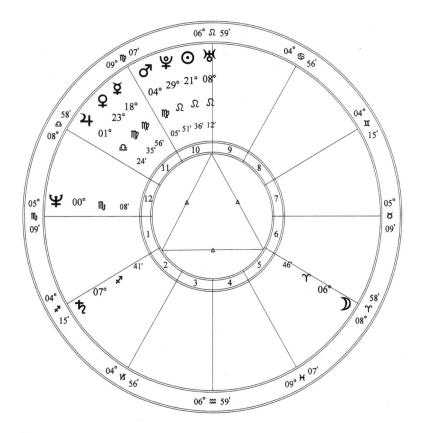

The Grand Trine. Uranus ♅ in Leo ♌; Saturn ♄ in Sagittarius ♐;
Moon ☽ in Aries ♈.

Our diagram demonstrates that aspects don't have to be exact to function. In this case, the Moon, which moves much faster than distant Uranus, is applying to, or forming, the trine aspect to both Uranus in Leo and Saturn in Sagittarius, the third fire sign. The Moon will continue moving along, at a speed of about a half a degree every hour, and when it gets to 9 degrees Aries, it will be separating from the trine of slow-moving Saturn and Uranus.

The configuration in our diagram, where three planets are in trine aspect to each other, is called a *Grand Trine,* and it forms an equilateral triangle within the chart. This figure does occur with some regularity in nature. The Grand Trine tends to link the three planets into a stabilized, self-contained, but free-flowing unit, the exact nature of which will depend upon the element (fire, earth, air, or water) and the planets involved.

Having divided our circle by three, our next step is to divide it by four. In doing so, we turn a hard corner and run right into the 90 degree, or *square,* aspect. The square puts planets at right angles to each other, where they tend to get in each other's way. Squares have a reputation for being difficult, for developing tension and manifesting as obstacles. The square aspect symbolizes life's challenges, which

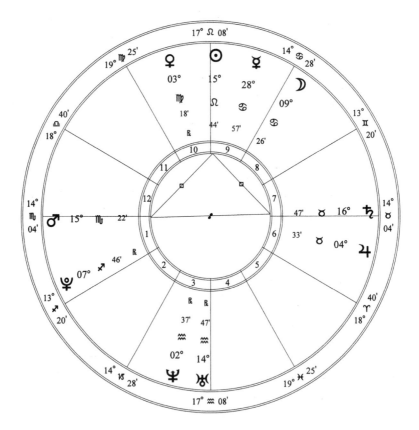

T Square. Mars ♂ in Scorpio ♏ opposes Saturn ♄ in Taurus ♉,
and both are in square aspect to the Sun ☉ in Leo ♌.

can either build character or destroy it. A square is not necessarily bad, for we all need challenges in order to grow. Much depends upon how the individual chooses to respond to the stress. The symbol for the square aspect is □, so if we want to write that Mercury is square Neptune, it would look like this: ☿□♆.

At 90 degrees, a square aspect is one-half of an opposition (180 degrees). It is not uncommon to see a configuration called a *T-square,* where two planets in opposition to each other are both squared by a third planet, forming a 90-degree angle to both ends of the opposition.

Occasionally, a fourth planet will join the configuration and create a *Grand Square,* or *Grand Cross,* wherein two oppositions square off against each other. The Grand Cross tends to manifest in a dynamic system of stresses and obstacles that keep life really interesting, but as with the Grand Trine, much depends upon the planets and signs involved.

The next step, after dividing our circle by four, would be to divide it by five, yielding the *quintile,* or 72-degree aspect. That doesn't sound very sexagesimal, does it? Five was not the favorite factor of the ancient Mesopotamians, and they didn't actually use the quintile. Johannes Kepler probably did the most to develop and promote the quintile aspect.[2]

Yes, Johannes Kepler was an astrologer! The same Kepler who inherited the observations of the great Tycho Brahe and used Brahe's data to unlock the secrets of planetary motion was also a hard-working astrologer who frequently corresponded with Galileo on the subject of astrology. Kepler used to make extra money casting charts and reading horoscopes, but then so did Brahe, for that matter. Brahe read for the Danish court when he wasn't preoccupied with wasting their money and expressing his general contempt—but I digress. Kepler, who relied heavily on the aspects in his astrological work, was very keen on the quintile, and used it to experiment with weather prediction and other fascinating hobbies.

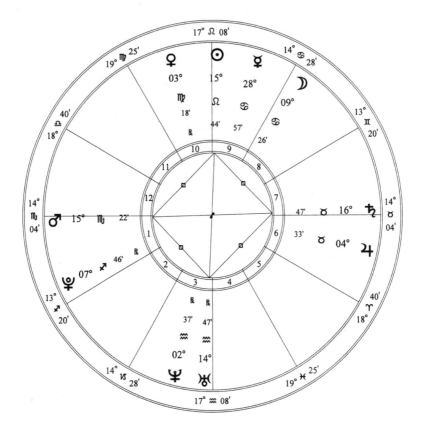

Grand Square. Sun ☉ in Leo ♌; Mars ♂ in Scorpio ♏;
Uranus ♅ in Aquarius ♒; Saturn ♄ in Taurus ♉.

Nevertheless, the quintile is considered a minor aspect by most, but not all, astrologers, being neither sexagesimal nor Ptolemaic. The Ptolemaic aspects are those listed by Claudius Ptolemy in his famous second century AD work on astrology, *The Tetrabiblos*. Ptolemy did absolutely nothing to unlock the secrets of planetary motion; in fact, he stalled the process for a good thousand years and everybody still thought he was brilliant. But then, Ptolemy wasn't an astrologer.

Even though he compiled the information in *The Tetrabiblos* and *The Almagest* from the works then extant in what remained of the famous library at Alexandria, borrowing heavily from Hipparchus in the process, Ptolemy demonstrates a lack of comprehension of the material. In fact, he made certain mistakes in his calculations that he surely would have noticed had he actually been using the information instead of merely compiling it. Newton himself passionately denounced Ptolemy and called him a fraud. Then again, Newton was pretty passionate about a lot of things that people don't like to talk about, like alchemy and eschatological biblical exegesis, which actually constitute the bulk of his life's work.[3]

And yet, for more than a millennium, Ptolemy's works were the bible of Western astronomy, and the adamant acceptance of his Aristotelian, geocentric order of the universe by the Roman Church severely impeded the progress of human knowledge. The real irony is that, in spite of the fact that Ptolemy's calculations and theories were just plain wrong, his systems actually worked—at least well enough to locate planets with the naked eye, which was more than sufficient at the time.

Perhaps that served as a disincentive toward detecting his errors, for even when Copernicus posthumously published his heliocentric theories, his nascent, but more correct system was still less accurate at predicting planetary positions than Ptolemy's. It wasn't until Kepler derived his revolutionary laws of planetary motion that Ptolemy and his epicycles were finally put out to pasture forever.

Still, Ptolemy did have access to the most impressive collection of texts ever assembled on the astrology of the ancient Mesopotamians and Egyptians, which is a lot more than we have today. In the successive sackings of the library at Alexandria, we lost the collected wisdom of the ancient world and are left with only Ptolemy, who lists the opposition, the trine, the square, and our next aspect, the sextile, as the preferred usage of the day. Ptolemy did advocate the use of the conjunction, but he didn't consider it an aspect, because planets in conjunction are too close together to be actually aspecting, or looking at each other.

The *sextile aspect* of 60 degrees divides our circle by six. The sextile completes our sexagesimal series of planetary relationships, and it is considered a positive, friendly linking of two planets. It's not quite as lucky or strong as a trine; in fact, it's half a trine. However, it's a comfortable, natural linking of planets that facilitates the exchange of influence between them. The symbol for a sextile is ⚹, so if we want to write that Jupiter is sextile Pluto, it would look like this: ♃⚹♇, and Jupiter and Pluto would be swapping stories like long-lost cousins.

Many years have passed since those far-sighted Babylonian astrologers first began to describe the interactions between planets with these harmonic relationships, but the aspects are still used routinely by modern astrologers all around the world, along with the twenty-four-hour clock and the sixty-second minute. Those lonely, sleepless nights were not in vain, for through their observations, our desert fathers laid a foundation for the measurement of time and space that remains with us still. So, bearing all of that in mind, it's time to move on to our next encounter with the Virgin.

Endnotes

1. The idea that precession was only rediscovered by Hipparchus, and that earlier civilizations possessed and utilized this knowledge, is the subject of a number of questionable, "fringe" publications, but it does get a more intelligent treatment in some quarters, that is, Giorgio De Santillana and Hertha Von Dechend, *Hamlet's Mill: An Essay Investigating the Origins of Human Knowledge and It's Transmission Through Myth* (Boston: Gambit, Boston, 1969); or Jane Sellars, *The Death of the Gods in Ancient Egypt* (New York: Penguin Books, 1992).

2. The following works cover Kepler's astrological pursuits: Johannes Kepler, *Concerning the More Certain Fundamentals of Astrology* (New York: Clancy Publications, 1942); Ken Negus, *Kepler's Astrology: Excerpts* (Princeton, NJ: Eucopia, 1987); Arthur Koestler, *The Watershed* (New York: Anchor Books, 1960); Bruce Scofield, "Were They Astrologers? Big League Scientists and Astrology," *The Mountain Astrologer* (2000), www.mountainastrologer.com/scofield.html.

3. For more information on Newton's obsession with alchemy, magic, and
   Arian Christianity, see Michael White, *Issac Newton: The Last Sorcerer*
   (Perseus Publishing, Helix Books, 1998).

Three

ST. CATHERINE LABOURE AND THE MIRACULOUS MEDAL

Zoe Catherine Laboure was, to all outward appearances, an average country girl, born and raised on a farm in the Burgundy region of France. It is in her very ordinariness, common sense, and devotion to duty that her extraordinary sanctity shines through. She was, after all, both a Taurus and a mystic, and reflecting the attributes of that earthy, practical sign, uncommonly grounded for such a world-class visionary. To our particular benefit, she had a habit of recording the time of important events in her life, beginning with her own mother's inscription of the time of St. Catherine's birth.

The evening Angelus bells were still ringing as Zoe Catherine came into the world. Her mother refused to rest afterward, and instead insisted the family call in a town clerk to properly record the event. This was something she had never thought of doing for any of her other children, and Madam Laboure gave birth to seventeen, in all. Sixteen faded into obscurity, but Zoe Catherine went on to join the ranks of the saints and incorruptibles. And so, the record stands that on May 2, 1806, at 6:00 p.m., St. Catherine Laboure was born in the little village of Fain-les-moutiers, near Dijon.[1]

Zoe Catherine was especially close to her mother, whose untimely death, when Zoe was only nine years old, left a painful void. A family housemaid reportedly found the little girl clinging to a statue of the Virgin Mary and crying, "It is you then, who are to be my Mother."

Born with the profoundly emotional Full Moon rising in Scorpio, Zoe Catherine identified intensely with her mother and was deeply transformed by her passing. The Scorpio influence often manifests in crisis or life-or-death experiences that provoke healing, rebirth, and

St. Catherine Laboure
May 2, 1806
6:00 p.m. -0:26:08
Moutiers, France

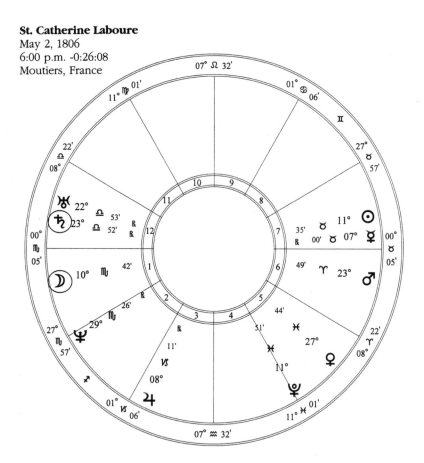

St. Catherine Laboure. Saturn ♄ rising in Libra ♎;
Full Moon ☽ rising in Scorpio ♏.

regeneration from the depths of the stinging sign. This close encounter with grief and the mystery of death at such an early age may have been instrumental in turning Zoe Catherine's feet to the religious path.

When St. Catherine decided to enter religious life is not exactly clear, but her sister, Tonine, is quoted as saying that after Zoe Catherine's first communion, when she was almost twelve, she became "entirely mystic." Before she was free to pursue her vocation, she was to spend over a decade in service to her father, managing his busy household.

Zoe Catherine's father, Pere, was a hard man. A prosperous farmer and old-world paterfamilias, he ruled his family with an iron fist. His daughter Zoe was cast in his own image. From the age of twelve, Zoe was mistress of the large Laboure household. With the younger Tonine, she cooked, cleaned, clothed, and cared for her father, her brothers, and the farm hands. In an age of microwave ovens and dishwashers, it is too easy to underestimate how much skill and judgment this required, but St. Catherine was a natural manager and excelled under the responsibility.

Saturn, the planet of discipline and limits, had a marked influence on St. Catherine's chart and character. Saturn is a bit of astrological bad news, for within the pressing confines of its ringed rulership fall the mature responsibilities and hard, cold realities that most of us would just as soon avoid: rules, regulations, restrictions, the impositions of karma, law and order, self-denial, deadlines, and other just desserts. Like St. Catherine's father, Saturn is the stern task-master of the solar system: not a tender father-figure, but rather that paternal principle that drives home the lesson that life is tough, winter is coming, and you better be ready to manage on your own.

Distinguished by both position and place, the Saturn in St. Catherine's birth chart rises just above her Ascendant in Libra, the sign of its exaltation. Planets in the sign of their exaltation tend to express their natures more completely, and St. Catherine manifested the qualities of a strong Saturn in her unflagging commitment to daily duty. She lived, by modern standards, a life of perpetual domestic drudgery with few distractions. Throughout her long life, she found her place performing the never-ending, menial tasks of keeping body and soul together. True to that Saturn nature even in her religious vocation, her lifelong assignment as a Sister of Charity was caring for the elderly, indigent men at the Hospice in Enghien, using the house-keeping and domestic skills she had mastered as a child in the farm-house in Moutiers.

St. Catherine mentions a very telling dream in her memoirs, one she dreamed when she was about nineteen years old. In this dream, she was in her parish church, and an old priest was celebrating Mass. Although the priest was a stranger to her, when the Mass was fin-ished, he beckoned her to come to him. She panicked and fled instead. She then found herself at the bedside of an invalid. The old priest was standing beside her.

He said, "My child, it is good to care for the sick. You run away from me now, but one day, you will be glad to come to me. God has his designs on you—do not forget it."

By the age of twenty-two, Zoe felt that the time had come to relin-quish her household duties and enter religious life. However, her father refused to consider it; she was much too useful to him on the farm. His denial of her lifelong dream sent a chill through the Laboure household. The daughter who had always been after his own heart was now estranged and distant. When one of her brothers asked the family for help in running his restaurant in Paris, Pere seized upon the opportunity to distract Zoe Catherine from her piety with the plea-sures of the city. And so in 1828, Zoe arrived in Paris, where her brothers had fled before her to escape the iron grasp of their father.

A family conspiracy was brewing, as her sympathetic siblings, more grateful than their father for Zoe's many years of service, rallied around her in support. Her sister-in-law ran an exclusive boarding school for young ladies in Chatillon, and she was able to prevail upon Pere to allow Zoe Catherine to reside there for a time, presumably to acquire some polish. It was in Chatillon, one fateful day, that Zoe paid a social visit to the convent of the Sisters of Charity. What she saw there was to change her life forever.

As she entered the parlor, Zoe noticed a portrait of an old priest. She was shaken to the core as she realized that this was the priest who had beckoned to her in her dream. She composed herself enough to question the sisters about it, only to learn that the painting was a likeness of their founder, St. Vincent de Paul, a holy man much loved for his works of charity among the sick and the poor.

With this realization that St. Vincent had called her to be one of his Sisters of Charity, Zoe Catherine was more determined than ever to pursue her vocation. As adamant as his daughter, her father gave her only a grudging consent, and actually refused her a dowry—a cruel slight, considering the family's wealth. Zoe's brother and sister-in-law in Chatillon pitched in, providing the newest bride of Christ with the dowry and trousseau she needed for her entrance into the order. The year 1830 found St. Catherine a novice at the order's mother house on the Rue du Bac in Paris. She never saw her father, or the farmhouse in Moutiers, again.

THE BIRTH CHART

St. Catherine's natal chart shares certain elements in common with those of other Marian visionaries, specifically, an emphasis on unusual relationships and a dominant lunar influence. These types of alignments would seem to indicate a tendency toward strange alliances in general, and special devotion to a maternal deity in particular.

In St. Catherine's case, the Moon was very full in Scorpio at her birth, and rising in the east, it dominates her chart from the first house. The first house begins at the Ascendant and is the most personal house, influencing the personality, the physical body, the appearance,

St. Catherine Laboure
Natal Chart
May 2, 1806
6:00 p.m. -0:26:08
Moutiers, France

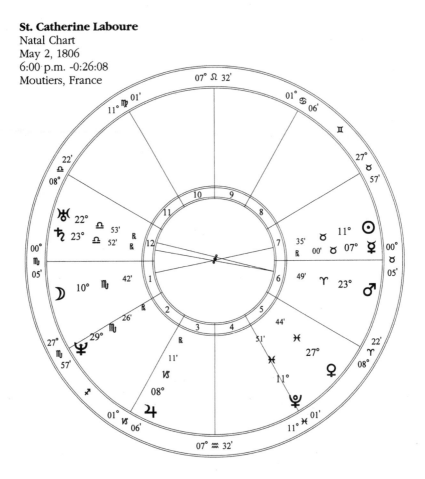

St. Catherine's birth chart. Saturn ♄ and Uranus ♅ rising in Libra ♎,
opposite Mars ♂ in Aries ♈ Full Moon rising in Scorpio♏,
opposite the Sun ☉ and Mercury ☿ setting in Taurus ♉.

and the subjective sense of self. St. Catherine personified that intensely
secretive Scorpio nature that confronts death and conquers it, or, at the
very least, refuses to surrender. She was passionately attached both to
her dying mother and to the spiritual regeneration of the maternal
archetype that she found in her devotion to the Mother of God.

St. Catherine's personality reflected both the light and the darkness
of that Full Moon simmering in the shadowy depths of Scorpio. Even

though she experienced a full revelation of the maternal deity, she spent her entire life in stubborn Scorpio secrecy on the matter, sharing her visions and messages privately with her confessor and only revealing herself as the fabled visionary in her last days.

There is a distinct emphasis in St. Catherine's chart on the Ascendant/Descendant axis, which is traditionally where the self comes into relationship with others. Her birth chart features a pair of oppositions lining the Ascendant/Descendant axis, emphasizing the importance of personal encounters and partnerships in her life.

Born at sunset with the Full Moon rising, her natal Sun and Moon oppose each other from the 1st to the 7th houses. The other opposition features the bizarre and brilliant planet Uranus rising in conjunction with her Saturn in Libra. Libra is generally considered to be the sign of relationships and close partnerships, and that unique conjunction is animated and inspired by an exact opposition to fiery Mars, strong in its own sign of Aries, and setting just below her Descendant.

Individuals born with a strong 7th house emphasis in their charts tend to gravitate toward intimate relationships, but St. Catherine never seriously considered marriage, even though she did inspire some proposals. Apparently she felt called to be the bride of Christ from an early age. Her Sun and Mercury in Taurus in the 7th house are stressed by that tight opposition to the Scorpio Moon. Her mother's death had left a deep scar.

Madeleine Gontard Laboure had married at twenty and died at forty-two, after seventeen pregnancies in twenty-two years. Catherine's perspective on marriage was probably different from that of a young woman today. With easy access to birth control and safe, legal abortions, the idea of forsaking romance for perpetual chastity now seems needlessly ascetic, but in Catherine's time, sex came with much more drastic consequences.

Marriage, even a sacramental union blessed by both families, was still an iffy proposition at best. Even the most tender of lovers eventually turned into a husband. Corrupted by his absolute power, he could drink, carouse, and spend his wife's money however he pleased. Child-bearing could be deadly, and divorce was hardly an option.

Catherine's own mother, Madeleine, had been an educated woman from a cultured family. Before her marriage, she had a brief career as a schoolteacher. After her marriage, she probably had little time for learning. The responsibilities of running a household and caring for children kept most married women too distracted to follow any other calling.

Religious orders offered medieval career opportunities to women who longed to be something more than the "biological pawn of nature." While more cloistered and restricted than the men's orders, the religious sisters did have more time and resources to devote to learning, to art and music, or to developing administrative and lead-ership skills. It wasn't much by today's standards, but it was more than many women of the time would ever hope to find in secular society.

Seen in this light, it might be easier to grasp the attraction of reli-gious life for young women, especially when, like St. Catherine, they had suffered through their own mother's hastened demise. I don't think it could be said that St. Catherine considered herself unmarried. She had chosen Christ, and He had chosen her. There is little to no doubt regarding her lifelong virginity.

THE VISIONS

Resuming our narrative, the summer of 1830 was a particularly hot one in Paris. The French capital was still reeling from the aftershocks of both the Revolution and the dramatic rise and fall of Napoleon. Constant feuding between rival monarchist and republican factions, coupled with the burden of heavy war indemnities imposed by the victorious European powers in the wake of Napoleon's defeat, cre-ated a uniquely unstable political climate.

The farm girl from Moutiers was hardly cloistered within this environment. Soon after St. Catherine's arrival at the order's motherhouse, the community launched into a rare celebration to honor the return of the relics of their founder, St. Vincent de Paul. St. Catherine attended daily liturgies and processions that put her back into the midst of Paris life.

During her return one afternoon from a community novena service, she began to experience a series of visions involving the heart of St. Vincent de Paul. At the height of the community's celebration, on the eve of the feast of their founder and saint, St. Catherine and her sisters went to bed full of anticipation for the high holy day ahead. During the course of that night, the young novice, on the path to sainthood herself, experienced one of the most famous visitations of the Blessed Virgin Mary in church history.

With her country common sense and usual exactitude, St. Catherine relates in her memoirs that she was awakened during the night of July 18, 1830, at the insistence of what appeared to be a dazzling little child standing by her bedside.

"Sister Labouré!" the child said, "Come to the chapel. The Blessed Virgin awaits you."

St. Catherine was afraid they would be discovered, but the child reassured her, "It is half past eleven; everyone is asleep. Come, I am waiting for you."[2]

St. Catherine followed the little fellow down to the chapel of the motherhouse, which she found blazing with lights. She waited for a few long moments at the sanctuary until the child announced, "Here is the Blessed Virgin."

She heard a sound not unlike the rustling of a silk dress, and suddenly a beautiful lady descended along the altar steps. The lady seated herself in the priest's chair and St. Catherine spent the next two hours kneeling at her feet, enraptured and adoring, while the lady discoursed on a wide range of prophecies and promises.

To the skeptical mind, it all sounds rather fanciful, too easily dreamed up by a backward young woman, alone in the big city. But let's pull back and look at the big picture, analyzing this event in an astrological context to see what the dominant psychological and spiritual forces were at this moment.

St. Catherine's historic encounter with her heavenly mother took place just before the New Moon in Cancer. Both the Sun and Moon were in Cancer, the Moon's own sign, and were straddling the IC (the

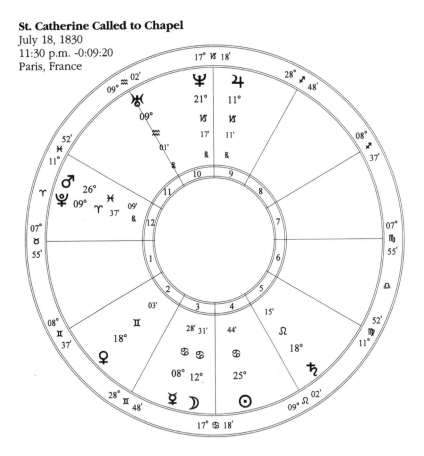

St. Catherine Called to Chapel
July 18, 1830
11:30 p.m. -0:09:20
Paris, France

St. Catherine called to chapel to see the Virgin Mary.
Neptune ♆ and Jupiter ♃ in Capricorn ♑ near the MC;
Sun ☉, Moon ☽, and Mercury ☿ in Cancer ♋ near the IC.

bottom angle of the chart). An otherworldly Neptune in Capricorn was culminating at the Midheaven, or MC, in wide opposition to the Cancer Sun. This opposition straddled the latter part, or third decan (20 to 30 degrees) of the signs Cancer-Capricorn, an area which, for some reason, seems to be frequently highlighted in these apparition experiences.

There were other planetary oppositions from Cancer to Capricorn as well. Both the Moon and Mercury were in opposition to Jupiter in Capricorn. The fast-moving Moon was just separating from the exact opposition while Mercury was just moving into range.

Even a cursory glance at the planets clustered about the MC/IC axis reveals that the dominant psycho-spiritual archetypes at that moment were of the mystical Cancer variety; that is, luminous and lunar, feminine and motherly, inspiring great emotion and devotion, while developing issues of security, especially concerning the family, motherland, and maternal providence.

While the planetary alignments within the event chart describe the environment, or the astrological weather, as it were, obviously, not everyone within range of this cosmic moment was experiencing these forces in the same way. However, St. Catherine's natal (birth) chart locked into the event chart through an intricate complex of exact planetary aspects, manifesting in her experience of a personal outreach and encounter with this maternal deity.

Let's insert St. Catherine into her environment by placing her natal chart around the event chart. As St. Catherine hurried to the chapel, her natal Full Moon alignment from Taurus to Scorpio was rising and setting on the current Ascendant-Descendant axis, amplifying the already considerable lunar influences.

A series of harmonic relationships, or aspects, was taking shape between the planets of St. Catherine's natal chart and the current, or transiting, planets of the event chart. Tight connections have formed between planets in the 10th through the 12th degrees of the earth

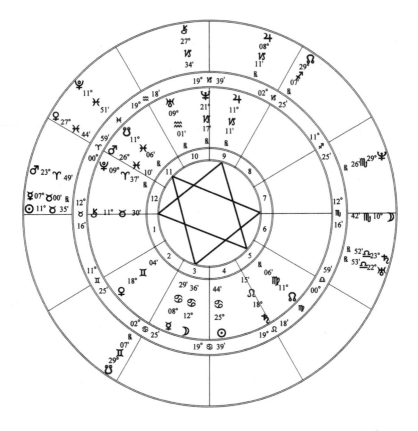

Planetary interactions form a Star of David.

signs (Taurus, Virgo, Capricorn) and water signs (Cancer, Scorpio, Pisces), linking them all into an interlocking, double Grand Trine (triangle), or Star of David configuration. This complex of planetary aspects uniquely linked St. Catherine's natal chart into this exact moment.

The current (or transiting) position of the planetoid Chiron was exactly conjunct St. Catherine's natal Sun at 11 degrees Taurus, and rising on the current Ascendant. Meanwhile, the transiting Moon's North Node formed a trine aspect (120-degree angle) to them both from 11 degrees Virgo. St. Catherine's natal Pluto is at 11 degrees

Pisces, conjunct the transiting Moon's South Node. Transiting Jupiter at 11 degrees Capricorn, opposite the transiting Moon at 12 degrees Cancer, completes the pattern.

All the elements were present: a strong emphasis on the Moon and the signs Cancer-Capricorn, and a Virgo-Pisces connection as well. Mystical, lunar archetypes predominate at that moment and lock right into St. Catherine's natal chart by aspect. When considered from the astrological perspective, it actually seems plausible that this young novice experienced a mystical encounter with a shining, motherly goddess figure, whereas others, with different charts, might have missed it altogether.

St. Catherine reports that she spent almost two hours at the Virgin's knee and their discussion covered a range of issues. The Virgin told St. Catherine that God had a mission for her, which would be revealed in due time. She also entrusted St. Catherine with the knowledge of some dire prophecies that concerned both France and the Vincentian communities. She warned St. Catherine that the French government would soon fall, and that the ensuing chaos would be a time of great danger for the leaders of the church. In revealing this, she promised her protection to the Sisters of Charity and the Vincentian Fathers. She also prophesied a worse time to come, in another forty years, with greater dangers and worse outrages. Again, she promised her continued protection to St. Catherine's order.

The lady also instructed St. Catherine to unburden herself to her spiritual director, and to him alone. She urged the novice to tell him everything, even though he would contradict and test her thoroughly. Mary assured her that her honesty and simplicity would win him over in the end. This was the origin of St. Catherine's lifelong secret. For forty-six years, St. Catherine told no one but her confessor about her visions.

This put the onus for action squarely on the unwitting Fr. Jean Marie Aladel. The country novice had already tried his patience with

her visions of the heart of St. Vincent de Paul, but in the days following July 18, 1830, her dramatic confessions became even more dis-
tressing. Much of what we know about the events on the Rue du Bac
in 1830 we owe to the diligence of Fr. Aladel. He published his own
account of the visions, and later directed St. Catherine to write her
versions, which were published anonymously in 1841, and again in
1856 and 1876. All the while, Sister Laboure lived a hard and humble
life of service, just like any other sister in her order.

Only a few days after St. Catherine reported her latest revelations
to her confessor, a sudden and unexpected revolt arose in Paris and
the reigning government was overthrown, just as the Lady had
prophesied. In a misguided attempt to reestablish the divine right of
the monarchy, the French King, Charles X, provoked open revolt by
arbitrarily dissolving the legislature and clamping down on the press.
He was driven from his throne in a matter of days, and in the ensuing revolutionary chaos, frenzied mobs terrorized the country.

The restored Bourbon monarchy under Charles X had ruled in a
united front with the Church, so much of the mob's anger was
directed at the clergy and religious orders. The corruption and privi-
lege of the ancient regime still tainted far too many of the clerical
offices. The greedier prelates, who enriched themselves at the
people's expense, may have deserved the wrath of the crowds, but
the enflamed mobs were not always so particular in their choice of
victims. Many innocent priests and religious people were beaten or
killed along with the rest. Mercifully, the house on the Rue du Bac
was spared.

Forty years later, St. Catherine and her sisters were again threatened during the Paris Commune, just as the lady had predicted. The
sisters feared for both their lives and their virtue at the hands of the
mobs, and eventually had to flee to the country for safety, but the
lady stood by her promises, and they soon returned to Paris to continue their work.

It must have been a great comfort for St. Catherine to believe that no harm would come to her community, for both revolts were frightening affairs. Other religious people and their orders were not so fortunate, and the gruesome stories of their deaths and torture at the hands of the revolutionaries would have been much more terrifying without those promises of protection.

THE MIRACULOUS MEDAL

As for the mission the Lady had promised her, St. Catherine was to serve as a special stimulus to Marian devotion throughout the world. This mission unfolded in the years between the rebellions. On November 27, 1830, at approximately 5:30 p.m. LMT, Paris, as St. Catherine knelt in prayer during an afternoon mass, she experienced yet another dazzling vision of the Blessed Virgin, the image of which has been preserved in the millions of medallions known around the world as the "Miraculous Medal." [3]

Initially, Mary appeared by the altar, holding a globe that symbolized the world. Her hands were emblazoned with brilliant jewels, and multicolored rays of light cascaded from her fingers. Then, she shifted her pose. The globe now appeared at her feet, and she lowered her arms to her sides, spreading them wide in a motherly attitude. The brilliant beams of light still poured forth from her hands, shining down upon the globe.

She instructed St. Catherine to "have a medal struck after this model. All who wear it will receive great graces; they should wear it around the neck. Graces will abound for persons who wear it with confidence." Revealed in this resplendent vision were distinct designs for the front and back of the medal.

The next day found St. Catherine back in the confessional with poor Fr. Aladel. The novice had been vindicated somewhat in the priest's esteem when the messages she had relayed from the Lady's previous visit in July had proven so prophetically accurate. Still, Fr.

Aladel never rushed into anything. He, like St. Catherine, was a Taurus, born May 4, 1800, and these two were to lock horns at every turn. That his penitent refused to testify in her own behalf or to allow him to reveal her identity did not help matters.

Over time, the two stubborn wills wore each other down. Eventually, Fr. Aladel came to know Catherine well enough to realize that she was entirely too unimaginative to have dreamed these things up herself. He also came to appreciate her simple goodness, especially when, time after time, even after vehemently disagreeing with his decisions, she submitted to them in humble obedience. Finally, in January 1832, Fr. Aladel took the opportunity to discuss the matter of the medal with the Archbishop of Paris, Hyacinthe de Quelen.

The archbishop liked the idea and gave his approval at once. However, a cholera epidemic intervened and delayed production temporarily, as the Sisters of Charity and their directors, true to their charter, busied themselves caring for the sick and bereaved. Finally, on June 30, 1832, the first batch of two thousand medals was delivered from the engraver. When presented to Sister Catherine, she simply said, "Now it must be propagated."

This date, with the Sun, Mercury and Venus in Cancer, stands as the "birthday" of the Medals of the Immaculate Conception, as they were officially known. In seemingly no time at all, the little sacramental had earned the nickname by which it is still known today, the Miraculous Medal.

St. Catherine's medal was a raging, overnight success. Its popularity spread like a spiritual wildfire across the continent, and within the first six years, well over twelve million were sold or distributed, hand to hand, passed along with the tales of the miracles attributed to their power. All around the world, people wondered about the mysterious nun whose visions had inspired this marvel, but St. Catherine kept her secret, day after busy day, tending to the needs of the sick and dying old men at the hospice in Enghien.

CONCLUSIONS

In St. Catherine's initial visit with her heavenly mother, at the New Moon in Cancer, we can trace the lunar themes of maternal reassurance. The Lady in white promises her protection to St. Catherine's order, which was like a family to the young novice, and she also promises protection to France, the motherland. St. Catherine spent the entire interview like a child at her mother's knee. That lunar maternal providence is further extended through the worldwide distribution of the sacramental talisman, the Miraculous Medal.

In contrast, the vision at La Salette, under the New Moon in Virgo, emphasized distinctly Virgo issues like the harvest, purity, work, and improvement. Another worthwhile comparison lies in the characters of the visionaries themselves. In St. Catherine, the Lady addressed a professed religious of admirable discipline and self-restraint, while the youthful visionaries of La Salette were of another stripe altogether. St. Catherine's "secret" probably facilitated her own spiritual development, while Maxim's and Melanie's lives took a downhill turn after their brush with fame, perhaps due in large part to the attention they received (which St. Catherine was able to avoid).

We are very fortunate to have such good data on St. Catherine Laboure, which is not always so easy to come by in these apparition events. We get so much more information out of a chart when we have an accurate Ascendant, Midheaven, and Moon position. We are equally fortunate to have St. Catherine's example before us of that steadfast Taurus nature: simple, patient, and provident. Day in and day out, humbly completing the same basic tasks, she carried the weight of the world on that big, broad back, and built a spiritual empire in the process.

Endnotes

1. In *St. Catherine Laboure of the Miraculous Medal,* pg. 4, Fr. J. Dirvin quotes, "Registre d'Etat Civil de la Commune de Fain et Saint-Just-les-moutiers, canton de Montbard (Cote d'Or)."

2. Dirvin quotes from P. Aladel, *Les Rayons,* and the autographs of St. Catherine for the time.

3. *St. Catherine Laboure of the Miraculous Medal,* pg. 92. Fr. Dirvin states that "At half past five, all the Sisters, professed and novices alike, gathered in the chapel for their evening meditation."

Four

LOURDES: OUR LADY,
THE WATER BEARER

THE EARLY YEARS: SCORN AND STARVATION

The story is almost too timeless, and too familiar: how one little girl, half-starved and illiterate, the sickly scion of disreputable stock, was blessed with a vision and the kind of natural nobility that eventually revolutionized her town, her country, and her church. The triumph of Bernadette Soubirous would be utterly unbelievable as fiction. As it is, her innocence and purity shine for all who have an eye to see, shaming the worldliness of the powers that be.

At the time the apparitions began, the Soubirous family was in dire straits, reduced to living in a wretched one-room cell, the abandoned remains of an old jail. The family had known better days in the mill trade, but Bernadette's father, Francois, had proven a notoriously bad business-man. The happy home by the churning wheel on the river was now only a fading memory. Francois had been reduced to day labor, and even that was hard to come by, particularly since his incarceration the previous year on charges of employee theft—charges that were never proven, but added their stain to what little remained of his reputation.

Bernadette's mother, Louise, was said to be overly fond of her wine. Perhaps her intemperance, as well as her husband's, played a part in reducing the family to this sorry state where she and her four surviving children were crammed into a derelict jail that even the inmates had long since abandoned. Hard pressed for food or warmth, the family was not without love, or so it was said. Lacking all else, at least they still had each other. Bernadette, at fourteen, was their oldest child, a position of some distinction in the mountain customs of the Pyrenees. Asthmatic and weakened from cholera, she had spent most of her childhood working as a servant or a shepherd, rather than in school.

We do have a birth time for Bernadette. Lois Rodden quotes Choisnard, who cites her birth record in Language Astral for the time of 2:00 p.m.[1] It has been my experience that babies are rarely born exactly on the hour, so there may be some rounding off behind that figure. Nevertheless, this presents an interesting chart, with a very angular opposition of the Moon in Leo to Venus in Aquarius straddling the Midheaven/IC axis. The Midheaven is the most prominent, public part of the birth chart, and that angular Moon-Venus opposition seems to have attracted a fair amount of attention into Bernadette's short life.

Bernadette was born on January 7, 1844, with both the Sun and Saturn in Saturn's own sign, Capricorn. Capricorn is the opposite and complimentary sign to Cancer. In the parlance of modern, Western astrology, under Saturn's crystallizing influence, Capricorn can be as hard and unyielding as Cancer is soft and vulnerable. Whereas Cancer represents the comforts and security of the home, Capricorn must leave the nest and take on the challenges of the world. A strange creature, this sea-goat, emerging from the enveloping depths of Cancer's ocean to scramble up the rocky mountain slope, Capricorn is perhaps the ultimate realist among the earth signs. More cynical than Taurus, possessing the broad scope that Virgo often lacks, he is the hardest worker and the best builder in the zodiac.

In Western astrology, which developed mainly in the northern hemisphere, the Sun passes through the sign Capricorn in the dead

Bernadette Soubirous
Jan. 7, 1844 NS
2:00 p.m. +0:00+12
Lourdes, France

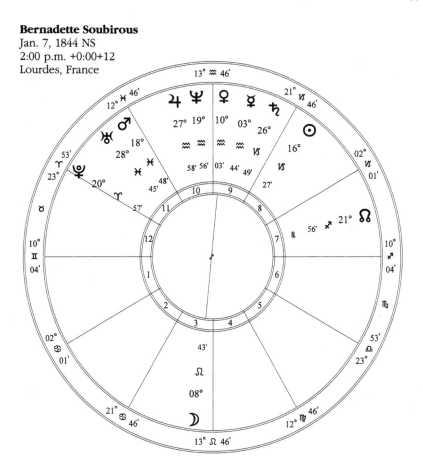

Bernadette Soubirous. Venus ♀ opposite Moon ☽,
straddling the MC/IC axis.

of winter, when newborn life must struggle against bitter cold, prolonged darkness, and relative scarcity to survive until the promise of
summer. Nothing comes easy for Capricorn, and those born under
the sign's influence often develop a somber maturity well beyond
their years to cope with the challenges of their early life. Bernadette
was already well acquainted with privation, shame, sickness, and
loss, but even at fourteen, still too ignorant and unlettered to qualify
for her first communion.

Capricorn is a social sign. Not particularly prone to introspection, it seeks itself in other people's recognition. Driven to achieve, often by deep insecurity, the sign imparts a knack for organization and administration; just the sort of traits that lead to success in business and politics. Capricorn wants to scale the hard, cold rock of ambition all the way to the mountaintop, the pinnacle of their chosen field. They see the big picture, the grand design, and have the tenacity to stick to their own master plan for as long as it takes. That perennial fear of winter motivates them to build the castles and amass the fortunes that will keep them and their loved ones safe and warm for one more season. Somehow, no matter how much they have, it is never enough. The fear never abandons them.

While Bernadette never was, or wanted to be, successful, she certainly was, and continues to be, fabulously famous. After that desperately harsh childhood, once the apparitions began, she became public property and had no private life at all. Sometimes Saturn and Capricorn are just cold and hard, keeping their natives on a very short leash, burdened with one responsibility and limitation after another. Even her *aquero,* the lady of her visions, couldn't promise to make her happy in this world, only in the next. Once the apparitions ended, she wisely secluded herself in a convent, where, still continually sought by her public but isolated from her family, she spent the remainder of her short life in a routine of painful illness and hard work.

We will return to this theme of Saturn and Capricorn, their influence on the powers that be, and the ambition that got them there, so hold that thought. But first, the story must be told.

THE STORY

On the cold morning of February 11, 1858, there was no wood in the Soubirous home, and no fire to warm them. Bernadette set out with her younger sister Toinette, and a neighbor girl, Jean Abadie, to scrounge in the forest for kindling. Maybe they would get lucky and find a rag or a bone to sell.

Heading out of town, the girls neared the foot of Massabielle, a massive, cliff-top rock formation, within view of the ancient hilltop fortress that served as the traditional landmark of the town. To reach the woods, they had to ford the river Gave at the bottom of the cliff. Bernadette's mother had warned her not to get her feet wet, for that would surely bring on the asthma, so while the other two girls scampered across the river, Bernadette reluctantly hung back.

According to her own accounts, as she lingered near the banks of the Gave, the girls calling after her as they hurried into the woods, she heard a sound like rushing wind. The sound seemed to be coming from a dark grotto in the rock wall under Massabielle. The noon Angelus bells were ringing from the town. As Bernadette turned to investigate the source of the wind, she saw what looked like a glowing young girl, tiny, white, and smiling brightly. She appeared to be standing above the eglantine, or wild rose, that draped the niche over the entrance to the grotto.

Bernadette rubbed her eyes and looked again. This time, the tiny demoiselle nodded, as if to greet her, and opened her arms, smiling all the while. Bernadette's initial reaction was fear, but she couldn't run away. She said she felt like she couldn't move, but she did manage to instinctively put her hand in her pocket and draw out her rosary for protection. She tried to make the sign of the cross, but found that she couldn't.

In response, the shining little maiden also produced a rosary, and crossed herself in a gesture of surprising beauty and grace. This time, Bernadette found she could respond, and after crossing herself, she began to feel calmer and a little less overwhelmed. Dropping to her knees, Bernadette began to pray with her rosary. The little lady fingered her beads along with her. When they had finished, the tiny thing beckoned her to come closer, but Bernadette was too awed to move. She then vanished, all smiles and delicate grace, leaving Bernadette to rejoin her companions.

The other girls had seen nothing of it, and teased Bernadette about praying while they did all the work. After considerable prying, Bernadette revealed to them what she thought she had seen. Once home, her sister Toinette told their mother. The Soubirous parents were not at all impressed with this news, and forbade the girls to return to the grotto. That Saturday evening, Bernadette told the local curate, Fr. Pomian, about the vision in confession. He asked for her permission to discuss the matter with the parish priest, Dean Peyramale.

Come Sunday, after Mass, several of the local girls urged Bernadette to return with them to the grotto. She pleaded with her parents for permission, which was not easily granted. Armed with a bottle of holy water, Bernadette returned to the grotto under Massabielle with a small host of childish companions. Arriving at the entrance to the grotto, she dropped to her knees and began to pray her rosary. As she began the second decade, her face changed and she announced the apparition's presence.

Bernadette sprinkled the holy water in the direction of the girl in white, asking her to stay if she came from God, but to go away if not. The more holy water she spilled, the more the apparition smiled. The little bottle was empty soon enough. Even though her companions could not see what Bernadette saw, they couldn't help but notice how serene and peaceful her face had become.

Suddenly, a large rock came tumbling down the cliff side and fell into the grotto, spooking the children. Jean Abadie, stationed above, had heaved it, hoping to frighten away the devil. The children panicked and scattered. Some tried to drag Bernadette away with them, only to find that they could not. She didn't seem to hear or respond to them at all, and in resisting their efforts to move her, her body seemed unnaturally heavy.

In their flight, several children encountered the family from the sawmill upstream. The adults followed the frightened children back to the grotto, where they had no more success at moving Bernadette out of her trance.

The miller himself, Antoine Nicolau, was summoned; a burly man, he still had no small trouble in leading her away. The incident deeply impressed Nicolau, seeing Bernadette so utterly enraptured, her eyes flooding with tears while her face shone with an otherworldly bliss. He kept trying to cover her awestruck eyes with his hand to dislodge her gaze from whatever it was that kept her so spellbound, but she wouldn't break contact. It took the efforts of the entire crowd to drag little Bernadette back to the sawmill, and it wasn't until she was seated in the mill kitchen that she came to herself. Then she excitedly told them all about the beautiful little girl she had seen.

IN THE IMAGE OF AQUERO

Bernadette's descriptions of the tiny, white maiden were consistent throughout the course of her visions. The apparition, whom she called aquero, or "that thing" in the local dialect, appeared youthful and girlish. There was nothing particularly matronly or maternal about her. Bernadette repeatedly said that aquero was about the same size as herself, if not a bit smaller. Bernadette was very small for her age. Although she had recently turned fourteen, the combined ravages of illness and malnutrition kept her about the size of an average ten or eleven year old. According to Bernadette's earliest descriptions, aquero looked to be about twelve years old. This is an important distinction, and one that the well-meaning supporters of Lourdes apparently prefer to ignore.

Aquero, according to Bernadette's initial descriptions, was a *jeune fille;* a *bien mignonette,* glowing in a white dress spun of a luxurious, soft, shiny stuff. Her head was covered in a white veil of the same magic fabric, so that only a tiny bit of her hair was revealed in the front. Her eyes were bright blue, and set in a long and very white face. The whole figure shone with a gleaming, white radiance. Around her waist was a blue girdle, which folded in the front and fell almost to the hem of her robe. Her tiny feet, barely visible beneath her robe, were bare, but each was adorned with a single, golden rose. Her rosary gleamed as well, with shining white beads and links of gold.

This costume is quite significant, for in this particular area of the Pyrenees, the locals maintained a tradition of fairy lore that told of the *petito damizela* in white who still lingered in the forests and grottoes of the region. When Bernadette first called the apparition a petito damizela, which translates as a petite, unmarried young lady, she may have actually been referring to aquero as a Pyrenean fairy woman. These Pyrenean fairies were tiny, enchanting ladies in glowing, white robes. Charming, helpful, and better natured than most fairy folk, they were recognized by their gleaming garments and said to spend much time washing them to snowy whiteness in the fountains outside their grotto homes.[2]

The roses on aquero's feet were yet another aspect of local fairy lore, as was Bernadette's reluctance to call her by any name other than "that thing." According to the tradition, these delightful fairy women sometimes married mortal men, making good wives and housekeepers—for a time. Eventually, the husband would slip up and call his fairy wife by her name, at which point she would disappear back into the fairy world forever.

Bernadette's apparition was distinguished from the local fairy folk by her rosary and the girdle of blue about her waist. Bernadette had initially presented her own rosary to the apparition in fear, probably as an instinctive reaction to ward off anything unholy, but the praying of the rosary became such an important part of each subsequent visit that perhaps we should assume Bernadette did equate aquero with the Blessed Virgin Mary, even if she continued for some time to treat her like a fairy woman. Can we trace the attempts to reconcile the two traditions within Bernadette's mind? In combining her catholicism with the local pre-Christian folk traditions in this image of aquero, perhaps she found some resolution and accommodation for them both.

By the same token, the ecclesiastical and civil authorities who promoted the matronly, more mature image of Our Lady of Lourdes, which bears so little resemblance to what Bernadette actually described, demonstrate, in their way, their attempts to resolve a similar interior conflict. Bernadette was rarely happy with the paintings and statues submitted for her appraisal. She was particularly frustrated with the design of the statue installed at the grotto itself in 1864, fashioned by the Lyonnais sculptor Joseph Fabisch. She thought it was both too old and too big, and yet, this image of a fully-grown, shapely woman, more in keeping with conventional ideas of the Virgin Mary, has become the standard image of Our Lady of Lourdes.[3]

THE VISIONARY TRANCE STATE

Another important feature of Bernadette's second apparition is the trance state; the spontaneous, involuntary condition of religious ecstacy. Bernadette, like many other Marian visionaries, entered into an altered state of consciousness at the approach of aquero. Her entire attention and vision were suddenly focused on something that no one else could see, while all her other senses retreated. Oblivious to anything else going on around her, she responded neither to sound, light, nor touch.

Onlookers deliberately subjected the entranced visionaries to disruptive, even painful stimuli, going so far as to stick them with pins or burn their hands to try to provoke a response. Bernadette certainly bore her share of these trials, and never seemed to notice. At Beauraing and Medjugorge, repeated experiments have been done on the visionaries that appear to demonstrate that they were not only insensible to pain while in trance, but also remained free from any after effects of the "experimental" burning or wounding upon their return to waking consciousness. We will return to this subject in later chapters, where the medical evidence is more modern and substantial than that which was available at Lourdes.

The trance state exhibited so spontaneously by Bernadette and other Marian visionaries has its parallels. The term "catalepsy" has been used since medieval times to describe a similar state of rigidity and unresponsiveness that was often associated with epilepsy. In the original Greek, the term implies a seizing, or to "seize down from." Patients experiencing a seizure were often thought to have been seized by a god or some other outside force.

Bernadette's trance state also bears some resemblance to the symptoms of anesthesia demonstrated by "hysterical" patients of her time. A popular nineteenth-century misdiagnosis, "hysteria" seemed mainly to afflict women, and could render patients oblivious to pain and other sensory stimuli. A somnambulist in a hypnotic trance, under the direction of a skilled operator, can be instructed to ignore pain. Surgical operations have been performed successfully using hypnosis as the only anesthetic.

This trance state is an ecumenical standard, and found in religious practices around the world. Saints and mystics of all faiths have been reported to exhibit symptoms of catalepsy during prolonged periods of prayer. Shamans or practitioners of voodoo deliberately invoke a trance state with drugs or rhythmic incantations to facilitate their communion with the inhabitants of other realms. A distinguishing feature of the trance state experienced by Marian visionaries is its spontaneity. The visionaries, like Bernadette, are usually children, not yogis or shamans. They are not so much seeking the trance state as it seems to be seeking them.

A distinguishing feature of Bernadette's ecstasies was the beauty and serenity of her face, and the inspirational effect this had on people. There was such grace in her extraordinary rapture that even those who came to scoff at the peasant idiocy were stunned into reverence at the sight of her. Some observers compared her to a great actress, with dramatic gestures and emotive expressions that commanded the crowd. Even the way she crossed herself, in imitation of aquero, was breathtaking. And yet she was hardly conscious, and focused not on the crowds, but on a vision that she alone could see.

FIFTEEN VISITS

After the tumultuous turn of events at Bernadette's second vision, Louise Soubirous was even more determined to keep her daughter away from that grotto. In town, gossip reigned, and Bernadette fast became an object of curiosity and scorn. The nuns at school were outraged, the children teased her, like children everywhere, and even some of the more self-righteous Lourdais confronted her rudely, demanding that she put a stop to the nonsense. Ironically, the week before Lent was traditionally a time for practical jokes. Many of the locals naturally assumed that Bernadette was up to some carnival trick.

It was on Shrove Tuesday, February 16, that a certain Madame Jeanne-Marie Milhet, a wealthy matron with a bit of time on her hands, took it upon herself to investigate the affair at the grotto. Like others in town, she wondered if the apparition wasn't some sort of *revenant,* a returning spirit of the recently departed. These unsettled souls were believed to come seeking prayers and masses from their loved ones to speed their deliverance from purgatory.

There was also speculation that aquero might be the ghost of Elisa Latapie, a young woman of exceptional piety, whose particularly "good death" the previous October had made a great impression on the parish priest, Dean Peyramale. Elisa had been very active in the local "Children of Mary," a devotional group for the young ladies of the parish. Their uniform, a flowing white dress with a blue sash, in which Elisa had asked to be buried, was so like the clothing of Bernadette's aquero that enquiring minds, like Madame Milhet, made the obvious connection.

Madame Milhet appeared at the old jail that Tuesday. As one who occasionally employed Louise Soubirous, Madame Milhet had some pull and was able to convince Louise to allow her to accompany Bernadette to the grotto. The plan was to take a pen and ink to the grotto and ask the apparition to write her name and requests. This was actually a common local practice in regard to revenants, for they were believed to be able to write their wishes. To ensure some privacy, they planned to go to the grotto very early on Thursday morning.

At 5:00 a.m. on Thursday, February 18, Madame Mihet and her seamstress, Antoinette Peyret, came knocking on the door of the old jail. Carrying a pen, paper, an inkstand, and a holy candle, they set out with Bernadette for the grotto. They had only just begun the rosary when Bernadette announced the appearance of aquero. The ladies urged Bernadette forward with the pen and paper. When Bernadette asked if the young lady would be so kind as to write her name, she replied that it wasn't necessary, in a voice that only Bernadette could hear. Instead, she had a request for Bernadette.

"Would you have the graciousness to come here for fifteen days?" she asked, using the most courteous form of address in the local patois. Bernadette immediately replied that she would, stunned by both the sweetness of aquero's voice and the respect aquero showed in addressing her that way.

Afterward, Bernadette was surprised to learn that the two ladies had not heard anything of the conversation, even though they had been standing close by. They thought that she had not even asked the lady to write her name. Bernadette told them of aquero's responses, adding that she saw no resemblance to the departed Elisa Latapie. Now Madame Milhet began to believe that it was the Blessed

Virgin who was appearing and she remarked on it as they made their way back to town. Antoinette was not so sure. Bernadette had no fixed opinion at all, at least none that she was willing to express.

And so began the fortnight of apparitions, from February 18 through March 4, 1858. Madame Milhet so wanted to be in charge that she insisted upon taking Bernadette into her own spacious home. That arrangement didn't last long, for in a few days, Bernadette's Aunt Bernarde stepped in to return the girl, her namesake, to the family. On Friday, February 19, the contingent going with Bernadette to the grotto before daybreak included eight people. On Saturday, February 20, their numbers had swelled to thirty. On Sunday, February 21, there were a hundred people waiting for Bernadette at the grotto.

These three apparitions followed a similar pattern. Bernadette arrived, dropped to her knees, and produced her rosary. Soon after she began praying, her face would change perceptibly and the crowd would know that aquero had arrived. Sometimes they could see Bernadette's lips move, sometimes she would sigh, but mostly, she was silent. What impressed the crowd most was the beauty of her face and the gracefulness of her few movements. Her physical appearance seemed sound testimony to the presence of the divine.

COMMISSIONER JACOMET

That Sunday evening, February 21, after vespers, M. Dominique Jacomet, the Commissioner of Police, detained Bernadette. He took her to his office for interrogation. Also present were Jean-Baptiste Estrade, the local tax collector, and his sister, who both shared the house with Jacomet. Their notes, and the notes of Jacomet, provide a detailed record of Bernadette's first official interview.

Jacomet was convinced the Soubirous girl was lying, and that someone had put her up to this business, probably her indigent parents. The growing crowds were also a legitimate safety concern. Jacomet

was an old pro at extracting confessions from the most hardened con-
sciences, but he foundered with Bernadette, who had already told
anyone who asked all that she knew. In fact, Bernadette rattled the
seasoned commissioner. After trying in vain to trip her up for a good
hour and a half, and failing to find any inconsistency or falsehood in
her story, he lost his temper and resorted to bullying the child with
insults and vulgar insinuations. Bernadette remained remarkably calm
throughout.

By that time a minor riot was shaping up outside the door, for
Jacomet did not have the right to examine Bernadette without the
presence of her parents. The people of Lourdes found Francois
Soubirous and brought him to the house to protect his daughter,
thrusting him through the crowd and then through the door.

In the throes of his temper, Jacomet greeted Francois with the pre-
posterous accusation that Francois and his wife, Louise, were forcing
the girl to go to the grotto and to lie about the apparition. Jacomet
even claimed that Bernadette had accused them, and he threatened
Francois with jail. Francois gladly promised to keep Bernadette away
from the grotto and left with his daughter as quickly as he could. His
previous experience with Jacomet made him take the threat of jail
very seriously, even though Jacomet's cell probably would have been
better than the one he currently occupied!

Far from being frightened, Bernadette appeared highly amused by
the commissioner's antics. She is reported to have laughingly said,
"He was trembling. He had a tassel on his cap which kept going ting-
a-ling."

Another intriguing aspect emerges from the line of questioning in
Jacomet's notes. Even after six apparitions, Bernadette professed no
opinion regarding the identity of her new friend. The commissioner
asked her straightaway about her visions of the Blessed Virgin, and
she immediately and repeatedly denied that it was the Virgin. The only
thing she would affirm, in spite of his attempts to trip her up on every

angle, was that she had seen a little, young lady (petito damizela), reiterating the same descriptions of her clothing and appearance that she had given previously.

Jacomet continued to refer to the apparition as the Blessed Virgin throughout the interview, and each time he did, Bernadette corrected him. In this interrogation, we get a sense of the pressure of public consensus, even among those who sought to discredit the apparitions. Bernadette's contemporaries already had fixed ideas about who and what she should be seeing, and did not seem to let the details of her descriptions deter them.

MARIAN TRADITIONS IN THE PYRENEES

Throughout the Pyrenees and southern France, there is a long, perhaps even timeless tradition of Marian appearances. In the immediate area surrounding Lourdes, there were at least forty shrines dedicated to her, and most of them had been inspired by either previous apparitions, or by the mysterious finding of her ancient statues. The medieval pilgrimage roads that led the faithful into Spain and on to Santiago de Compostela ran right through the Bigorre region. Wherever the zealous pilgrims wandered, miracles followed, spilling over on both sides of the road. Many of the shrines in the area surrounding Lourdes eventually took on the function of mini-pilgrimage sites, serving those who couldn't undertake the full trek into Spain.

From the thirteenth century through the seventeenth century, in particular, comes evidence of local Marian apparitions that could be said to have set the "pattern" for the public perception of Bernadette's story. At the fountain in nearby Garaison, the Virgin appeared in the early sixteenth century to a twelve-year-old shepherdess named Angleze de Sagazon. There are distinct parallels between this story in the local lore and the details of Bernadette's experiences.[4] Like Bernadette, Angleze was also poor and uneducated, and only she could see and hear the Lady during her appearances. Just as at Lourdes, the Virgin requested that a chapel be built outside of town, at the site of the apparitions near the fountain. The chapel at Garaison became a popular pilgrimage site, and, like Bernadette, Angleze eventually retired to a convent.

In the nearby grottoes of Medous, a popular pilgrimage destination until at least the end of the eighteenth century, a shrine commemorated a much earlier apparition of the Virgin to a little shepherd girl named Liloye. The faithful can still, with a little imagination, make out the image of Virgin and child in the tangled rock formations hidden within the mysterious caves.[5]

The local shrine of Betharram has an intriguing history. According to the legend, young shepherds, out grazing their flocks, saw a mysterious light that looked like flames coming from between the rocks at the foot of the mountain. As they came closer to investigate, they found a marvelous statue of the Virgin hidden in the bushes. The locals decided to place the statue in a niche on a bridge over the river Gave, but after installing it there, come the morning, the statue was gone. It had fled back to its rocky home. They tried to move it again, this time securing the statue in a nearby church, but it refused to stay there as well. The image escaped and reappeared again where it had been found. Thus it was decided to build a chapel on the wilderness site, which soon became a popular pilgrimage center. It is said that Bernadette got her own rosary at Betharram.[6]

Another story from Betharram explains the origin of the site's name. A young girl had fallen into the Gave, and was in danger of drowning, when she prayed to the Virgin for help. Mary appeared on the bank of the river, holding out a flowering branch, which she used to pull the girl to safety; hence the name, Betharram, which means "beautiful branch" in the local Bernaise dialect. This name raises another interesting parallel, for in 1931, a series of approved Marian apparitions took place in a Belgian town called Beauraing. The Virgin repeatedly appeared to a group of children from the branches of a hawthorn tree. We will be examining these apparitions in detail in a later chapter, but it is worth mentioning here that the name Beauraing also means "beautiful branch" in their local dialect.

As Ruth Harris points out in her excellent book *Lourdes: Body and Spirit in the Secular Age,* in the Pyrenees, the Virgin had a particular affinity for both the hawthorn and the wild rose. Harris mentions twenty-eight shrines to the Virgin in the region surrounding Lourdes that involve either a hawthorn or wild rose.[7] Bernadette's aquero always appeared standing on the wild rose branches draped above the entrance to the grotto. These thorny plants played a role in the traditional medicine of the area, and were considered to have some unique healing virtues, but their special connection to the Virgin Mary and her miraculous statues may lead us much further back into pre-Christian traditions.

In the nearby town of Sarrance, due west of Lourdes, is a splendid and treasured Marian shrine. Legend has it that a beautiful bull suddenly began to appear in town each day, only to disappear at night. Everyone tried to catch him but it was impossible. No rope could hold him. One fellow decided to follow the bull at night, and it led him to a mysterious spring, deep in the woods. There, the bull bowed down and prayed to an image of the Virgin Mary, which stood on a stone at the spring's source. Word spread, and soon everyone wanted to worship at the miraculous statue. The bishop of the nearby town of Oloron came to see it, and decided to move the marvelous image to the cathedral, but come the morning, the statue was gone! Like the Marian image at Betharram, it had made its way miraculously back to the spring. That was where the statue wanted to be worshiped.

A shrine was built on the site and the statue stayed put. Meanwhile, the stone at the source of the spring, where the statue had originally been revealed, gained a special reputation for helping pregnant women. They would actually eat tiny pieces of the rock to ensure an easy delivery.[8]

This theme of cattle finding a miraculous image of Our Lady in the wild is very popular in the area around Lourdes. At the shrine of Notre-Dame de Bourisp, the Marian image was revealed when a shepherd followed a steer into the forest and found it licking the statue with its tongue. At Notre-Dame de Nestes, a calf had revealed the statue in a bush, necessitating the building of yet another wilderness shrine.[9]

This was the spiritual and psychological atmosphere in which Bernadette lived and learned, where a respectable Roman Catholic veneer overlaid thousands of years of Basque traditions. Inspired livestock and the worship of miraculous statues in the wild intertwined freely with a passionate devotion to the Mother of God. Her ancient images, possibly older than Christianity itself, were buried and forgotten, but not gone. Sleeping just below the surface, like the old beliefs that originally inspired them, these statues resurfaced unexpectedly, calling worshippers out of their towns and back to the wilderness, for this heavenly Mother did not want to be worshipped in the proper places, in churches or Christian sanctuaries; she wanted the faithful to come out to the mountains, to the caves and rivers, to springs and hawthorn bushes to pay her their proper respects. In return, she granted grace and healing, and the protection of a good mother goddess.[10]

BELIEFS OF THE BASQUES

In the Basque population of the Pyrenees, we have a unique link into the mindset of our most distant ancestors. There is reason to believe the Basques have occupied the Pyrenees region from the remotest antiquity, possibly even to the time of the Cro-Magnon cave painters. The inaccessibility of their mountain fastness kept them relatively isolated from the Indo-European influences that swept the rest of the continent. Consequently, the Basques have retained a unique language and a culture that, while not entirely untainted by foreign contact, still reveals roots reaching down into our most shadowy origins.

Furthermore, the Basques, with their extensive folklore and mythology, are relative latecomers to Roman Catholicism. Religious writers of the 1400s and 1500s continue to speak of the Basques as "gentiles" or "pagans." The widespread persistence of their ancient beliefs and practices provoked the full wrath of the Spanish Inquisition.[11] The brutal repression of centuries of witch hunts has left its mark, and clearly, some of the tradition that remains is highly adulterated and Christianized, but we can still trace religious and cultural influences extending far back into the Neolithic period, and perhaps beyond.

Basque beliefs are rooted in the landscape, in the rugged mountains, the waters, and the caves reaching deep into the earth. They held to that most primitive fundamentalism, the belief in the divinity of the masculine Sun and the feminine Moon. The terms "Ost" or "Eguzki" refer to the light of the Sun and their god of the firmament. This masculine force, similar to Zeus or Thor, ruled the day and the world of light, but the night belonged to Ilargia, the Moon. Ilargia ruled the hidden, dark side of nature, the underworld of the dead. The Basques were forever fascinated with her mysterious phases and cycles.[12]

However, the Basque people's deepest and most widespread devotion, long before the arrival of Christianity in the Pyrenees, centered on their female deity, the great goddess who lived in the caves. Her name, perhaps the ultimate irony, was Mari. Devotion to Mari spanned the entire Basque territory, and any respectable hilltop boasted a shrine to Mari, and a statue as well, but the caves remained her favorite habitation.

Within the vast lore and ritual dedicated to her worship, the image of Mari emerges, complex and glorious. She moved like a fireball from mountaintop to mountaintop, trailing wild storms from the subterranean caverns in her wake. She demanded honor and charity from men, punishing those who failed to keep their word or refused to help others. Oddly enough, tradition holds that Mari must only be addressed in the familiar pronoun, putting a unique twist on Bernadette's surprise at being addressed formally by her aquero. Mari commanded legions of fairy spirits, with varying titles in different locales: the Mairi, or Maide of the mountaintop cromlechs and stone circles, and the fey laminak, often spotted combing their hair in the caverns.[13]

This great and very ancient goddess spawned a vast body of tales and traditions, and the rituals of her devotees in the caves of the Pyrenees kept the Spanish Inquisition busy for years. One of her most vicious persecutors was Juan de Zumarraga, who, in 1528, assisted in the biggest Basque witch hunt. Zumarraga eventually moved on to Mexico, where, as bishop, he persecuted and destroyed the native Aztec culture and religion just as vigorously as he had brutalized his Basque brethren.

One of Mari's more popular minions is a creature known as Beigorri, a red-haired bull or calf. One of several cattle deities associated with her worship, Beigorri's chief function is to serve as the guardian of the houses, or shrines, of Mari. Seen in that light, the tales of a magical bovine unearthing a long-lost statue of a female divinity, which then refuses to be worshipped in a Christian sanctuary but instead draws her devotees back to congregate at her wilderness origins, starts to make a certain kind of sense. Perhaps, in these unique Marian traditions, which continue to spring up so freely, even after centuries of repression, we can trace both the reemergence of the Basque Mari, and her conflation, in the aftermath of the Inquisition, into the all-encompassing image of the Christian Mary.

BACK TO THE GROTTO

The morning after Bernadette's interrogation by Commissioner Jacomet, her parents firmly forbade her to go to the grotto. She was torn between obedience to her parents and the promise she had made to aquero. She stayed home during the dawn hours, when she would normally have made her trek to Massabielle, and later reported to school, where the sisters continued to treat her with contempt. A large crowd had gathered to see her at the grotto, but eventually dispersed.

It was during her lunchtime break that the inner compulsion became too intense, and she found herself heading down the path to the banks of the Gave. Her detour did not go unnoticed, for try as she might to be inconspicuous, poor Bernadette would never again have another moment of private life. The police began to follow her immediately, and another crowd quickly gathered at the grotto. Even after saying her rosary and bearing up under the taunts of police Sergeant D'Angla, aquero still did not appear. Bernadette was desolate as her aunt led her away to the mill to rest.

Stricken in conscience, Bernadette once again visited Fr. Pomian in the confessional. "They do not have the right to stop you," he told her. He was right. That same night, the local authorities conferred together and agreed that they had no legal grounds to prohibit her from visiting the grotto, and that doing so would only provoke resentment among the people. Constant surveillance certainly was in order, and they determined to watch the entire Soubirous family around the clock, but from that evening on, Bernadette was finally free to go to the grotto whenever she chose.

The following morning, Tuesday, February 23, Bernadette was back at the grotto by 5:30 a.m. Almost 150 people waited there to see her, and they were not disappointed. On the next morning, with almost four hundred in attendance, in addition to her usual routine, Bernadette fell to her face and kissed the ground after saying her rosary. She explained later to her aunt that aquero had asked her to do this as penance for sinners.

THE MIRACULOUS SPRING

On the morning of Thursday, February 25, Bernadette's behavior took a bizarre turn. People had been arriving from 2:00 a.m. on, for it was getting harder and harder to get a good spot at the grotto. Bernadette began her rosary and entered her trance state as usual, but then she began to crawl about toward the back of the grotto, kissing the ground as she went along. Her lips were moving as if in conversation, but the crowd could hear nothing. Then, still on her knees, she turned and began moving toward the Gave. The crowd dispersed to give her room. She stopped and reentered the grotto, going to the very back wall. She seemed to be looking for something and experiencing some confusion in finding it.

After more fumbling, she bent down and scooped up a handful of dripping mud from a depression at the back of the cave. Bringing it up toward her face, as if to drink it, she stopped just short of doing so, and dug around a bit more. Four times she brought handfuls of the filthy stuff to her face, finally tasting a bit of it on her fourth try and smearing her face as she did. The crowd was shocked, and murmured that she had gone mad.

Her supporters were even more dismayed when, dripping and dirty, Bernadette then crawled over to eat some leaves from a saxifrage plant growing along the fringe of the mud hole she had just dug. As Bernadette came up out of her trance and headed back into town, the crowds she left behind were outraged. Many who had believed and stood by her felt betrayed. Bewildered and angry, they bore the abuse of the scorners and curiosity seekers who now felt justified in their skepticism.

As strange as Bernadette's behavior seemed to observers, in her own words and from her own perspective, her actions have their own inner consistency. Bernadette explained that aquero told her to go and drink at the spring and to wash herself in it. This was when she left the grotto on her knees and headed for the Gave, for that was the only water she could see. But aquero beckoned her back into the grotto and directed her to look under a rock at the rear of the cave. She did find a little trickle in the mud there, and after some digging, was able to scoop out a muddy handful. She threw the mud aside three times because it was too dirty to drink, but did try to drink the fourth handful. Aquero also told her to eat the leaves of the plant. Her only explanation as to why was that it was done "for sinners."

Lourdes was frothing over with gossip after Bernadette's performance, but when some of the onlookers returned to the grotto that afternoon, they were surprised to see that the hole Bernadette had dug in her trance had grown. A stream of water was now gurgling out of it. They dug out the hole a bit more, as Bernadette had done, and the water flowed more fully and clearly than before.

Such was the origin of the famous healing waters of Lourdes. The mudhole Bernadette dug that day at the back of the grotto has since poured its water all around the world, and draws pilgrims by the millions every year to drink and bathe in it. The spring itself did not miraculously appear on that day. Locals familiar with the area were aware of its prior existence, but the source had been blocked up for some time by the rubble washed in from the Gave. Bernadette's entranced reactions to aquero's instructions lead me to believe that she probably had no knowledge of its presence. Once the area had been dug out more, and the floor of the grotto cleared, the spring actually flowed from the area in front of the grotto entrance; a fitting fountain for a fairy to launder her gleaming white gown.

While many in town continued to speculate upon the subject of the Soubirous girl's sanity, others rushed back to the grotto to dig about for themselves, carrying bottles of the spring water back with them. Meanwhile, the authorities intervened again. That night, Bernadette answered a summons from the Imperial prosecutor, Dutour. He had some questions for her.

ANOTHER INTERROGATION

The interview that took place in the prosecutor's house that night went much the same way as the interview with Commissioner

Jacomet. Dutour was convinced that Bernadette was lying before he even saw her, but the child's simple honesty again triumphed over his every attempt to trip her up. Like Jacomet before him, the exasperated Dutour resorted to bullying and coarse intimidation, and ordered Bernadette to keep away from the grotto. Bernadette's mother Louise broke down sobbing under the pressure.

Dutour had kept the two standing for two hours of intense interrogation. When he begrudgingly offered them a seat, Bernadette sidestepped his condescension, refusing the chair with, "No, I would soil it." She continued the interview sitting cross-legged on the floor, "like a tailor."

Where did this child find the poise, the character, and the courage to withstand the intimidation, the threats of prison, and worse? Later in life, while at the convent in Nevers, she told Sister Vincent Garros, "There was something in me that enabled me to rise above everything; I was tackled from all sides, but nothing mattered. I wasn't afraid." [14]

She left the imperial prosecutor's office laughing at Dutour, just as she had laughed at Jacomet. He had cut a comic figure, so flustered by her intransigence that he kept jabbing his pen at his inkstand and missing, while crossing out what he had written and making a mess of his notes.

The following morning, February 26, a crowd gathered around Bernadette's door as the family debated whether she should go to the grotto or not. Aunt Bernarde stepped in again, declaring, "If I were in Bernadette's place, I would go!"

When Bernadette arrived at the grotto, a crowd of nearly six hundred awaited her, but although she recited her rosary and performed her usual supplications, aquero did not appear. Heartbroken, she resorted to the mill, blaming herself. However, the next morning, aquero was back and the crowd was even larger.

On Sunday, February 28, 1,150 people were gathered around the grotto. The situation was potentially dangerous, for the crowd was wedged between the cliff and the river, an accident waiting to happen. The constabulary forces were about, but crowd control was difficult to enforce. After Mass, the Warden of Springs detained Bernadette and conducted her to yet another interrogation, this time with the examining magistrate, Judge Clement Ribes. He also ordered her to keep away from the grotto, but when Bernadette explained that she had promised to visit aquero for a fortnight, he had no legal grounds to prevent her.

A MEDICAL MIRACLE

It was on the following day, Monday, March 1, that the first of the many miracles attributed to the healing waters of the spring occurred. The water had been carried far and wide by the faithful, and rumors were beginning to spread about healings wrought by its power, but the first cure that was officially investigated by medical authorities and accepted by the Episcopal commission as evidence of the "work of God" took place on this wise.

A young mother named Catherine Latapie set out in the middle of the night for Lourdes, taking her two youngest children with her. She seems to have gone on impulse, for she was a full nine months pregnant, but desperate for help. She had fallen from a tree back in October of 1856, seriously injuring her right arm. The broken arm had mended, but two fingers of her right hand remained paralyzed and gnarled, making it painfully difficult to perform her spinning, knitting, and other household tasks.

She had arrived at the grotto at about 2:00 a.m. and stayed to witness the morning apparition. Afterward, climbing to the back of the grotto, she plunged her hand into the icy spring waters. As she did, she felt a wave of healing come over her. Her fingers were suddenly loosened and her hand made whole again. No sooner had she begun a prayer of thanksgiving than she was wracked by the onset of labor. Gathering her children together, she hurried them over the six kilometers back to their home. There she delivered a baby boy, not fifteen minutes after they crossed the threshold. The child was christened Jean-Baptiste, and grew up to become a priest. Both the healing of her hand, which was whole from that day forward, and her relatively effortless delivery were attributed to divine intervention.

WHAT AQUERO WANTS

The following day, March 2, there were almost 1,700 people gathered at the grotto to wait for Bernadette. As she came out of her ecstasy, she headed for the rectory, for aquero had made a special request that morning. In the tradition of the apparitions and miraculous statues that preceded her, she had told Bernadette to go to the priests and ask that a chapel be built on the spot, so the people could come in a procession. Having shared this news with the crowd around her, they rushed ahead of Bernadette to the rectory, already convinced that a grand procession was in store for the "big day," Thursday, marking the end of the fortnight of apparitions. This was probably not the best way to approach the clergy on this sensitive matter, and things got really awkward afterward.

Bernadette's meeting with the priests later that day did not go well. The parish priest, Dean Peyramale, was not about to authorize any processions, particularly while the local gendarmerie was only just sorting out the problems presented by the crowds, and he was certainly not inclined to entertain any requests from some mysterious apparition who refused to identify herself. Whereas Bernadette stood firm and confident before the worldly authorities, the wrath of the parish priest made her feel confused and timid, shrinking her to the size of "two grains of birdseed."

Peyramale was angry that day, and he railed at Bernadette. Striding up and down, he accused her of manipulating the crowds and the circumstances for her own ends. He was even less impressed with the two aunts who accompanied her to this ill-fated meeting, for he had driven them both out of the Children of Mary years ago for getting pregnant before marriage. After assaulting them with an unpleasant tirade, he ordered them out. As they were leaving, Bernadette realized she had been so confused by his reaction to the procession that she had completely forgotten to relay aquero's request for a chapel. Now she would have to go back and face him again.

Dominiquette Cazenave, the sister of the station-master, agreed to go with her and booked another appointment with the priests for 7:00 that evening. She pleaded with Peyramale to go easy on the child this time. When the two arrived, Bernadette promptly delivered aquero's request for a chapel, and once again, the priests attacked, like dogs on a wounded deer. Peyramale insisted that aquero make that wild rose bush bloom before he would believe in her, and ordered Bernadette to deliver his counter-demands to her. The other priests questioned why aquero hesitated so long to identify herself. They all wanted to know who she would claim to be. As the tone of the interrogation escalated, Dominiquette took Bernadette and left. Once outside the rectory, Bernadette was greatly relieved, for she had at least completed her commission, and done what aquero had asked.

The next morning, March 3, over three thousand people were waiting at the grotto. When Bernadette first arrived among the throng, aquero failed to appear. Bernadette was deeply grieved and retired to the mill to escape the crowds, which she blamed for the disappointment. Her cousin, Andre Sajoux, convinced her to go home and try again later, which she then did. Returning to Massabielle around 9:00 a.m., she found aquero waiting for her and all her tears were soon forgotten.

That afternoon found Bernadette knocking on the rectory door. She happily informed the curé that aquero still wanted her chapel. When Peyramale demanded again to know aquero's real name, Bernadette told him that she had asked her name, in obedience to him, and had also asked about making the rosebush bloom, but aquero had only smiled in reply.

As Thursday, March 4, approached, the whole region was caught up in the preparations for the "big day." While Bernadette had never made any promises or projections, the people expected some grand miracle to occur. The police commissioner took great pains to inspect the grotto throughout the night to ensure there would be no trickery or special effects. Dozens of police and military personnel were on hand, both in town and at the grotto, to manage the expected crowds and to prevent accidents on the treacherous footpaths over the Gave.

When Bernadette arrived on the scene, shortly after 7:00 a.m., the size of the crowd ranged from an estimated eight thousand to twenty thousand. Aquero appeared as Bernadette began the second decade of her rosary. It was a fairly long apparition, lasting about forty-five minutes, and Bernadette spent some time inside the grotto in silent conversation with aquero. Saying another rosary outside the grotto, Bernadette blew out her candle and headed back to town, leaving the silenced crowd behind. There was no miracle, no roses, no naming of names; it was just like any other apparition that preceded it, and indeed, Bernadette had promised nothing more. It was the popular imagination that had been overrun with wild ideas about miracles.

And so it ended. The fourteen days of apparitions were done and the disappointed crowd dwindled away. The press made much ado about the nothing in their reports, scoffing at the people's deflated expectations. But Bernadette was free; she had kept her promise to aquero, visiting the grotto every day and faithfully delivering her requests to the priests. She could return to school and her home; except that her home was now overrun with strangers who sought her out constantly, carrying on as only the frenzied faithful can. Time and time again, Bernadette had to remind these importunate seekers that she wasn't a priest, and yet the crowds still pressed her to bless their rosaries, their children, and to touch and heal them.

Naturally, there were those who sought to profit from all the excitement, and those who accused the Soubirous clan of similar motives. Regardless of how desperately poor and starving Bernadette's people were, there appears to be no evidence that they ever tried to use the child for gain. Bernadette herself was as incorruptible in life as in the grave, adamantly refusing every coin that was pressed upon her. The local authorities even tried to set her up in a string of "sting operations," but she never took the bait.

And so the fifteen days of apparitions came to an end. While certainly entertaining, they had proven a big disappointment overall. There had been no dramatic miracles at the grotto, the lady had never shown herself, the rosebush never bloomed. There was no great revelation, other than the spring, and while there were certainly rumors of miracle cures, the medical evidence was not yet forthcoming. Oddly enough, the parish priest, Dean Peyramale, who had been so hard on Bernadette, had done an about-face on the healings, becoming an enthusiastic miracle hunter. He hastened to champion some rather dubious cures that later cost him credibility.

As the talk of miracle cures increased, Bernadette testified during yet another interrogation on March 18 that she did not believe she had the power to cure anyone. Meanwhile, the people kept coming to the grotto, littering the area with the candles and votive items they left behind. But the apparitions were not over yet for Bernadette.

THE IMMACULATE CONCEPTION

In the early morning hours of March 25, the feast of the Annunciation, Bernadette awoke with a compelling urge to go to the grotto. When she arrived, about 5:00 a.m., and began saying her rosary, aquero appeared to her. This time, Bernadette pressed her point, asking aquero four separate times to reveal her identity. Finally, after the fourth request, it happened. Aquero dropped her hands down to her sides, palms forward, fingers extended, assuming for a brief instant the pose of the Virgin of the Miraculous Medal with the parti-colored graces streaming from her fingers. Bringing her hands back up to her accustomed pose, prayerfully poised over her breast, she then uttered the words that would ensure her emphatic acceptance by the Roman Catholic authorities: *"Que soy era Immaculada Councepciou,"* or "I am the Immaculate Conception."

Dean Peyramale was thunderstruck when Bernadette delivered these words to him at the rectory. She had rushed directly from the grotto, repeating the strange phrase over and over to herself so she wouldn't forget. "A woman cannot have that name!" he roared. Once again, the parish priest lost his temper with poor Bernadette and sent her away.

But Peyramale's enthusiasm for the apparitions in his parish had suddenly been lit with a brand new flame. The Immaculate Conception? Finally, the apparition was speaking his language. This announcement changed everything, elevating aquero above the dim mists of peasant superstition, and instantly transforming her into a Godsend; a miraculous justification of a new and troublesome church dogma.

The Immaculate Conception was officially promulgated as church dogma in 1854 by Pope Pius IX. While only recently formalized, it had a long history, representing the culmination of centuries of debate as the Roman Church struggled to rationalize its instinctive devotion to the Mother of God. After absorbing so many of the traditions, rituals, and imagery of pre-Christian goddess worship into their impassioned deification of the Virgin Mother of Christ, the Church was left with some thorny theological issues. Wrestling with this innate need to worship God as mother within such a distinctly patriarchal and male-dominated system required genuine mental gymnastics.

You have to catch the train of Roman Catholic theology at the first station; otherwise, you'll never get aboard. There are certain first principles that must be accepted, without which, the rest makes no sense. The doctrine of original sin is one such first principle. In summary, it teaches that we are all born tainted by the fall, unwittingly separated from God and His grace, and in thrall to the lord of this world. Adam and Eve are to blame for this sad state of affairs, for according to scripture, it was they who succumbed to the original temptation. However, after describing the circumstances of the fall, Genesis 3:15 contains this cryptic prophecy, in the words of God addressed to the accursed serpent:

> . . . I will put enmity between thee and the woman, and between thy seed and her seed; they shall bruise thy head and thou shalt bruise their heel.

An eventual redemption seems almost implicit within the fall itself.

In order to be fit to carry God incarnate within her, theologians determined that Mary had to be free from any taint of original sin, even from the very moment of her conception—not like the rest of you women! Mary was the antithesis of Eve; even a new Eve, never knowing the separation from God's love that has haunted us since the fall. She was fully human, and yet the first and highest among all mankind, chosen and specially consecrated before she came into being for this extraordinary task of bringing God into the world.

The Immaculate Conception is a truly lovely idea, and lends itself to the most exalted and poetic interpretations. Still, I can't help but wonder, what if God decided He wanted to be born of a perfectly awful woman instead; some lying, thieving prostitute, for instance? Wouldn't that be even more miraculous and Godlike, transforming the basest elements into the purest good? What would creative theologians make of that?

Even though the doctrine of the Immaculate Conception is a fairly recent development in church dogma, we can actually trace its main tenets back to some of the earliest sources. The apocryphal Gospel of the Birth of Mary, of unknown authorship but of a certain antiquity, describes the conception of the Virgin Mary in terms that clearly presage the doctrine of the Immaculate Conception. This gospel figures into the works of St. Jerome in the fourth century, so it is at least that old.

In this version of the story, Mary's father, the Levite Joachim, is reproached by the High Priest for his wife's barrenness. He retreats to the wilderness in despair, where he is blessed with a visit from an angel. The angel tells Joachim that, like Abraham and Sarah before them, his wife's womb has been closed all these years that the Lord may be glorified in its miraculous opening.

According to Chapter II, verse 9:

> . . . Anna, your wife, shall bring you a daughter, and you shall call her name Mary.

Verse 10 continues:

> She shall, according to your vow, be devoted to the Lord from her infancy, and be filled with the Holy Ghost from her mother's womb. She shall neither eat nor drink anything which is unclean, nor shall her conversation be without among the common people, but in the temple of the Lord; that so she may not fall under any slander or suspicion of what is bad.

Afterward, the angel appears to Joachim's wife, Anna, bearing a similar message. In chapter III, verse 2, the angel says:

> . . . a daughter will be born unto you who shall be called Mary, and shall be blessed above all women.

Verse 3 continues:

> She shall be, immediately upon her birth, full of the grace of the Lord ... and being devoted to the service of the Lord, shall not depart from the temple, till she arrives to years of discretion.

Verses 4 and 5 continue:

> In a word, she shall there serve the Lord night and day, in fasting and prayer, shall abstain from every unclean thing and never know any man; But being an unparalleled instance without any pollution or defilement . . . [15]

It would seem from this text that by the fourth century, this rather Nazarite idea that Mary had been especially consecrated and pure, even before her birth, already had a strong grasp on the Christian

imagination. In the very early apocryphal gospel, the Protoevange-
lion, commonly attributed to the apostle James, the brother of Jesus,
and the first bishop of the Christians in Jerusalem, we find this
charming tale from Mary's infancy in chapter 6, verses 1–3:

> And the child increased in strength every day, so that when she
> was nine months old, her mother put her upon the ground to try
> if she could stand; and when she had walked nine steps, she
> came again to her mother's lap. Then her mother caught her up,
> and said, "As the Lord my God liveth, thou shalt not walk again
> on this earth till I bring thee into the temple of the Lord."
> Accordingly, she made her chamber a holy place, and suffered
> nothing uncommon or unclean to come near her . . . [16]

This obsessive emphasis on the purity of the Virgin Mary is as much
a part of the proverbial "Age of Pisces'" as the message of the Christ
himself; that is, if you accept the idea that the precession of the
equinoxes (introduced in chapter 2) is linked to the evolution of religious ideas. The revelation of the suffering, sacrificial Christ, the Pis-
cean IXTHUS and his fishers of men, forever turning the other cheek
and forgiving seventy-times-seven times, has always been accompanied and counterbalanced by the puritanical and nitpicking tendencies of the sign Virgo. Wherever you find the disciples of the Christ,
abandoning their egos in martyrdom and agape, you also encounter
their fanatical devotion to chastity.

The ideal of virginity was one of the chief distinguishing features
of early Christianity, setting Christians apart from their pagan and
Jewish neighbors. This was a radical concept in the days before birth
control. Foregoing marriage and sex not only demanded terrible sacrifice and self-control, it also liberated Christians from the endless
duties of the householder and parent, freeing them to seek and serve
the kingdom of God. The presence of so many self-proclaimed virgins within the early church led to the development and regulation of
the religious orders, which to this day are peopled with the modern
virgins of the church.

But is the doctrine of the Immaculate Conception true? Is it even necessary? I'm certainly not fit to judge, but it does shed a beautiful light. I find it uplifting that men should even rouse themselves to think such things. The case could be made that the doctrine does represent an evolution, even a revolution, in the definition of female divinity, one that is perfectly in keeping with, if not impelled and inspired by, the very impetus of the age. Whatever its metaphysical merits, it certainly represented a turning point in the declining fortunes of the nineteenth-century Roman Catholic Church.

So when little Bernadette stumbled over these strange words as she delivered her message on the rectory doorstep, she could hardly have imagined their implications on the institutional church. To the common people who worshipped at the grotto, aquero had merely identified herself with one of the many popular titles of the Virgin Mary. Most of them had assumed she was their heavenly Mother all along. But for servants of the institution of the Church of Rome, like Dean Peyramale, her choice of words sounded more like a heavenly justification of some recent and rather controversial papal decisions.

The political subtext underlying the proclamation of the doctrine of the Immaculate Conception was there for anyone who had an eye to see. Once the single, most dominant force in European society, the Church had come down in the world; a long way down. The authority of the Church had been undermined by enemies on all sides, but the scourge of "modernism" was chief among the papal plagues. Ideas like original sin and redemption were losing ground against the onslaught of nineteenth-century materialism and the rampant secularization of society.

In 1854, Pius IX had proclaimed the doctrine of the Immaculate Conception solely on his authority as pope; alone and acting without the cooperation of the bishops of the world. This was deliberate on his part, and probably undertaken to expand and enforce papal authority. In fact, his actions set the tone for the ensuing declaration of papal infallibility in 1870.[17]

The pope was not without his critics. They couldn't necessarily contend with the doctrine itself, for the feast of the Immaculate Conception was actually quite popular, especially since the success of St. Catherine Laboure's Miraculous Medal. It was already accepted and enthusiastically celebrated in communities throughout the world. What rankled within the ranks was the high-handed manner in which the dogma had been proclaimed. The pope seemed to be picking exactly the wrong time to propagate such a sentimental dogma; one that could only widen the growing divide between the Church and modern society, between faith and rationality, and between Catholics and Protestants. It seemed reckless to flaunt his authority at a time when that authority had become so tenuous. And now, Bernadette's aquero had seemingly offered the pope the ultimate justification for his actions. Dean Peyramale began corresponding feverishly.

It was this identification of Bernadette's aquero with the Immaculate Conception that made all the difference. It brought the Roman Catholic Church's utmost attention to bear on the apparitions at Lourdes. With the speedy approval of the apparitions by the Episcopal Commission of Inquiry in 1862, the grotto under Massabielle was miraculously transformed from yet another local, Marian shrine into the busiest and most important Catholic pilgrimage site in the world. Popular devotion to the Virgin Mary saved the institutional church in nineteenth-century Europe. The enormous success of Lourdes, following close upon the success of the Miraculous Medal, inspired a new wave of Marian Catholicism that proved to be an effective antidote to the skeptical materialism of the modern world.

THE SIGNS OF THE TIMES

Today, as millions of pilgrims regularly pour in and out of Lourdes, it is a Lourdes that St. Bernadette would hardly recognize. While there is no mistaking the spiritual aura of the place, its crass commercialism is equally unavoidable. That is the price you pay for success I suppose, but now that we are hovering about the realms of material success, crass commercialism, and the institutional church, this might be a good point to return to the here-to-fore suspended subject of the sign Capricorn.

Saturn's sign is conspicuous not only in Bernadette's birth chart, but also in the chart for the beginning of the apparitions at Lourdes.

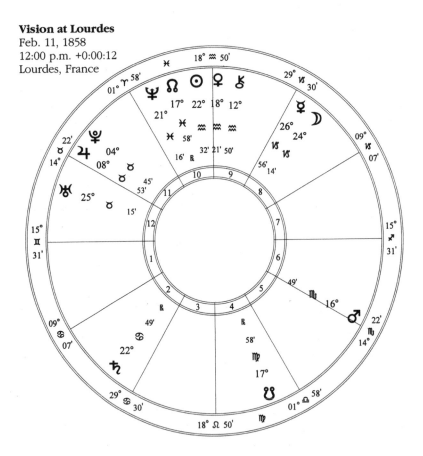

Vision at Lourdes
Feb. 11, 1858
12:00 p.m. +0:00:12
Lourdes, France

Vision at Lourdes. Moon ☽ and Mercury ☿ in Capricorn ♑ opposite Saturn ♄ in Cancer ♋; Venus ♀ in Aquarius ♒ on the Midheaven.

An earth sign and prone to both deep insecurity and vaulting ambition, Capricorn builds, seeking validation in structure and achievement. Capricorn represents worldliness and the powers that be, expressing both the sense of adult responsibility and the will to control that drives people to seek positions of authority in the first place.

In this chart, set for the ringing of the Angelus bells at noon on February 11, 1858, the beginning of the Lourdes phenomena, we find an unusual link between the Moon's sign, Cancer, and its opposite sign, Capricorn. The Moon is conjunct Mercury in Capricorn, and both oppose Saturn in Cancer. This opposition spans the third decan, or the latter third of the Cancer-Capricorn axis. That same area was also highlighted by planetary opposition in the chart for the Virgin's appearance to St. Catherine Laboure on the Rue du Bac, linking these two events together in the influence they would both have on modern Marian devotion, on the doctrine of the Immaculate Conception, and its impact on the institutional church. This same Cancer-Capricorn area was again highlighted by planetary oppositions in the chart for the 1871 apparition at Pontmain, France, which is included in a later chapter.

With such an emphasis on Saturn and Capricorn in the chart for its inception, the Lourdes story is not exactly one of maternal solicitude. There wasn't anything particularly motherly about aquero, but there is something decidedly institutional about Lourdes. Once aquero became the Immaculate Conception, Lourdes was big business. By the time Bernadette was safely stowed away in her convent, Lourdes belonged to the world.

Both the parish and the diocese undertook grand building plans that totally transformed the wild, pagan ambiance of Massabielle into the very image of the established church. But even the oppressive and occasionally tasteless architecture could not deter the thousands of pilgrims pouring in. The healing waters of Lourdes were a powerful magnet, drawing people from all over, rich and poor, laymen and

Inner Wheel: Vision at Lourdes   Outer Wheel: Bernadette Soubirous
Feb. 11, 1858 NS   Jan. 7, 1844 NS
12:00 p.m. +0:00:12   2:00 p.m. +0:00:12
Lourdes, France   Lourdes, France

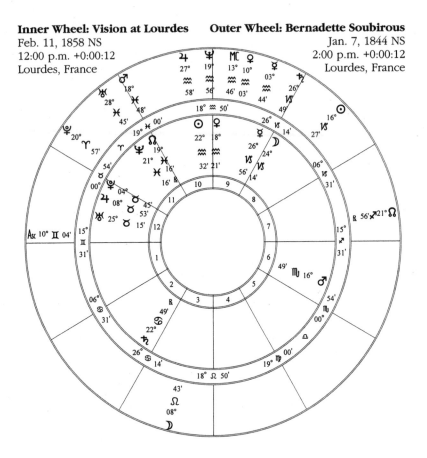

Inner wheel: vision at Lourdes; outer wheel: Bernadette Soubirous.
Concentration of planets in Aquarius ♒ at the Midheaven;
transiting Saturn ♄ in Cancer ♋ opposite transiting Moon ☽
and Mercury ☿ in Capricorn ♑, which is conjunct
Bernadette's natal Saturn ♄.

clergy, peasants and nobility alike. They shared together in the rituals
of caring for the sick and dying; the bathing, carrying, and countless
acts of charity and brotherly love. Never before in Christendom had
there been such a thing; these massive gatherings of souls, united in
prayer around the pools of healing waters at the shrine. I cannot
think of a finer illustration of the humanitarian principles of Aquarius,
the Water Bearer, in action.

It is the sign of the Water Bearer that dominates the Midheaven in both the birth chart for Bernadette and in the chart of the first apparition, and Aquarius is well-tenanted with planets in both cases. The apparition chart boasts the Sun, Venus, and Chiron on its Aquarius Midheaven, while Venus, Neptune, Mercury, and Jupiter in Aquarius are perched on the Midheaven in the birth chart for Bernadette.

Both charts feature an angular Venus in Aquarius closely conjunct the Midheaven. Venus is the other starry goddess of the solar system and her attributes reflect the qualities of her mythological namesake. Whereas the Moon, as heavenly mother, is maternal and protective, Venus, the goddess of beauty and love, is charming, graceful, friendly, and fun—like Bernadette's aquero. Aquero was tiny and delightful, and about the same age as Bernadette—more like a magical friend than a parental figure. She was a beautiful water bearer, indeed, and the beauty and grace of Bernadette in her ecstasies helped to popularize the apparitions.

It's not that the Moon isn't influential in the apparition chart. It's in Bernadette's sign, Capricorn, and with Mercury, it is tightly conjunct Bernadette's natal Saturn in Capricorn; a conjunction further emphasized by the opposition to transiting Saturn in Cancer. This alignment says a lot. Not only are the Moon and Saturn in opposition in the apparition chart, they are both in each other's signs. The Moon rules Cancer, and Saturn rules Capricorn. This type of arrangement is known as *mutual reception,* for each planet is "receiving" the other. This links the two influences more closely together and further facilitates the exchange of energy between the two.

But there's more—any planet in the sign opposite its rulership is a long way from home. It is considered to be in detriment, for it can be detrimental to its normal functioning to be in a sign of such opposite qualities and character. The Moon is in detriment in Capricorn, and Saturn is in detriment in Cancer. So the Moon and Saturn in the apparition chart are in (1) opposition, (2) mutual reception, and (3) detriment, all at the same time. This is an emphatic astrological emphasis on the Cancer-Capricorn polarity, and on their rulers, the Moon and Saturn, but it is also a somewhat distorted emphasis, developing the more problematic aspects and issues of these signs.

That difficult Saturn influence is evident in the pressure and responsibility laid upon Bernadette, and the surprising maturity she showed in facing up to the challenges of her mission. Aquero never promised Bernadette peace and protection. Her public life (Capricorn) destroyed her private life (Cancer), cutting her family and roots (Cancer) right out from under her. When she did try to return to her home, she found little comfort there, for it was overrun with pushy strangers and the poor child never had another moment she could call her own.

In the wake of all the embarrassment Melanie and Maxim had caused the Church after their vision at La Salette, it was thought to be in the best interest of both Bernadette and Lourdes that Bernadette retreat to the protection of a convent, but doing so severed the last of her family ties. Through it all, Bernadette was constant. A real Capricorn's Capricorn, she demonstrated genuine character and integrity, forsaking the world for the ultimate prize.

In packaging the apparitions for public consumption, the ambitions of the present (Capricorn) distorted the history of the past (Cancer), especially where the hard facts conflicted with sentimental imagination, or failed to serve the needs of the institutional authorities. The ancient traditions that were bound up within the image of aquero, linking the faithful back into the old ways of their ancestors, were once again repressed, denying the people access to their rightful spiritual heritage.

But these alignments also augured success: worldly success, material success, great buildings, impressive structures, fame, and renown. The Church prospered, public worship prospered, business and civil authority prospered, and Lourdes prospered, going from fairy tale to success story in seemingly no time at all, as each passing year brought more and more people in procession to the grotto, just as aquero had wanted.

The underlying Cancer-Capricorn influence is unmistakable, but the most popular and obvious impact of Lourdes is symbolized by the planets clustered about the Midheaven in both charts, where the Water Bearer pours out his libations on a thirsty world. The holy water of Lourdes is both its biggest attraction and most popular export. Who hasn't been moved by the dramatic pictures of rows and rows of crutches, left beside the spring in testimony to healing? The sick and desperate, the hale and hearty, the faithful and the merely hopeful, stream in from all corners of the earth to drink and bathe in aquero's magical fountains beside her grotto home.

The association of the sign Aquarius with the outpouring of the gift of living waters seems so obvious, but there is more to the symbolism of this sign. Like Capricorn, Aquarius is also a social sign, seeking itself through friends and like-minded associates. It is not a practical earth sign like Capricorn, and not, despite its name, a feeling water sign like Cancer. Aquarius is an air sign, intellectual and communicative, preferring the abstractions of ideas and ideologies, and the more detached loyalties of friendship. Aquarius likes nothing better than to join together with other idealistic individuals in the pursuit of a common goal or interest; the more progressive and outré, the better, and the more, the merrier. Aquarius actually enjoys being another face in the crowd, finding validation in popularity and safety in numbers, while strongly identifying with its own special interest group.

The pilgrimage groups that began to converge upon Lourdes in the years following the apparitions were devoted, not only to the Church and our Lady, but to a range of social and political causes that grew out of the instability of the times, including the ideals of a Catholic state, the restoration of the Bourbon monarchy, and the political agenda of the Assumptionist order in particular. It is hardly an exaggeration to say that, for that time, these gatherings represented the largest popular massing of people in Europe, if not in the world. That stellium of Aquarian planets in both charts continues to operate to this day, as more and more pilgrims come in procession every year, sharing together their hopes and dreams by the streams of living waters.

CONCLUSIONS

As we approach a tentative conclusion to this never-ending story, I propose that in following this course of events, we are actually tracing very ancient and indigenous religious habits, ones that embody such instinctive and deep-seated devotion that they are recycled from age to age and yet still remain vital and meaningful. The caves of the Pyrenees have hosted female deities and mother goddesses, in communion with their chosen visionaries, since long before the arrival of Christianity, and perhaps even before the beginning of history. Each generation experiences similar phenomena and exhibits similar responses. The differences lie in the meanings inferred; the definitions, context, and interpretation. At Lourdes, these larger historical parallels have been repressed, and important evidence was ignored to make the story fit within the limited, and distinctly non-Catholic vision of the Roman Church. It remains for us, blessed with unprecedented freedom of thought and information, to retrace the lost threads and piece the puzzle back together.

While I'm certainly not fit to judge what aquero meant when she said she was the Immaculate Conception, one thing is for sure: if she wanted a chapel to be built, and wanted the people to come in processions, and to bathe in and drink the spring waters, she said the one thing that would most readily assure it would all come to pass. Whoever or whatever she was, aquero wasn't stupid.

The belief in the healing powers of rushing spring waters seems to have been part of our spiritual heritage for so long that perhaps we can only hope to trace its origins back to somewhere deep within our own history. We still come, in greater numbers than ever before, to worship and purify ourselves by the riverside, where a heavenly goddess returns to rereveal an ancient source of salvation. In the older forms of devotion that reemerged at the apparition sites, the Roman Catholic Church tapped into the people's unconscious longing to worship the feminine aspects of God, ensuring its own survival into the twentieth century. How ironic, that the church that once prospered by destroying the pagan goddess cults should come, in time, to thrive on their remains.

The message of Lourdes is timeless, at once ancient and modern. It is a message of community, of miracles we can share. It is a message of hope, even against hope, when all else has failed, when the combined powers of materialism and science must part ways to clear a path for faith. It is also a testament, among the thronging crowds, to the power of one; one little girl, who couldn't lie, and wouldn't be swayed from her vision. It is that innocence, that honesty, that purity of purpose, springing from contact with genuine divinity, that still captures the imagination and thrills the heart.

Endnotes

1. Lois Rodden, *Profiles of Women* (Tempe, AZ: AFA, 1988), 288. "Luc de Marre," from Birth Record Given by Choisnard in "Language Astral" (1922), 218.

2. Ruth Harris, *Lourdes: Body and Spirit in the Secular Age* (New York: Viking/Penguin, 1999), 77–78.

3. Fr. Rene Laurentin, *Bernadette of Lourdes* (Minneapolis: Winston Press, 1979), 112–114; and Margaret Gray Blanton, *The Miracle of Bernadette* (Englewood Cliffs, NJ: Prentice-Hall, 1958), 209–210.
   My version of the storyline of Bernadette's apparitions draws upon and synthesizes the accounts in the above sources, and other relevant texts cited within these notes and in the bibliography.

4. Harris, *Lourdes,* 39–42.

5. www.campan-pyrenees.com/medous/eng/navia.htm (accessed May, 2003).

6. www.geocities.com/~betharram and www.betharram.org (accessed May, 2003).

7. Harris, *Lourdes,* 68.

8. Harris, *Lourdes,* 36–37, and www.concentric.net/~Bluesox/day28.html (accessed July 3, 2002; site now discontinued).

9. Harris, *Lourdes,* 37–38, and Blanton, T*he Miracle of Bernadette,* 45–46.

10. Pamela Berger elaborates on this point in *The Goddess Obscured* (Boston: Beacon Press, 1985), 37. In Gaul, Christian leaders routinely destroyed statues of goddesses as part of their missionary duty. "During the era of conversion, from the fourth through the eighth centuries, some rural pagans no doubt hid their statues, perhaps even buried them. Legends concerning the finding of statues of stately females, immediately christened the Virgin, abound throughout Europe. The sites of the discoveries have often been what archaeologists now know to be ancient mother goddess shrines."

11. Max Dashu, "Secret History of the Witches, Xorguinas Y Celestinas," www.suppressedhistories.net/secret_history/xorguinas.html (accessed July 3, 2002; site now discontinued).

12. Angel Murua, "Folklore and Traditions, The Basque Country: Come and then Pass the Word," www.buber.net/Basque/Folklore/folk1.html.

13. Michael Everson, "Tenacity in Religion, Myth and Folklore: The Neolithic Goddess of Old Europe Preserved in a Non-Indo-European Setting," *The Journal of Indo-European Studies* 17, nos. 3–4 (Fall/Winter 1989), 277–95.

14. Andre Ravier, *Bernadette* (London: Collins, 1979), 21.

15. *The Lost Books of the Bible and The Forgotten Books of Eden* (World Bible Publishers, 1926), 19.

16. Ibid., 16.

17. Charles E. Sheedy, C. S. C., *Immaculate Conception* (Danbury, CT: Encyclopedia Americana).

Five

FATIMA AND THE MIRACLE OF THE SUN

THE GUARDIAN ANGEL OF PORTUGAL?

By the time Lucia dos Santos and her young cousins, Francisco and Jacinta Marto, received their first visit from the Virgin Mary in May of 1917, they were already experienced visionaries. While tending her family's flock two years earlier, Lucia and three other girls had seen a strange, white figure floating in the air above the trees on the northern slope of the hill they called Cabeco. In her memoirs, written in 1937, Lucia described it as resembling "a statue made of snow," or a "person wrapped up in a sheet."[1]

The girls saw this same specter on three separate occasions. In fact, whenever they returned to the same place, even after deliberately avoiding it for a while, they saw the same thing. Lucia claims that she told no one about it, but the other girls were not so reticent. As gossip spread about town, Lucia struggled with the insinuations and contempt she received from her family and neighbors. Normally an affable child, she could turn stubbornly sullen under pressure.

In the following year, 1916, little Francisco and Jacinta began to herd their family's sheep with Lucia. The three had been close for years, and Jacinta and Francisco had missed Lucia's companionship so much when she left with the flock every morning that they begged their parents, Olympia and Manuel, to let them be shepherds too. They were much too young, but after a year of begging, their parents finally relented. Six-year-old Jacinta and eight-year-old Francisco met cousin Lucia and her flock every morning at the watering hole. They avoided the other shepherds for the most part and kept to themselves on their families' lands.

One day, they stopped at the foot of the eastern slope of the same hill, Cabeco. A misty rain drove them into a little hollow among the rocks. As they were playing, they heard a strong wind shake the trees. Coming toward them, over the treetops, was the same strange, white figure. This time, Lucia was able to make out its features. It looked like a young man; a teenager who was about fifteen years old. He was snowy white and brilliantly translucent, shining like a crystal suffused with sunlight.

He landed on the ground in front of them and introduced himself as "the Angel of Peace." He then instructed the children to pray with him. He taught them a special prayer, which he made them repeat three times: "My God, I believe, I adore, I hope, and I love You! I ask pardon of You for those who do not believe, do not adore, do not hope, and do not love You."

From then on, according to Lucia's memoirs, the three children devoted more of their time to praying as he had taught them. They also agreed, at Lucia's insistence, to keep the matter entirely to themselves.

Several months passed before the children saw the angel again. It was on a sweltering summer afternoon, when they were playing at the well at the bottom of Lucia's garden. Suddenly, the Angel appeared, admonishing them to pray even more. According to Lucia's memoirs, written twenty years later, the Angel told the children that Mary and Jesus had special designs on them and that they should offer prayers and sacrifices constantly.[2]

The idea of offering up their own sufferings as a sacrifice to speed the salvation of sinners was firmly pressed upon the children by the Angel. He told them to make a sacrifice of everything they could, and to offer it up to God as reparation for the sins by which He is offended, and for the conversion of sinners.

Six-year-old Jacinta particularly took this practice to heart, offering up constant prayers and her every childish disappointment as a karmic deterrent to the divine justice that would otherwise descend upon the unjust.

This very Christian concept of a pure soul taking on the moral burdens of others is epitomized in St. Paul's message that Christ died to save sinners; the spotless lamb and only Son of God, sacrificed to save a fallen race. However, throughout Roman Catholicism, we frequently encounter other "victim souls" who bear the burdens of nameless sinners in their innocent sufferings. While this type of mysticism is not really acknowledged in Protestant Christianity, the idea is also fairly common in Hinduism,[3] where gurus can take on the suffering arising from the karmic complexes of their students in order to speed their development. Even St. Bernadette was urged by her aquero to kiss the ground and to humble herself for the sake of sinners. The idea seems to be that there is a great moral debt to be paid, and no matter who ran up the charges on the karmic credit card, anyone with some grace to spare can send in a payment.

Returning to that well at the bottom of the garden, in her later memoirs Lucia reported that during his second visit the Angel identified himself to the children as the Guardian Angel of Portugal. He appeared to them the third time, many months later, again on the slopes of Cabeco. This time he offered the children Holy Communion, admonishing them again to make reparations to God for the crimes of ungrateful men, and to pray for the conversion of sinners. Lucia vividly describes a sacred Host dripping with blood.

Bear in mind that the year was 1916, and the place was the western edge of a continent engulfed in bloodshed and mayhem. While Lucia and her little cousins entertained an angel, millions of young lives were being thrown away in meaningless sacrifice as the war of attrition raged at Verdun and the Somme. It would take a lot of prayer to ever find sufficient forgiveness.

So by the time the children received their first visit from the Virgin Mary, on May 13, 1917, they were no ordinary children and it was no ordinary time. And the Cova de Iria, where the Virgin appeared, was no ordinary place.

IRIA, GODMOTHER OF THE RIBATEJO

The Cova de Iria, or cove of Irene, is a hollow, wooded depression among the hills of Fatima, probably the remains of an extinct volcano. Lucia's father, Antonio Abobora, owned the land at the time. While the origins of the name are obscure, it was most likely named for Santa Iria, and tradition holds that she, or someone like her, once had a hermitage there. Iria is the godmother and patron saint of the Ribatejo, the local region where the river Tagus (Tejo) and the confluence of its tributaries dominate both the landscape and the imagination.

One of the most unique and often overlooked areas of Europe, the wealth of traditions expressed in the customs and folklore of the Ribatejo reveals a rich blend of cultural and historical influences. In the centuries before Christ, these lands were Ibero-Celtic strongholds, peopled with the sort of Celts who sailed with the bard Amergin across the waves to settle in Ireland. The Roman conquest followed, and Christianity in its wake, sparking a cultural revival that was all too soon smothered in dark ages after waves of successive "barbarian" invasions by Vandals, Visigoths, and Sueves. The eighth century brought the Muslims and the occupation of Islam, converting by the sword and forcibly uprooting the Christian and indigenous influences. The Moors were eventually driven out in the Reconquest of Portugal, in the aftermath of the Crusades.

The successive influences of all these different peoples and beliefs are layered into the popular myths and legends of the region, in almost the same way that the strata of sediment along the banks of the Tejo retains the history of the land. The older legends form the basis, the foundation, onto which the later influences have compiled, collapsed, and fallen in their time. A careful excavation reveals the fragile artifacts among the debris.

Nowhere is this more evident than in the legends of sweet Santa Iria, who reveals in her riparian martyrdom her misty origins as a water goddess, or divine anima, of the River Tagus. She is the very spirit of the Ribatejo, and is particularly revered in Fatima's neighboring towns, Tomar (Nabancia) and Santarem, her ancient namesake.

According to local tradition, Iria was the gifted and beautiful daughter of a noble family of Nabancia, presumably born in or around the seventh century. She had several aunts and uncles in the religious life directing her education, and under their influence, Iria opted for the veil herself while still in the purest bloom of youth. Her beauty and charm did not go unnoticed, and it was on her regular forays to the village church that she caught the eye of the handsome Britaldo, favorite son of the local governor.

Poor Britaldo was literally sick with love for her, but Iria's choice to live as the bride of Christ left him wasting away, courting death rather than the reluctant maiden. In an act of great compassion, Iria agreed to meet with her cavalier, and gently explained her decision to him. The holy rendezvous healed Britaldo's broken heart, and sparked his own faith. He was honored to sacrifice his love to the Lord, and truly loved Iria more than ever. However, he could not help but extract a promise from her to never love another, and to this she swore.

Britaldo was not the only one captivated by Iria's charms, for her uncle, the monk Remegio, began to harbor a dark passion for her as well. As her spiritual director, he saw the girl regularly, and took advantage of this relationship to make passionate advances to her. When she refused him, he grew bitter and jealous.

Remegio was an educated man, and not only in the ways of the church. He dabbled in the dark arts as well. He brewed up a magical potion, which he served to Iria as a tea. The herbs caused her body to mimic the signs of pregnancy. Soon her womb began to swell and ugly rumors began to swirl, tarnishing her sterling reputation. The bad news reached the ears of Britaldo and when he heard that his virtuous Iria was pregnant, he flew into a rage, and commanded his servant, Banao, to kill her.

At this point, our overtly Christian story begins to reveal roots reaching much deeper into the pagan past. Iria was overtaken while praying on the banks of the river Nabao. After decapitating her, Banao, which means "the banisher," threw her body into the river. Her mortal remains flowed with the tide into the waters of the Tagus, which carried her down to the banks of Escalabis, the settlement that would become her city, Santarem. There, she became imbedded in the sands just below the surface.

Meanwhile, God revealed the truth to another of Iria's uncles, the good Abbot Celio. Celio vindicated his niece, restoring Iria's honor, and then set out along the riverbanks to search for her. What he finally found was a miracle. Iria's perfectly preserved, innocent body had been enshrined by the angels in an alabaster tomb, just below the waters, mercifully beyond the reach of all who sought to possess her in life.

Try as they might to remove the relics, the waters would always rise up and protect her, and so Iria remained, safe in her sanctuary among the waters of the river Tejo. Many miracles and healings were attributed to the shrine, and churches and convents were established thereabouts to commemorate the local saint.

Centuries later, her fame attracted a visit from another Portuguese saint, Queen Isabel. Legend has it that when St. Isabel approached the riverbanks, the waters parted so she could walk across dry shod to pay her respects at the tomb of Santa Iria.[4]

The idea of a riverbank haunted by an innocent but powerful female spirit is a common motif in these parts, and the scattered threads of this and other ancient traditions are delightfully rewoven into the enchanting story of Iria of Nabancia. As Alexander Parafita has pointed out in his excellent work on the traditional legends of Portugal,[5] the popular stories detailing the tragic martyrdom and burial of innocent Iria stem from a dense nexus of pre-Christian mythology. Echoing distinctly through this elaborate story are the songs of the nymphs, who have inhabited the mythical landscape of the Ribatejo for millennia. These charming female spirits guard rivers and water sources, tempting the unfortunate men who cross their paths.

In his landmark book *Voyages in My Land,* Almeida Garrett makes a fine point in noting that the Santa Iria of monastic legend and the Santa Iria of the troubadours seem like two different persons. A recurring strain in both story and song, the fragile but enduring spirit of the Tejo reappears, cut and pasted into Portuguese romances that tell of the seduction of an innocent maiden who is ravished, killed, and then buried in the riverbed by her heartless lover. The popularity of this heroine among the troubadours may represent an attempt to reclaim and repatriate her ancient legacy within the resurgence of Christian nationalism that followed the Reconquista and the expulsion of the Moors.

While the details of the life of the Christian Santa Iria don't indicate whether she ever made it up to the Cova, there is a tradition that a female mystic or visionary had a hermitage there.[6] The name Cova de Iria reflects the association of this little hollow with the most popular and pervasive female divinity of the surrounding area. It may be mere coincidence, but the feast of Santa Iria, and her annual festivals, which are still celebrated throughout the land, are held on or around October 20, the anniversary of her martyrdom. The famous miracle of the sun, at the final apparition in the Cova, took place on October 13—not exactly the feast of Santa Iria, but within the octave, as they say.

THE FIRST APPARITION ON THE AZINHEIRA

So on that fateful day, May 13, 1917, when the children decided to pasture their sheep in the Cova de Iria, they were entering a hollow already mysteriously hallowed. It was a Sunday, and they went after Mass. It was a bit of a trek to the Cova and Lucia reports in her memoirs that they didn't arrive until almost noon. Soon enough, the sheep set about grazing, and Lucia and her cousins set about to play.

Like the visionaries at La Salette, the children had begun to build a little "house" out of stones, when a blinding flash of light suddenly burst from the sky. Mistaking it for lightning, they took off running in the direction of a sheltering oak tree. Arriving under its branches, they were greeted with another blinding flash, which set them off running again. As they darted out from under the holm oak, it was then that they saw her, balanced within a ball of light, atop a small evergreen the locals call an *azinheira*.

She was shining white, and her face was so blindingly brilliant and beautiful that it hurt to look upon it. Her garments shone as if they were made of white light, and consisted of a simple tunic and a white mantle draped over her head. The bright edge of her gleaming mantle glowed with intense golden light. The ball of light around her extended for perhaps a meter and a half, and the children stood absorbed and surrounded within it, unable to move or utter a word. Then the Lady addressed them.

"Don't be afraid," she said in her unforgettable voice. "I won't hurt you."

The security this reassurance brought prompted Lucia's question—not "Who are you," but "Where do you come from?"

"I am from heaven," she replied.

Emboldened, Lucia then asked what the Lady wanted of them. She said she wanted the children to come to the Cova for six months in succession, on the thirteenth day of the month and at the same hour. She promised that she would then tell them who she was and much more besides. She also promised to come again a seventh time.

The children eagerly wanted to know if they too would go to heaven, and the Lady assured them each, in turn, that they would, although Francisco was advised to say some extra rosaries. Lucia wanted to know about some neighbors who had passed away, and the Lady told her that one was in heaven, but one would be in purgatory until the end of the world.

Then the Lady repeated the request of the angel who had come before her, that the children should offer up all their suffering as a sacrifice to God for the conversion of sinners. Little did they know at the time that Francisco and Jacinta would see heaven sooner than later, and they would all have more than their share of innocent sufferings to offer up in sacrifice.

The Lady could only promise them that they would suffer, but that the grace of God would comfort them. As she spoke these words, she opened her hands toward the children and great beams of light streamed forth from them, light that pierced their hearts and souls, making them, as Lucia said, "see ourselves in God." The three fell to their knees and began to pray.

The Lady admonished them to pray the rosary every day for peace in the world and an end to the war. Then she began to ascend from the little azinheira tree, disappearing slowly into the eastern sky.

THE CHARTS

After the children recovered from the initial shock, Lucia insisted that they tell no one what they had seen and heard. Francisco would not be a problem, for in fact, he had only seen the Lady. But Jacinta was so excited that as soon as she returned home and saw her mother, Olympia, she told her everything right away.

Jacinta was a bit of a chatterbox, and found it hard to keep anything to herself. With her outgoing Mercury, the messenger of the

Jacinta Marto
March 11, 1910
4:37 p.m. GMT +0:00
Aljustrel, Portugal

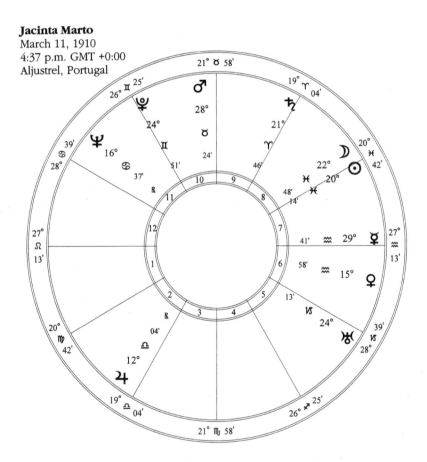

Jacinta Marto. Venus ♀ and Mercury ☿ in Aquarius ♒;
New Moon ☽ in Pisces ♓.

gods, perched on her descendant in Aquarius, she was a regular her-
ald to the masses. Born at the New Moon in the self-sacrificing and
spiritual sign of Pisces, in the 8th house of death and debt, she was,
according to Lucia, the most committed of the three children to offering up the suffering and acts of sacrifice that would offset the karmic
debts of others. Deeply sympathetic and mystical, this little Pisces
would live only a brief life of sickness and pain before escaping to
her promised place in heaven.

The chart for this initial apparition reveals both an angular Moon
and a strong Venus. It is set for 12:10 p.m., based upon Lucia's accounts
of their arrival at the Cova. Throughout the series of apparitions, the
Lady generally arrived at the noon hour, if not shortly thereafter. The
angular Moon in Aquarius is setting in the west, and only a few degrees
from the Descendant in Aquarius. The Descendant is the angle opposite the Ascendant (or Rising Sign), where meetings, encounters, and
important relationships take place.

Both Jacinta and Lucia were born with Venus in Aquarius, like St.
Bernadette. The Aquarian Moon in this apparition chart, at 14 degrees
of the sign, is conjunct the Venus of both girls. In the chart for the initial apparition at Lourdes, we saw a similar concentration around
Venus in Aquarius on the Midheaven. At Fatima, as at Lourdes, that
Aquarian popularity and attraction would soon draw huge crowds of
people, gathered together around their common ideals and aspirations.

The event chart for the first apparition at Fatima is top-heavy with
a stellium of five planets, including Venus in Taurus dominating the
chart from the 10th house. Taurus is Venus's home, the sign of her
rulership, where the bright goddess of love is able to more fully
express her beautiful and bountiful nature. Venus wields a strong
influence in this apparition chart, being both in the sign of her rulership and elevated in the 10th house. Venus also disposits, or rules,
the four other planets in her sign (Mars, Jupiter, Sun, and Mercury),
expanding her influence and making her a kind of cosmic den
mother or landlady to that Taurus brood.

First Vision at Fatima
May 13, 1917
12:10 p.m. -1:00
Fatima, Portugal

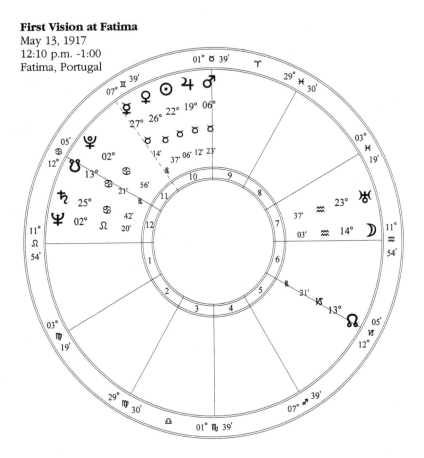

First vision at Fatima. Concentration of planets in Taurus ♉,
with Saturn ♄, Pluto ♇, and the South Node ☋ in Cancer ♋.
Note that Moon ☽ is in Aquarius ♒.

The loving providence of Venus in Taurus was certainly needed at
the time, for something dark and sinister was stirring in the primordial
depths, troubling the waters of Cancer, the Moon's sign. Saturn, the
cosmic timekeeper and taskmaster, had returned. In fact, Saturn, strait-
ened within the sign of its detriment, at 25 degrees Cancer, was only 3
degrees from the position it occupied during the first apparition at
Lourdes! Meanwhile, Pluto, the dark lord of the underworld, had also

advanced into the Moon's demesne, where he was headed for a rendezvous with the Moon's Nodes. Pluto would conjunct the Moon's South Node in Cancer over the coming months, an alignment that would further integrate the painful forces of death and dispersion.

In 1917, the existence of the planet Pluto was a secret unknown by most, but not all. Still lurking in the underground, at least one person, the American astronomer Percival Lowell, was doing the digging that would eventually reveal the shadowy influence of this 9th planet. By 1905, Lowell had completed most of the calculations that would lead to the eventual discovery of his mysterious Planet X. Even though Lowell would die before the war was over, in 1930, using Lowell's calculations and telescopes, in the observatory that Lowell's money had endowed, Clyde Tombaugh would finally pinpoint the exact location of this insurgent, dark force we have since come to know as the planet Pluto.

This combination of difficult planets in the highly emotional and feeling sign of Cancer contributed to the general sense of despair throughout the world. All the joy had fled from Europe in the bloodbath of World War I. The maternal instincts of Cancer had been so utterly thwarted that instead of nurturing the young, their protectors were shipping them off to slaughter in wave after wave of uniformed human sacrifice. At the senseless height of the war of attrition, whoever could afford to lose the most men, might win. No one seemed to know exactly why, or how to make it stop.

Only eight days earlier, on the fifth of May, in a voice that echoed the general despair, Pope Benedict XV had written a memorable letter, lamenting "the cruel war, the suicide of Europe." To his heavenly mother he cried, "To Mary, then, who is the Mother of Mercy and omnipotent by grace, let loving and devout appeal go up from every corner of the earth—from noble temples and tiniest chapels, from royal palaces and mansions of the rich as from the poorest hut—from every place wherein a faithful soul finds shelter—from blood-drenched plains and seas. Let it bear to her the anguished cry of mothers and wives, the wailing of innocent little ones, the sighs of every generous heart: that her most tender and benign solicitude may be moved and the peace we ask for be obtained for our agitated world."

In this passionate appeal to the Mother of God, the pope eloquently elaborated on the painful Cancer themes of the time; troubled homes that afforded no security and war-weary women weeping for their loved ones. He may have also solicited a surprising response.

To summarize, the chart for the first apparition at Fatima features an angular Moon that conjuncts the natal Venus of both girls in Aquarius, a dignified and elevated Venus in Taurus, and some serious trouble in the sign Cancer. While little Jacinta was the self-sacrificing Pisces of the group, both Lucia and Francisco were born with a stellium of planets in Cancer, and were deeply affected by the temper of the times, even if they didn't understand it all. Francisco had a brother already in uniform, and Lucia's family was fighting the conscription of their only son. Even though the tiny town of Fatima seemed worlds away from the front, the big news of the war had directly impacted their little lives.

The birth times for Jacinta and Francisco are quoted from their official birth records,[7] while the birth time for Lucia is from her baptismal record.[8] Lucia was born with a prominent stellium in Cancer, near her Midheaven, in the 9th house. Uranus in Capricorn is in opposition to her natal Cancer stellium.

During the first apparition, transiting Pluto at 2 degrees Cancer, was exactly conjunct her natal Jupiter, while the transiting Moon's Nodes, at 11 degrees Cancer (and moving backward) were closing in on Lucia's natal Moon and Neptune conjunction (9 degrees Cancer). The Moon's South Node passed over Lucia's Moon-Neptune conjunction during the following months, as the series of apparitions unfolded.

Lucia dos Santos
March 22, 1907
7:00 p.m. 0.61 +0:36:32
Aljustrel, Portugal

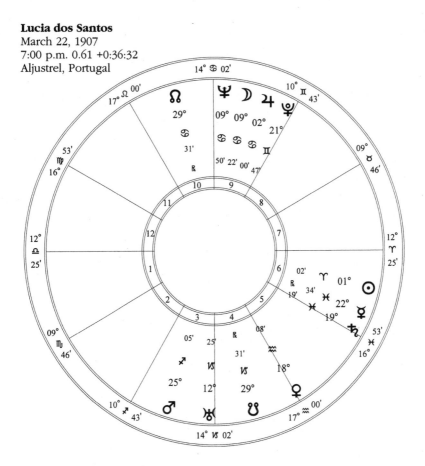

Lucia dos Santos. Jupiter ♃, Moon ☽,
and Neptune ♆ in Cancer ♋ in the 9th House.

This concentration of planets in Cancer in Lucia's birth chart puts a significant emphasis on the Moon. The Moon is the ruler of the sign Cancer, so when beaming down from the security of her home sign, the Moon is free to be herself, to give full expression to her uniquely sensitive, dreamy, and maternal nature. In Lucia's chart, the Moon is also tightly conjunct the mystical planet Neptune, the mythical ruler of the sea, further reinforcing the capacity for great depth of feeling and spiritual sensitivity, but also potentially clouding the mind with excess emotion.

The planet Jupiter, the larger-than-life king of the gods, traditionally rules philosophy and religion, and is also very strong in Lucia's chart. Her Jupiter is in Cancer, which is the sign of its exaltation. As we saw in the charts for the apparition at Lourdes, planets fare better in some signs than in others. We have seen how planets can thrive when in the sign of their rulership, and how their nature can be inhibited when in the opposite sign of their detriment. A planet's

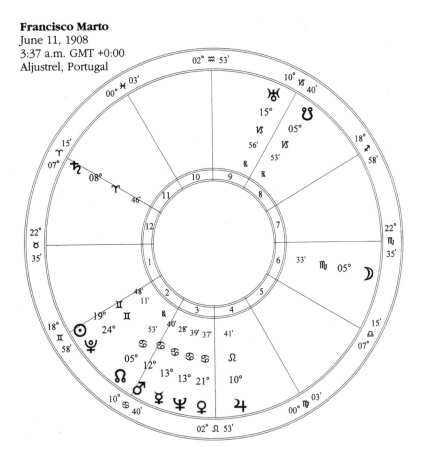

Francisco Marto
June 11, 1908
3:37 a.m. GMT +0:00
Aljustrel, Portugal

Francisco Marto. Concentration of planets in Cancer ♋.

traits and tendencies are actually amplified in exaltation, making it potentially even stronger than when in the sign of its rulership, all other things being equal. So with both the Moon and Jupiter in Cancer, Lucia was born with the two strongest planets in the sign Cancer; a distinct astrological emphasis on the Moon's sign and qualities.

The astrological 9th house, which holds Lucia's natal Jupiter, Moon, and Neptune in Cancer, is the traditional sector of religion, philosophy, and higher knowledge. The 9th house also rules long distance travel, publishing, and publicity; the art of developing a message and spreading it far and wide. How fascinating then, that this girl, the only visionary of Fatima to survive to adulthood, with such a distinct emphasis on the Moon, Cancer, and the 9th house, has become a figure of such worldwide importance in Marian Christianity. In many quarters, Lucia is considered a mouthpiece of sorts for the Blessed Virgin, and her every utterance regarding the famous "secrets" is received with the utmost reverence and attention.

The birth chart of Francisco Marto shows another preponderance in the sign Cancer; specifically, Francisco was born with the Moon's North Node, Mars, Mercury, Neptune, and Venus in Cancer, opposed by Uranus in Capricorn. His Moon is in Scorpio, forming a tight trine (a harmonious 120-degree angle between two water signs) to the Moon's North Node in Cancer. Like his sister Jacinta, Francisco would live only a brief life, centered about his vision of his heavenly mother.

THE AFTERMATH

You can well imagine the clamor that broke out in the village once Jacinta's story spread about. Tio Marto, her father, took a sympathetic view, but Lucia's mother, Maria Rosa, was decidedly hostile to the whole idea. She was convinced the children were lying, and that her Lucia, the eldest of the three, was the ringleader in the charade. Conditions in Lucia's home and family were disintegrating rapidly, as the stress of her father's drinking and gambling wore away at her mother's good nature. Maria Rosa seemed to focus all of her own emotional desolation into an unholy campaign against Lucia and her lies. What had once been such a happy home was turning into a source of endless torment.

In the month between the first two apparitions, life changed in many ways for the three little shepherds. They still met each morning at the watering hole they called "the barreiro," and pastured their flocks throughout the day, but they met now with a grave sense of duty and purpose. According to Lucia's memoirs, while all three children immediately stepped up their program of sacrifice and prayer, it was Jacinta who truly took these acts of penance to heart.

One of the first sacrifices they agreed to make was to forego their daily lunch for the salvation of sinners. Initially, they thought of giving their lunches to the sheep, but decided instead to share them with the poorer children of the village. Those children began waiting regularly by the roadside each morning to beg for the handouts. Having unburdened themselves of that sacrifice, when their hunger became too overwhelming, Lucia and her two cousins would forage in the brush for roots and berries, bitter acorns or wild olives. Parched and dry in the heat of the afternoon, they abstained from water, intent on pursuing their own discomfort to counterbalance the weight of sin in a world at war.

As the children waited for the next appointment with the Lady, they became the focus of a lot of attention in their village, none of it good. Lucia suffered the most, for while Maria Rosa raged in her home, the Marto parents were considerably more patient. Lucia grew more secretive and sullen under all the pressure.

As the appointed day, June 13, drew near, it dawned on Maria Rosa that the children's next meeting with the Lady was scheduled for the same day as the biggest festival in the parish. St. Anthony of Padua, the patron of the parish church, was a native of Lisbon, and much loved throughout his native Portugal. The children of the village eagerly anticipated his feast on the thirteenth of June each year, for the celebrations would last all day.

Maria Rosa was sure that the children wouldn't want to miss all the fun just to go to the Cova, and she focused her efforts on this point to try to distract them from their purpose. It was no use. The appointed day dawned and the children would not be dissuaded.

THE JUNE APPARITION

Lucia took the sheep out to graze much earlier than usual, and hurried them back into their pens by 9:00 a.m., so she could attend the Missa Cantata in town. Returning home, she was dismayed to find a small crowd waiting for her; they were visitors from the nearby towns, both the faithful and the merely curious. They wanted to accompany her to the Cova, and she unwillingly agreed, but asked them to wait until she returned from Mass.

It was almost 11:00 a.m. when she returned from the church and set out for the Cova with this small entourage. Maria Rosa did not miss the opportunity to unleash a torrent of abuse upon their departure. Lucia was devastated and wept as she walked to the Cova.

"I felt very, very bitter that day," she later wrote in her memoirs. "I recalled the times that were past, and I asked myself where was the affection that my family had for me only a little while ago?"

Waiting for them at the Cova was another crowd of almost fifty people, mostly visitors from other towns in the region. Once the visionaries arrived, they all sat down together to wait the approach of the noon hour, talking and praying the rosary together. Suddenly, Lucia arose, and called to Jacinta. The three ran together to the little azinheira tree, for she had come again, at the same hour, to the same place.

While the children communed with her in the privacy of their trance, the onlookers had things to say about what they saw that day in the Cova. Some of them thought the light of the sun seemed to dim during the apparition. Others thought that the top of the azinheira

seemed to bend under some invisible weight. One witness, Maria Car-
reira, who lived nearby, reported that after she heard Lucia greet the
apparition, she heard a strange sound in response, like a very faint
voice, but she couldn't make out the words. She compared it to the
buzzing of a bee.

The three children were the only ones who saw her, and once
again, while Francisco could see her, he could not hear what she said
and relied on the girls to tell him. Lucia greeted the Lady by asking
what she wanted of her. The Lady told her to come to the Cova on
the 13th day of the coming months, at the noon hour. She also told
the children to pray five decades of the rosary every day and asked
them to learn to read. She hinted at more requests to come, and
promised to tell them later exactly what she wanted.

Again, Lucia asked if the Lady would take them to heaven. Her
answer was specific and seems startlingly prophetic. She replied that
she would take Francisco and Jacinta very soon, but that Lucia would
have to stay on earth for a while, for Jesus wanted to work through
Lucia to establish devotion to his mother's Immaculate Heart throughout the world. Francisco died in 1919 and little Jacinta followed him
soon after, in 1920. As I write this, Lucia is ninety-six years old and
still going strong. As we saw earlier when analyzing the configura-
tions in her birth chart, she has been a prominent figure in the spread
of Marian devotion throughout her entire life.

After the children's second visit with the beautiful Lady, the Marto
family maintained a bemused, but benign, skepticism, while the reaction of Lucia's family was more critical than ever. After hearing Lucia's
account of the second apparition, Maria Rosa decided to take her little liar to the parish priest, convinced that he alone could get the
truth out of her.

Fr. Ferreira was courteous and patient with Lucia, questioning her
thoroughly on every aspect of her story, trying to ferret out any
inconsistencies. He had already interviewed Francisco and Jacinta,
and was forearmed with the details of their version of events.

His subsequent remarks made quite an impression, for while he didn't think the children were lying, and found no inconsistencies in their stories, he also concluded that this was no revelation from heaven. He put forth the opinion that perhaps it was all the work of the devil, playing tricks on the children.

This thought so unnerved Lucia that she decided she wouldn't return to the Cova for their next appointment. Reasoning that the devil was the author of discord, she began to believe that only a diabolical force could have driven all the love from her family and caused them to turn so bitterly against her.

THE JULY APPARITION

As the thirteenth day of July drew near, Lucia began to hide from everyone: her cousins, her family, and especially the crowds who began to arrive on the 12th, hoping to accompany the children to the site. Still, when the day dawned, Lucia felt an irresistible urge to go and meet the Lady. She conceded to the inevitable and made her way to the Marto home, where she found her two little cousins crying at the thought of going without her. They were overjoyed at Lucia's change of heart and together they set off for the Cova, where a crowd of two to three thousand people awaited them. In this immense crowd was Tio Marto, who had come to protect his children. His wife Olympia, and Maria Rosa, Lucia's mother, were there as well, armed with holy candles and intent on driving away the demon that had been deceiving the children.

Crushed within the crowd and sweltering in the July heat, Tio Marto heard Lucia say, "Take off your hats, for I see our Lady already." Like many of the other witnesses, Tio Marto reported that he saw something cloudlike and nebulous descend upon the little azinheira, and that the sunlight seemed to dim perceptibly. He also heard the buzzing sound that others reported, which he said sounded like "a horsefly in an empty water-pot."

Lucia once again asked the Lady what she wanted, and her reply was much the same as before. She again asked the children to come to the Cova on the thirteenth day of the next month, and to pray five decades of the rosary every day to obtain peace in the world and an end to the war.

Like Bernadette before her, Lucia pleaded with the Lady to reveal her name, but was put off for the time being. The Lady promised that in October, she would tell all, and produce a miracle to silence the scorners. Again, she encouraged the children to sacrifice and pray for sinners, and then opening her hands as before, the revealing light streamed down, penetrating the children's hearts.

The light warmed and illuminated them as before, but this time, it seemed to pass down through them into the earth, revealing a terrifying vision of lost souls in the torments of hell. Lucia only revealed the details of this vision years later, in her third memoir, but witnesses at the scene reported that the children did seem terrified at one point during that July apparition.

PROPHECY OR HINDSIGHT?

There were several other important, even prophetic, messages revealed in that July 13 (Cancer) apparition, particularly the reference to the end of World War I, the promise of a worse war yet to come, and the warnings regarding the emergence of Russia as a powerful threat to Christianity. Much has been made of the prophetic accuracy of the Lady's statements, and they are usually well woven into any narrative account of the Fatima story, but in all fairness, little to nothing was said of them at the time. The children did speak of receiving "secrets," and refused to divulge them, but Lucia made no public admission of these prophetic messages of the Virgin until much later.

For instance, the Virgin's prediction that Francisco and Jacinta would soon join her in heaven, while Lucia would remain on earth, is usually included in accounts of the second apparition (on June 13).

However, Lucia made no mention of this until late in 1927, almost a decade after their passing. The revelations regarding the three visits the children received from the Guardian Angel of Portugal were not published until 1937.[9]

One of the most famous of the Fatima prophecies, regarding the end of World War I and the promise of a worse war yet to come, was not made public until 1941, when World War II was well underway. It was published in Lucia's third memoir, which also included the account of the famous "night illumined by an unknown light," which the Lady had reportedly said would presage the outbreak of this second war. Lucia not only revealed this prophecy for the first time in the 1941 memoir, but also explained that she had seen this "unknown" light in late January 1938, referring to a time when the aurora borealis had been particularly spectacular.

Memory is a funny thing, and hindsight is always 20/20. I am not accusing anyone of fabricating after the fact, and I don't intend to pass judgment on Sr. Lucia. However, as an astrologer, I am keenly aware of the difference in relative value between predictions boldly proclaimed before the evidence is in, and backhanded "predictions" made afterward. Lucia herself makes the excuse in her third memoir that she did not publish these things before because God did not choose to use her as a prophet. I am certainly in no position to argue with that.

However, these messages that Lucia reportedly received during the Cancer apparition on July 13, 1916, form the backbone of what the devotees of Fatima like to call "Our Lady's Peace Plan from Heaven." While the apparitions of Fatima remained relatively unknown outside Portugal until 1941, the publication of these "prophetic" revelations in Lucia's memoirs resulted in worldwide recognition and the development of a fascinating branch of Roman Catholic political activism. The major tenets of this Peace Plan include the conversion of Russia, the revelation of the secrets in three parts, and the call for the pope to consecrate the world to Mary's Immaculate Heart. The visionaries are cast as the personal envoys of the Blessed Mother, and the pope as the guardian of their secrets.

Much is made of the quality of Lucia's memory in retaining this detailed information over the intervening years. Certainly someone with a Moon-Neptune conjunction in Cancer could have a retentive and enduring memory. It is equally likely that she could be given as much to fantasy as to divine illumination. Again, I'm not passing judgment on these matters, but I think it would be irresponsible not to at least raise some of these questions.

There may have been just as much repackaging of the details of the vision at Fatima as there was of Bernadette's aquero at Lourdes. Sister Lucia wrote these definitive memoirs within the protective confines of the cloister, and under direction from her superiors. The first memoir was undertaken in 1935 on orders from the Bishop of Leiria, at the time when Jacinta's mortal remains were being transferred from Ourem to the cemetery at Fatima. Preparations were being made to request Jacinta's beatification, and Lucia's memoirs played a role in establishing an exalted hagiography for her.

Her second memoir was composed in 1937, again under orders from the Bishop and the Mother Provincial of her order. Her superiors believed Lucia was still guarding secrets that she would only reveal under obedience, so obedience was demanded. This second memoir contains the details about the visions that took place before the initial apparition of Our Lady, incidents that have become a standard part of the Fatima story. There was an undeniable pressure to produce underlying these narratives, and Lucia did her best to please her superiors, who exercised significant control over her destiny. How much editing and direction she received behind the convent walls is something we may never know.

Lucia's third memoir was written in 1941, again under orders of the Bishop. A new biography of Jacinta was about to be released, and the Silver Jubilee celebration of the 1917 apparitions was approaching. This called for something big, and Lucia did not disappoint. The third memoir opens with the secrets, and contains the earliest published account of the Virgin's request that the pope consecrate Russia to her Immaculate Heart. The Virgin's actual request was made within the context of another vision Lucia experienced in 1929, but in this memoir, Lucia writes that in the July 1917 apparition, presumably presaging the Russian Revolution, the Lady said that she would come later to ask for the consecration of Russia.[10]

I'm not implying that there either was or wasn't some great conspiracy afoot, but rather pointing out the usual foibles of human nature, writ large. Marian Catholicism is a very emotional religion, learned at the mother's knee, and the faithful are often as deeply attached to it as they are to their own parents and children. We all tend to process new information in the way that best supports our own cherished notions. The most hardened skeptics are as guilty of that as any religious fanatic. The truth gets lost on both ends of the spectrum. While it would be irresponsible to try to deny the long history of institutional coercion and the deliberate repackaging of the truth on the part of the Roman Church, a compassionate eye can see that a good many of those responsible really believed they were doing the right thing.

THE MINISKIRT FROM HELL

Just as at Lourdes, church officials found it necessary to ignore certain aspects of the children's initial description of the Lady's appearance. In their earliest interviews, when asked to describe the Lady's dress, the visionaries said that it went down to her knees. Our Lady's miniskirt almost stopped the Fatima Peace Plan dead in its tracks.

In his book *Origens Orientais da Religião Portuguesa,* sociologist Moises Espirito Santo quotes from the interviews conducted by Dr. Manuel Nunes Formagio regarding the skirt that nearly discredited the apparition. The priest wrote, "The angel of darkness sometimes transforms himself into the angel of light to fool the believers. The Lady could not appear unless she were the most decently and modestly dressed. The dress would have to go down to her feet. The opposite constitutes the most serious obstacle to the supernaturalism of the apparition and makes us believe that we might be dealing with a mystification prepared by the spirit of darkness."[11]

Under pressure, in subsequent interviews, the children's descriptions of the Lady's hemline underwent significant alterations until November of 1917, when a priest of the Diocese of Leiria declared in an article, "The skirt reached her ankles and she was wearing white stockings."[12] That is the only description that has survived into the modern accounts.

OFFICIAL INTERROGATIONS

The civil authorities had some very tough questions for the visionaries after the July apparition. The revolution of 1910 left Portugal under the control of a left wing and anti-clerical government. A number of secular reforms had already been introduced, alarming the faithful. It was only a matter of time before the children received a summons to appear before the administrator of the nearby town of Ourem.

Tio Marto absolutely refused to bring his two children, and prepared to go in their stead. He reasoned that the two were much too young to stand before a court or be held responsible for their actions. Also, the distance of nine kilometers was too far for them to walk, and neither Francisco nor Jacinta could ride a donkey without falling off. Lucia's family had a different reaction, and hoped the administrator might be able to get the truth out of her. On the morning of Saturday, August 11, her father loaded her up on a donkey and led her off to Ourem.

The administrator, Arturo de Oliveira Santos, was not impressed with the dusty entourage that presented itself for his examination. He bullied Lucia with questions, demanding to know her "secret" and threatening her life if she didn't tell. He eventually dismissed them, ordering Lucia to stay away from the Cova.

On her return to Aljustrel, Lucia found Jacinta and Francisco in tears. Lucia's sisters had told them that the officials in Ourem had executed her. Lucia would never forget the difference between her family and the Martos; how Manuel and Olympia trusted and protected their children, while her own family seemed so ready to throw her to the wolves.

On Sunday, August 12, the village once again began filling with the faithful. These seekers badgered the children mercilessly. Among them was Arturo Santos, the administrator of Ourem. Apparently, his interest in the apparitions had deepened, and he now insisted on both attending at the Cova, and on taking the children to the parish priest for further questioning in the morning.

That, in itself, was a ruse, for after loading the children in his wagon on the morning of the thirteenth, Santos cracked the whip and drove his horse right back to Ourem, running against the throngs of people streaming down the roads into Fatima. As the noon hour approached, some six thousand people waited in the Cova, but the three visionaries were nowhere to be found.

Oddly enough, at the appointed hour, something did happen. Bystanders reported hearing a thundering rumble, or a murmur. Some saw a flash of light to the east, while many others claimed they saw the cloudlike presence descend upon the little tree, and heard that strange buzzing in the air. It didn't last long, but it left the impression that the Lady had at least tried to keep her appointment.

The realization that the authorities had made off with the children began to spread through the crowd and a riot seemed imminent. The anger was directed not only at the officials in Ourem, but the people also suspected the parish priest of complicity in the matter, for the children had been taken from his residence. Fortunately, there were a few dedicated Christians among this vast mob of believers, Tio

Marto among them, who discouraged violence and defused the anger, urging the people to wait on the Lord and trust that His will would be done. Eventually, they dispersed.

Meanwhile, where were the children? Santos hurried them back to Ourem and secreted them away in his own home. You can well imagine their fear and disappointment as they heard the noon hour come and go. Santos kept them locked in overnight, and then hauled them off to a hearing at the town hall at ten o'clock the following morning.

There, he threatened the children with prison, torture, and death if they wouldn't admit their lies and reveal their secrets. How the children withstood this brutality is perhaps one of the most overlooked miracles of Fatima, but they did. When they refused to cooperate, Santos threw them into the Ourem jail.

Imagine, if you will, the three little shepherds cast into a dark, stinking cell with the town thieves, cutthroats, drunkards, and other assorted lowlifes. After a bit of a cry, and a vain, longing gaze out the one, tiny window, the children began to pray, and to offer up this new, expanded suffering as a sacrifice for sinners.

The other inmates couldn't help but notice, and soon gathered around, consoling them, asking questions, and offering advice. Even the worst of the lot were charmed by Jacinta's earnestness and Francisco's boyish bravery. The three then decided it was time for the rosary, and taking an image of Our Lady from around her neck, Jacinta asked one of the detainees to hang it up on the wall. The children began to pray to it, like a shrine, and as they did, more of the inmates gathered around and joined in the responses, briefly transforming the ugly, desolate cell into a house of prayer.

When the rosary was finished, Jacinta began to cry for her mother. One fellow produced a little concertina to console the new prison pet, and then the music and dancing began! The peasants of the Serra love to dance, and in no time, the jailhouse was rocking with singing and laughter and all tears were forgotten. Suddenly, the door opened and a guard entered to take the children away from their new friends and back to the offices of the administrator.

Having failed in all his attempts thus far, Santos made one last, desperate effort to break the children. He actually threatened to put them in a cauldron of boiling oil if they wouldn't tell their secrets and admit to their lies. When he got the same answer as before, he instructed the guard to take Jacinta away and deep-fry her.

This he presumably did, leaving Lucia and Francisco to face the administrator. The two prayed fervently, believing they were all about to suffer a horrible death. When they still wouldn't crack, Santos ordered the guard to take Francisco and cook him to a crisp, leaving Lucia standing on her own. She still wouldn't give in, and actually seemed eager to rejoin her companions in the paradise they had been promised.

Finally, Santos gave the order to dispatch Lucia, but when the guard escorted her back to the chamber of horrors, no cauldron of death awaited her. Little Jacinta and Francisco greeted her instead, and they were overjoyed to be reunited again. It had all been a cruel trick, but they had won, and bested Santos at his worst.

Santos locked the children in his house again for the night, and then freed them the following morning, after a final interrogation. While it is easy enough to find fault with the church's handling of the affair, at least they didn't throw the children in jail or threaten them with boiling oil. The church hierarchies and the ranks of secular government are more similar than not, as both are filled with human beings. Inconsistent, incomplete, and often needlessly cruel, there is no need to point fingers when we have only ourselves to blame.

It was August 15, the Feast of the Assumption, when the three returned to Fatima. The townspeople, most of whom were gathered at Mass during their arrival, were not at all pleased with this presumptuous kidnapping on the part of the officials. Another riot would surely have ensued, but Tio Marto had the presence of mind to forestall the crowd by feigning a friendly accommodation of the officials. In the popular narratives, Tio emerges as a man with profound faith and a love of peace that transcended the anger he must have justifiably felt, but any violence or insurrection on the part of the people would have only made matters worse.

Lucia's family seemed unmoved by either her absence or her return, and sent her right back out with the sheep. While grazing the flock later that afternoon at Valinhos, on the hill Cabeco, in the same spot where she and the other children had originally seen the vision of the floating, white figure, the Lady appeared to her again. It was only a brief, consolation prize of an apparition, but her message was the same: to seek her at the Cova on the 13th of the month, to continue to pray the Rosary every day, and to expect a miracle in October.

THE SEPTEMBER APPARITION

September found the children perfecting their penances as they awaited the Lady's next appearance. The crowds began arriving early again, badgering the visionaries incessantly with requests for an interview, prayers, cures, a touch, a kiss, a relic, and so forth. On the morning of the thirteenth, the road to the Cova was so jammed with pilgrims that it was nearly impassable.

This was the briefest apparition. The Lady repeated her main messages, urging the children to continue to pray the rosary every day and promising to return in October with a miracle.

In the Cova that day were several priests, including Monsignor Joao Queresma, who later reported that as the crowd responded to Lucia's announcement of the approach of the Lady, he and his companion saw a luminous globe moving from east to west across the sky.[13] Many people saw or heard some manifestation of the presence in the Cova, but many saw nothing at all.

BLESSED NUNO AND THE BIRTH OF PORTUGUESE NATIONHOOD

As the fateful day in October drew near, the news spread throughout Portugal that the people of Fatima were expecting a miracle at the Cova. This promise struck an ancient chord in the heart of every patriot, for Lucia and her cousins were not the only ones to be blessed with visions and extraordinary experiences in Fatima. The remains of an old hermitage at the Cova, attributed to Santa Iria, already marked it as hallowed ground. Even though the land was only fit for grazing sheep in 1917, this spot represents a nexus, a meeting point of the molding forces of Portuguese history.

Legend has it that Blessed Nuno knelt to pray to Our Lady in a tiny chapel just eight miles west of the Cova before he set off to fight the historic Battle of Aljubarrota. The Holy Constable, Nuno Alvares Pereira, is a national hero of Portugal, renowned as much for his sanctity as for his battlefield bravery. Known as the "Precursor of Fatima," he was the local duke, with his headquarters in the nearby Castle of Ourem.

In August of 1385, the Portuguese crown was in dispute. Portugal was under attack from the forces of the king of Castille, who was pursuing his wife's claim to the throne. Knowing that his men were badly outnumbered, on August 13, Nuno prayed to the Blessed Virgin for a miracle to save Portugal from the Spanish invaders. Nuno had already vowed to carry the image of the Virgin before him into battle on his standard, and his sword had always been hers. Nuno's sword, "Maria," is still proudly displayed in the Carmo at Lisbon. Facing what seemed like certain death, both Nuno and his upstart king, Joao of Avis, earnestly petitioned the Queen of Heaven and St. Michael, the Guardian Angel of Portugal, pledging dramatic displays of gratitude if they would just grant this crucial victory.

Soon after, Nuno was struck with a brilliant idea and made a significant change in his battle plan. He had received artillery support from the English that would allow him to make use of the most sophisticated tactics of his time. On the following day, the Eve of the Assumption, he inverted his front lines, forging an impenetrable defensive stronghold. The Spanish troops, after much argument, were foolishly drawn in to attack. The Portuguese troops, numbering about seven thousand, out-manned but divinely inspired, routed the Castilian army of nearly thirty thousand in a miraculous turnabout.

Returning to the ancient chapel that had sheltered their pleas in their most desperate hour, Nuno and King Joao built a new church and the magnificent landmark of a monastery, Batalha (battle), which still stands today in remembrance of the miraculous victory that saved Portugal. After a noble life of military service to his country, Blessed Nuno retired to a Carmelite monastery to end his days in prayer. Meanwhile, the new dynasty established by the miraculous victory and under the protection of the Mother of God and the Archangel embarked on the age of navigation and exploration that marked the high point of Portuguese history. Prince Henry the Navigator was the son of Joao I of Avis and the wife he won through his crucial English alliance, Phillipa of Lancaster.

In a sense, Blessed Nuno and his king were both reenacting and re-creating Portuguese history, for this region was already sacred in the national consciousness. The historic monastery Alcobaca stands only a few kilometers from Fatima, built by Alphonso Henriques, the first Christian king of Portugal, in gratitude to Our Lady and St. Michael for their divine help in freeing the land from the Moors in 1139. His victory over the Moors at Ourique consolidated the throne beneath him, and when Alphonso Henriques was crowned, he officially and formally dedicated Portugal to the protection of the Blessed Virgin Mary as its patron, and named St. Michael the guardian of its armies. Then, in their honor, he built the beautiful Alcobaca, a world heritage site.

So this area around the plain of Fatima has been central to the development of the Portuguese national identity. The roots of their

Christian nationhood, under the special protection of the Virgin Mary and Michael, the Guardian Angel of Portugal, run deep beneath this land, in a dense network of faith, tradition, legends, miracles, and Muslims. Here, according to Lucia's memoirs, in the Cova de Iria, between the Batalha and Alcobaca, at a time of national crisis, when a socialist government threatened their faith from within and the raging world war threatened their lives from without, the Archangel Michael, Guardian of the Armies of Portugal, and the Blessed Virgin Mother of God returned to protect their people.

THE OCTOBER APPARITION AND THE MIRACLE OF THE SUN

All of Portugal awaited the big day, either with great expectations or, like Lucia's mother, Maria Rosa, with a sense of impending doom. She was convinced the crowds would turn on Lucia and kill her when she didn't produce the required miracle. The weather was miserable, as a huge storm blew in from across Europe, drenching the Serra da Aire. The muck and mire did not deter the faithful, who came sloshing down the roads to Fatima, driven by a force that transcended all class distinctions, and united in this great quest for a miracle.

As the noon hour approached on the 13th, between fifty to one hundred thousand souls waited in the Cova. Shivering and soaked to the skin, many had waited for days to get the choice spots. The visionaries made their way through the throng to take their place by the little azinheira, or what little the relic hunters had left of it. The redoubtable Maria Rosa was in attendance, convinced they were all going to die. In the pelting rain, the sea of impatient souls scanned the skies, searching for Our Lady. The noon hour had come and gone.

Suddenly, Lucia cried, "Put down your umbrellas!" The people obeyed, and then stood for several minutes, exposed to the rain. Some of the bystanders began remonstrating with the children, and pushing, amidst a groundswell of grumbling. Then, the children saw her! Their faces changed noticeably, and it was clear to all who could see them that they were immediately enraptured with a vision they shared among themselves.

As the Lady alighted on the scant remains of the azinheira, Lucia once again asked her what she wanted. This time, the Lady had some definite answers. She wanted a chapel built on the site. She also identified herself as the Lady of the Rosary and predicted an end to the war and a homecoming for the soldiers.

According to Lucia, she then said, "Let them offend our Lord God no more, for he is already much offended." Again, she opened her hands to send forth the familiar light, but this time, the light seemed to shoot up into the sky, toward the sun. At this moment, while only a few in the crowd could see the Lady, they all saw the clouds suddenly part and expose the sun. Lucia cried out in ecstasy, "Look at the sun!"

Lucia later reported that she then beheld a trio of visions, one after the other, of Our Lady with the Holy Family, as the Mater Dolorosa, and as the Queen of Mt. Carmel. What the crowd saw was a lot more interesting. According to the testimony of thousands, they witnessed a miracle of cosmic proportions.

Well over fifty thousand people all saw something, but each in their own way. Many of the eyewitness accounts include the following outline of details, with some variations. As the clouds suddenly parted to reveal the sun, it shone forth like a silvery disk. It seemed as bright as usual, but it actually invited the gaze, for they could look on it without burning their eyes. Then the sun began to "dance," or at least that is the term the witnesses thought best described the movement they saw. Soon, it was whirling rapidly like a giant pinwheel on fire. It stopped, and then began spinning again.

The sun was ringed with a crimson border and began to spew streams of blood-red flames across the sky. Eventually all the colors of the rainbow were reflected to earth and everything was awash in a swirling spectrum of color. Next, many saw the sun tremble and shudder, before it began a horrifying plunge to earth, streaking through the sky in a jagged course as if it were about to fall into the Cova.

At this point, thousands cried out and fell to their knees, expecting a fiery apocalypse and the end of the world. The atmosphere seemed suddenly much warmer, as if flames were descending upon them. The whole episode lasted perhaps ten minutes, but even that is difficult to pin down. The sun then began to climb back up in the sky, on the same jagged, zigzag path. It stabilized, becoming the familiar daystar that burned too brightly to behold. Thousands of people in the Cova noticed that their clothes, some of which had been wet for days, were suddenly dry.

This is what they say they saw. Over fifty thousand people, thanking God, and still reeling from the shock of the sight of the sun crashing to earth, huddled together, dumbfounded at the significance of what they had just experienced. No one was disappointed in the Lady's promises that day. The dance and fall of the sun were seen forty kilometers away in the town of S. Pedro de Moel by the poet Afonso Lopes Vieira, and nineteen kilometers away by startled witnesses in the village of Alburita, who were convinced the world was coming to an end.[14]

Something extraordinary happened in the Cova that day. Perhaps it was a miracle of perception, for there was no astronomical evidence that the sun or earth had done anything out of the ordinary, but thousands of witnesses in the Cova and elsewhere were convinced the sun was falling on them.

Mass hallucination is frequently offered as an explanation, as it is for other kinds of unexplainable occurrences, but I'm not sure that anyone has ever defined mass hallucination in a way that made it seem any less supernatural than whatever it was supposed to be debunking. If that crowd of thousands all saw the same imaginary thing at the same time, and other witnesses nineteen kilometers away saw it too, that would be pretty miraculous in its own right, wouldn't it? There are fakirs who are adept at inducing illusions within the minds of their audiences, but there were no hypnotists or fakirs present to focus this crowd's attention, only three illiterate children. Who was the operator who induced the hallucination? If it occurred spontaneously, both in the Cova and at a distance, how would you explain that? What sort of mechanisms would be operating?

Miracle of the Sun
Oct. 13, 1917
1:15 p.m. BST -1:00
Fatima, Portugal

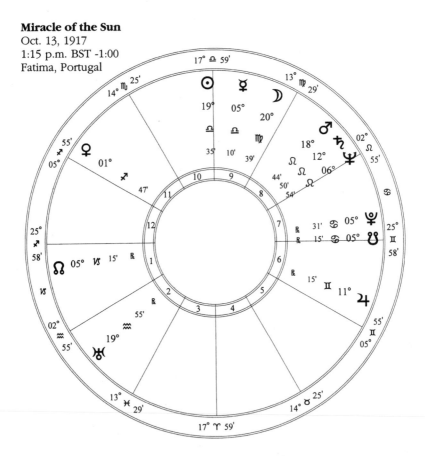

Miracle of the Sun. Sun ☉ in Libra ♎ trine Uranus ♅ in Aquarius ♒, which is opposite Mars ♂ in Leo ♌; Moon ☽ in Virgo ♍; Pluto ♇ conjunct South Node ☋ setting in Cancer.

The chart for the event does involve the Sun in an unusual alignment. While it may be mere coincidence, the Sun is at 19 degrees Libra, which traditionally was the degree of the fall of the Sun. (A planet is in its fall when it is in the sign opposite its exaltation. The Sun is exalted in Aries, the opposite sign of Libra. The exact degrees of each planet's exaltation and fall are found among the writings of the Greeks but probably originated in Mesopotamia.) The Sun is also forming an exact trine, or 120-degree aspect, to Uranus at 19 degrees Aquarius. This sets up an easy, flowing exchange of "influence" between the Sun and the offbeat, rebel planet Uranus, the oddest eccentric of the solar system. Uranus specializes in surprise, and its influence is often shockingly unexpected, striking like a bolt out of the blue.

Opposing Uranus is volatile Mars in Leo, the Sun's own sign. So there is a unique and potentially explosive emphasis on the Libra Sun, which could suggest the possibility of the seemingly impossible. The Marian emphasis is present throughout the chart, with the Moon elevated in Virgo and the angular conjunction of Pluto and the South Node in Cancer.

In all fairness, I think it would take a lot more than astrology to really explain what happened in the Cova that day, just as I think it takes more than Roman Catholicism to fully explain the significance of what was going on in the apparitions at Fatima.

WHO IS FATIMA?

The town of Fatima is now famous the world over because of the appearances of the Virgin Mother of God. Each passing year brings millions of pilgrims to visit the shrines, but more and more of them aren't even Christian, they are Muslims, and the site holds an entirely different attraction for them. The name of the town itself, Fatima, presents a mystery. Fatima is not a Portuguese word, but the name of the holiest woman in Islam; the youngest and favorite daughter of the prophet Mohammed. Mohammed himself declared that only the Virgin Mary held a higher place in paradise than his Fatima.

Mohammed was no stranger to the Virgin Mary. She is the only woman ever mentioned by name in the Koran, and he refers to her in no less than thirty instances.[15] Chapter (surah) 19 of the Koran dedicates forty-one verses to her. Mohammed expressed faith in the virgin birth of Christ, the Immaculate Conception, and the special "ever-virgin" status of Mary, a status he also conferred upon his daughter, Fatima, even after the birth of her four children.

This set up a special connection between the two in the minds of the faithful, as the two holiest women among the many servants of the God of Abraham. As Islam grew, the image of Fatima expanded, like the Virgin Mary in Christianity, gathering up divine attributes along the way—very often the attributes of the goddesses that had held sway within the lands converted by Islam's sword. So every time we say "Our Lady of Fatima," and unknowingly reconnect the two, what are we really saying?

How did a tiny village in Portugal come to bear the name of the holiest woman in Islam? The answer probably lies in the Almohad invasions of the eighth and ninth centuries. The Islamic armies conquered all of Spain and Portugal, converting by the sword, and renaming towns and villages to commemorate their conquest. It's quite possible that the name dates back to this era. However, the popular Christian version of the story behind the name takes us forward to the days of the Crusades, to the time of the troubadours and the traditions of courtly love.

In the reconquest of Portugal, European Christians fought to recapture the land from the Muslims, who had held it for four-hundred years. As the Christian hidalgos swept through the region, driving out the Islamic rulers, a Templar Knight named Goncalo Hermingues fell in love with one of his captives, the beautiful daughter of the sultan of the Castle of Ourem. Her name, like many Muslim girls, was Fatima. The couple wed, and she converted to Christianity, taking the name Oureana. She didn't live long, pining away for her family and the life she left behind. Upon her death, her heartbroken husband renamed the nearby town Fatima in her honor. He then retired to a monastery.

It makes a lovely story, but reeks of twelfth-century political correctness. It also enfolds elements of the popular tales that developed around the enchanting, but elusive, magical Mouras. The legendary Fatima Oureana of Ourem was surely a Moura, but just how magical was she?

THE MAGIC OF THE MOURAS

Mouras are otherworldly fairy women who haunt the old ruins, caves, and mountaintops where the Iberian Celts and earlier inhabitants of the land would have worshipped. The site for the castle of Ourem, a rocky hilltop fortress that dominates the surrounding landscape and has been occupied since prehistoric times, has been home to legendary Mouras through the ages. Mouras are also associated with hollows, like the Cova de Iria; for instance, a hollow near Lisbon is called the "hollow of the Moura." Like the nymphs, Mouras are also depicted as seductive temptresses lingering near water or water sources.

Mouras tend to crop up in places where older, ancestral ways have been abandoned, or suppressed, hence their more recent conceptualization as the lingering spirits of Moors in the wake of the Christian reconquest. Generally pictured as dark-eyed Muslim beauties, in fact, the Mouras considerably predate the Moors in Portugal. The name itself could come from older Celtic words like *Mahra* or *Mahr*, meaning "spirit."[16]

The Mouras, like the Mari of the Pyrenees, have a great propensity for spinning, especially deep within their caverns and remote mountain hideouts, which has led some to speculate upon an association with the Greek Moiras, the spinners of fate. Mouras are often associated with buried treasure, as if they were guarding some secret wealth hidden deep within the earth.

Further south, in the Algarve, the Castelo de Lamego, like the daunting Castle of Ourem, sits high on a rocky hilltop. Dominating the local landscape in the same way that the Castle of Ourem caps the plain of Fatima, the Castelo de Lamego is the dramatic setting for ancient tales that bear intriguing parallels to those of Ourem and Fatima.

During the Christian reconquest, the Castelo de Lamego was also home to a legendary Muslim princess, named Ardinia. Besieged by the Christian Crusaders, she fell in love with a handsome knight named Tedon. She agreed to convert and eloped with him to a nearby abbey, where the two were united in Christian marriage by the local abbot. Their story ends tragically, for her father, the Moorish king, did not approve, and fighting ensued, which ultimately cost the lovers their lives. Some say the ghost of Ardinia still haunts the castle at night. While Ardinia was surely an enchanting Moura in her own right, her story is but another layer in a rich strata of lore piled atop this timeless fortress.

An even older story tells of an ancient king and his encounter with a magical Moura. She revealed to him three tunnels and chambers under the Castelo, deep down into the rock. These chambers were filled with treasure, and sealed with a spell to repel intruders.

When the Castelo came under attack, the king fled, leaving his three children behind with the fairy woman. She hid them in the secret caverns under the castle, where they, and the treasure, remain to this day, under a powerful enchantment.[17]

So these stories of enchanted Mouras and Christian knights and their intrigues within the ancient hill forts are not an uncommon fixture in the Portuguese mythological landscape. Consequently, I think we have to take that Christian story of the naming of the town of Fatima with the proverbial grain of salt.

A minor uproar occurred in 1995 when hundreds of Shi'ite Muslims in Iran suddenly began booking pilgrimages to Fatima. These Muslim pilgrims believed that it was their Fatima who appeared to the children in 1917, not the Virgin Mary. Obviously this claim is not supported by the testimonies of the visionaries, but perhaps it harkens back to something deeper.

They were inspired by the work of Moises Espirito Santo, a Portuguese sociologist. In his book *The Almohad Invasions and Fatima*, Espirito Santo made the case that the Muslim Almohad Invaders had named the town for the Islamic Fatima as early as the ninth century, and that the Roman Church had twisted the facts. His book was translated and widely distributed throughout Iran.[18] Naturally, Church officials discounted his research, but my personal opinion is that the Muslims did name the town for Fatima, the holiest woman in Islam. Maybe someone had a vision in the Cova.

THE SECRETS OF FATIMA

Who is Fatima? She is a complex and fascinating character. The holiest woman in a religion with a seemingly unholy disregard for women, she shares important qualities and attributes with the Virgin Mary. These parallels have arisen over the centuries in the course of the development of their respective worship and give us unique insight into the way feminine holiness is perceived within a predominantly masculine religion.

Like the Virgin Mary, Fatima was the product of an immaculate conception, albeit Muslim-style. Islam does not share the Christian obsession with purity and sexual abstinence and promotes a more natural attitude on the whole subject. Mohammed and his first wife, Khadijah, had four daughters and two sons. The two boys unfortunately died in childhood, but the four daughters all lived to a marriageable age. Fatima was the youngest of the four, and according to tradition, Mohammed was forty-one at her birth, so Khadijah would have been about fifty-six years old.

Mohammed taught that the angel of the Lord led him away from Khadijah to fast and pray for forty days, commanding him to abstain from any relations with his wife. As the forty days came to a close, Mohammed was transported to paradise in a vision. The Angels Gabriel and Michael appeared to him, offering a meal of fruit and water. Mohammed broke his fast with this heavenly food. They then ordered Mohammed to go to Khadijah, for "Allah ordained upon Himself to create noble progeny from you tonight!"[19]

Khadijah conceived Fatima that night. The Islamic reasoning is that the sperm from which Fatima was generated was formed from that heavenly food, and she was therefore not an ordinary woman, but holy above all others. This holiness is reflected in her long list of traditional attributes, by which the Shi'ite Muslim faithful still extol her virtues. Her most popular epithet is Fatima Al-Zahra, the radiant one, but she is also known as as-Siddiqah (the Righteous), at-Tahirah (the Pure), al-Muhaddathah (the one spoken to by angels), and a score of other honorary titles.

Her most interesting attributes, for our purposes, were conferred upon her by her father, and reflect distinct similarities between her worship and the popular cults of the Virgin Mary. Mohammed himself declared proudly that Fatima was al-Batoul, meaning that she was above menstruation.

In the voluminous writings of the Shi'ite Imams, we find many references to Fatima's special condition. For instance, in Bihar, verse 10, Imam Abu JaafarAl-Baqir says, "When Fatima was born, Allah (Exalted Is His Name) revealed to an angel to speak the name Fatima with Muhammad's tongue. Allah then said: 'I have bestowed knowledge upon you and safeguarded you from menstruation.'"

In *Fatimah: The Radiant, Daughter of the Apostle of Allah,* by Abu Ali al-Fadl ibn al-Hasan, the author cites the Musnad (a collection of transmitted sayings) of the eighth Imam ar-Rida for this quotation from Mohammed: "Fatima is not like the women of human kind, nor does she suffer the illness (bleeding) you women suffer!"

Al-Amr-Tasri narrates in Arjah Al Matalib that the Prophet was asked about the meaning of Batoul. Someone said to him, "Messenger of Allah, we have heard you say that Maryam (the Virgin Mary) is Batoul and Fatima too, is Batoul!" The Prophet replied, "Batoul is she who never sees blood, meaning that she never discharges menstrual blood; because menstruation is resented if it occurs in Prophet's daughters."

We might gather from this that Muslim Imams considered menstruation to be a bad thing, and indeed, Allah, the Almighty, is quoted as saying, "They ask thee concerning women's menstruation. Say: They are a discomfort and a pollution, so let women alone at such times and go not into them until they are cleansed."[20]

In many primitive societies, women's monthly cycles were terrifying to men, and very strict taboos were imposed to isolate women during this time.[21] Even modern, Orthodox Judaism still requires a ritual bath at the end of a woman's period before she is considered clean enough to come near a man. In all fairness, until quite recently, this would have been a sanitation issue, and the proper disposal of all emissions a matter affecting public health. That in itself does not even begin to explain the amount of superstitious prohibitions that arose, and lurk among us still. In the mind of the Muslim faithful, a truly holy woman would be free from such evil and uncleanliness, or, al-Batoul, like Fatima and the Virgin Mary.

Fatima, like the Virgin Mary, was also declared ever virgin, or Aladhra. Mohammed explained that, even after the birth of her children, Fatima was still a virgin, because having been conceived from heavenly food, she was actually a human huri. A huri, or houri, is a woman of paradise, and dozens of them await the Muslim faithful upon their death, eager to attend to their every need. Mohammed was not as clear about what awaits faithful Muslim women in paradise, but he taught that each righteous man gets his own stable of beautiful houris in his eternal reward, and each one is both a consummate domestic servant and sexual goddess.

In the Holy Koran (surah LVI, verse 35), Mohammed states, "We have created the huri of special creation; and made them virgin-pure and undefiled." Commentating on this verse, Majma-Al-Bayan explains that "[What is meant by virgin-pure] is that whenever their husbands come near them, they find them virgins."

Imam Sadiq was asked, "How can a huri always be a virgin, no matter how many times her husband comes near her?" The Imam answered, "Because huris are created from pure goodness where no blight can alter them, nor does decrepitude inflict them . . . menstruation does not pollute them . . ."[22]

According to the traditions of the Imams, Mohammed did not just consider Fatima to be a human huri, but to be *his* human huri. The sixth Imam as-Sadiq, Ja'far ibn Muhammed, is quoted as saying:

> We are told that our forefathers said that the Messenger of Allah often indulged in kissing the mouth of Fatimah, the mistress of the women of the world, so that Ayisha (Mohammed's wife) finally protested, saying, "O Messenger of Allah, I see you indulge so often in kissing the mouth of Fatimah and placing your tongue in her mouth."

He answered:

> Yes, O Ayisha, when I was taken up to heaven, Gabriel took me into Paradise and brought me near the tree of Tuba (beatitude). He gave me an apple of its fruits, which I ate, and which became a sperm in my loins. Thus when I returned to earth, I laid with Khadijah, and she conceived Fatimah. Whenever, therefore, I yearn for Paradise, I kiss her and place my tongue in her mouth, for I find in her the fragrance of Paradise. I also sense in her the fragrance of the tree of Tuba. Fatimah is thus a celestial human being.[23]

That sounds a bit incestuous to our modern ears, but we can be very quick to judge. These Islamic beliefs may not be any more ridiculous than some of our own pet Christian assumptions. The Virgin Mary, like Fatima, is also considered "ever virgin" by Roman Catholics, even after the birth of her son, Jesus.

This seems particularly odd in light of the gospel stories about the brothers and sisters of Jesus. In the Gospel of Matthew, chapter 12, verse 46–50, Mary appears along with Jesus' brethren, trying to have a word with him. The Roman Church claims the problem lies in the translation. They explain that the word for brothers also means cousins, implying that the cousins of Jesus followed Mary around as if they were her sons. The same story is repeated almost verbatim in the Gospel of Mark, chapter 3, verses 31–35, and in the Gospel of Luke, chapter 8, verses 19–21. James, the brother of Jesus, was a leader in the early Church in Jerusalem. Is contradicting the Gospels in order to perpetuate Mary's "ever virgin" status really any less irrational than declaring her a human huri? Protestants tend to believe in the brothers.

In this parallel between the Muslim and Christian traditions, we behold the pervasive sexism of the soul. Men's fascination with women's bodies is not only timeless and universal, but their shame at the ungodliness of their fascination is equally widespread. Just for the sake of comparison, there is precious little ink or argument wasted on the genitals or reproductive functioning of Jesus, whereas the subject of the Virgin Mary's intactness was bandied about for generations. Mohammed, Moses, Abraham, or any other great prophets of monotheism all seem to have had the normal equipment and kept it in good working order, for there was nothing unholy about male sexuality. Women, on the other hand, with their discomforts and pollutions, were so fundamentally unclean that they had to be neutered and denatured before being elevated to the pantheon.

What is truly worshipful about Fatima is not her unnatural virginity or freedom from monthly periods. It could be that the Shi'ite Imams, like Roman Catholic theologians, were highly imaginative in defining the objects of their worship. As Dr. Ali Shariati has pointed out in his book, *Fatima is Fatima*,[24] she should be respected in her own right for who she was. Her strong character and integrity set her apart. Her loyalty and devotion to her father, and to his revolutionary worship of the one God, her honesty and bravery, her charity, her untiring service to her family and faith, her complete surrender to the will of Allah, and the courageous manner in which she stood up to her father's enemies after his death—these are the things that make Fatima an exalted symbol of Islamic womanhood, especially now, as Muslim women struggle to define themselves in a new millennium. Fatima did not hide behind the veil. She was a woman who took on the world.[25]

THE POPE AND FATIMA

In recent years, perhaps the most surprising proponent of the link between the Virgin of Fatima and Islam has been Pope John Paul II. Ever since the assassination attempt on May 13, 1981, the anniversary of the initial apparition, the pope has taken an increasing interest in both Our Lady of Fatima and in reaching out in friendship to the people of Islam. On that fateful day in 1981, as his Muslim assassin was taking aim, the pope's head was turned by the sight of a little girl wearing a Fatima medal. He bent over to greet her just as the gunman fired, causing the bullet to miss his head, and probably saving his life.

As the pope convalesced from his wounds, he had a lot of time to meditate upon the meaning of it all. He came to believe that Our Lady of Fatima had saved his life, and once he recovered, he traveled to the shrine at Fatima to show his gratitude, even placing one of the gunman's bullets in the crown of Our Lady's statue.

The recent release of the details of the mysterious Third Secret of Fatima have led many to speculate that it includes a prediction of the assassination attempt. It contains imagery referring to a man "clothed in white" who "falls to the ground, apparently dead."[26] However, that statement is embedded within such a complicated context that its meaning is really subject to interpretation.

The pope's increasing interest in our Lady of Fatima has coincided with his push for a radical ecumenism within the church. He has made significant overtures to Orthodox Christians and Jews, becoming the first pope to visit Orthodox territory since the Great Schism of 1054, and apologizing to Jews in the Holy Land for Christianity's history of anti-Semitism. Meanwhile, he has tried to reverse the tide of history by reaching out to Christianity's staunchest enemies, the Moors.

His more recent efforts, in light of the repolarization of Muslim and Christian interests in the aftermath of the September 11 attacks, seem almost prophetic. On May 6, 2001, he became the first pope to enter a mosque, praying together with Muslims in a truly historic ceremony in the Umayyad Mosque in Damascus. Later, during that fateful September, he announced while on a trip to Kazakstan, "I wish to affirm the Catholic Church's respect for Islam, for authentic Islam: The Islam that prays, that is concerned for those in need." The pope has repeatedly emphasized the message that the two religions both worship the one God, the God of Abraham, and he has continued to call for cooperation and friendship between Christians and Muslims, to the alarm of many Protestant fundamentalists.

In this instance, Our Lady of Fatima, whose very name bridges the two faiths, has been instrumental in helping to reunite the divided worshippers of the one God; the many and varied "people of the Book," as Mohammed called them, all claiming allegiance to the same ultimate, all-knowing deity, but murderously antagonistic toward each other in pursuit of His favors. While many devotees of Fatima look to the day that their particular brand of monotheism will conquer the world, perhaps the Lady's real "Peace Plan from Heaven" is more far-reaching and inclusive.

While the Church has carefully packaged and managed the events at Fatima to their own ends, just as they did at Lourdes, a careful analysis of the astrology and the local lore reveals a more universal significance that really shouldn't be co-opted or controlled by any single, self-serving sector.

Unfortunately, the Roman Church got out of the business of being "catholic" a long time ago, confining itself instead within a narrow bandwidth of orthodoxy. Having defined their position, they must constantly defend it by editing reality, for God will always transcend our misguided attempts to claim Him or Her for our own, or to confine His or Her infinite being within the limits of our imagination and pride. By very definition, God is unknowable. Our language cannot possibly encompass It, our minds are too limited to ever fully grasp Its truth. In which case, what is the point of orthodoxy, when our ideas are so incomplete, other than to enforce compliance?

And yet, no matter how infinite and unknowable this author of the universe may be, He or She or It keeps reaching out to us in love. It catches us when we fall, seeks us when we hide, enlightens us in our darkness, loves us when we are hateful, and It appears out of the blue to little children in a form they can recognize and respond to; as a loving and beautiful mother, for even motherly love is born out of the depths of Its own being. When we peel back the layers of legends surrounding these apparitions, a timeless spirit is revealed that belongs to us all, and binds us back together out of our self-imposed separateness. In this case, Pope John Paul II, with his far-reaching ecumenical initiatives, may be way ahead of his flock. But how long before the sheep catch up with their pastor?

Endnotes

1. Fr. Louis Kondor, SVD, ed. *Fatima in Lucia's Own Words: Sister Lucia's Memoirs* (Fatima: Postulation Centre, 1976), 59.

2. Ibid., 64.

3. Paramahansa Yogananda, *Autobiography of a Yogi* (Los Angeles: Self-Realization Fellowship Publishers, 1973), 490.

4. This version of the legend of Santa Iria is drawn from the website for the town of Leiria (www.members.tripod.com/~Leiria/) and the excellent and informative "Echoes of the Ribatejo" website (www.ribatejo.com). Also from Almeida Garrett, "Voyages in My Own Land," www.ig.com.br/paginas/novoigler/livros/viagens_garrett/cap29a31.html.

5. Alexander Parafita, *O Maravilhoso Popular: Lendas, Contos, Mitos* (Lisbon: Platano Publishing Company, 2000).

6. William Thomas Walsh, *Our Lady of Fatima* (Doubleday: Image Books, Doubleday 1954), 49.

7. Lois Rodden quotes Luis Ribiero for the birth times for Jacinta and Francisco. He quotes the times from the birth certificates.

8. Kondor, *Fatima in Lucia's Own Words,* 9. Quoting from the baptismal record, Lucia was born "at 7 in the evening."

9. Sandra L. Zimdars-Swartz, *Encountering Mary* (New York: Avon Books, 1992), 197–201.

10. Kondor, *Fatima in Lucia's Own Words,* 112, 118.

11. Ray Vogenson, www.geocities.com/fatimaforagnostics/FAT.05.FATIMA.2.htm (accessed July 3, 2002; site now discontinued). Commentary on the questioning by Dr. Manuel Nunes Formigão, in Documentos, 67, quoted in Moise Espírito-Santo's Origens Orientais da Religião Portuguesa.

12. ibid.

13. William Thomas Walsh, *Our Lady of Fatima* (New York: Image Books, Doubleday, 1954), 126–127.

14. Ibid., 149.

15. Fr. Ladis J. Cizik, "Our Lady and Islam: Heaven's Peace Plan," *Soul Magazine* (Sept.–Oct. 2001), 6.

16. Max Dashu, "The Serpent in the Mound," www.Suppressedhistories.net, 2002. Dashu quotes Menendez-Pelayo for this translation.

17. Bruno Melo and Paulo Monteiro, www.planeta.clix.pt/castelos/vis/lmg/lamego.html (accessed July 3, 2002; site now discontinued).

18. www.datafileportugal.com (accessed Nov. 27, 1995). "Lisbon newspapers attributed the confusion to a Jewish Portuguese sociologist Moisés Espírito Santo (Moses Holy Ghost in its literal translation) whose recent

study: "The Almohads and the Apparitions at Fatima," was published by the New University of Lisbon, translated by the Iranian embassy in Lisbon and circulated widely in Iran. The sociologist attempted to prove a link between the site at Fatima, where illiterate shepherds allegedly had a vision of the Virgin Mary in May 1917, with the prophet Mohammed and the Almohad crusade of the ninth through the eighth centuries. Espirito Santo, a descendent of the new Christians who converted to Catholicism from Judaism to escape the worst excesses of the Spanish inquisition and its vestiges in Portugal, said Fatima had been named by Berber followers of the Almohad during the Moorish occupation of the Iberian peninsula (they were finally expelled in the twelfth century) and the significance of the area was 'much later perverted by the Roman Catholic hierarchy.'"

19. Abu Muhammed Ordoui, *Fatima, the Gracious* (Qum, Iran: Ansariyan Publications, Qum, Iran), chapter 5, "Transcendental Events."

20. *The Holy Koran,* surah II, verse 222.

21. Dr. Lotte Motz, *The Faces of the Goddess* (Oxford: Oxford University Press, 1997), 55, 60.

22. These translated quotes of Majma-Al-Bayan and Imam Sadiq come from Arakmulla Syed's Al-Shi'a Webring, www.ezsoftech.com/islamic/Fatima3 .html (accessed July 3, 2002; site now discontinued).

23. Abu Ali al-Fadl ibn al-Hasan ibnal-Fadl at-Tabrisi, 'Fatimah: The Radiant Daughter of the Apostle of Allah, Her Birth, Names, and Epithets" (I'lamu 'l-Wara bi A'lami 'l-Huda), Dar al-Ma'rifah, Beirut, 1979. A translation of this twelfth century author's work is available at www.home.swipnet .se/islam/A_Personality/Fatima(a.s.).html (accessed July 3, 2002; site now discontinued).

24. Dr. Ali Shariati, *Fatima is Fatima* (Tehran: Shariati Foundation and Hamdami Publishers, 1980). This is the theme of Shariati's book, and he makes the point throughout.

25. Mohammed briefly advocated the worship of the three daughters of the Arabic moon god, Al Ilat, in the "Satanic Verses" later stricken from the Koran. Fatima may have seemed a more acceptable substitute.

26. David Willey, "Fatima's 'Third Secret' Revealed," (Europe: BBC News). May 13, 2000.

Six

BEAURAING AND BANNEUX:
THE VIRGIN OF THE POOR

A LADY IN WHITE

In late autumn of 1932, in a small town in southern Belgium, a group of neighborhood children routinely went out after 6:00 p.m. to fetch thirteen-year-old Gilberte Voisin from the local convent school. The town bears the intriguing name of Beauraing, which means "beautiful branch" in the local dialect. The group of children consisted of Gilberte's brother, Albert, eleven, her sister Fernande, fifteen, and their neighbors, fourteen-year-old Andree Degeimbre and Andree's little sister, also named Gilberte, who was nine.

On the evening of November 29, as the children arrived at the convent yard, young Albert surprised them all by exclaiming, "Look! The Virgin, dressed in white, is walking above the bridge!" The others were slow to turn and look, knowing Albert's reputation as a trickster, but when they did, they too beheld a glowing woman in white walking above the railroad bridge over the convent yard. They could see her legs moving beneath the folds of her gown, although her feet seemed to be hidden in a cloud.

Soon the nuns inside the convent school heard the frightened children screaming and banging on the door. Gilberte was always dismissed

151

at 6:30 p.m., and the children were just a bit early. When Gilberte arrived at the door, she saw the lady too. She stopped suddenly at the threshold, pointed at the bridge, and gasped. Sister Valeria saw nothing at all, except a hysterical group of children who quickly ran off for home.

The five frightened children burst into the Degeimbre kitchen, out of breath and barely able to gasp out their news. Germaine Degeimbre, recently widowed, couldn't help but notice that the children were genuinely frightened, but she was skeptical, and dismissed their story. The Voisin parents had a similar reaction, as did the nuns at the school. No one believed the wild tale, but the next evening, the children saw her again.

As they left the schoolyard with Gilberte, the beautiful Lady in white was walking over the railroad bridge, just as before. She walked to the end of the bridge toward the railway station, then turned and walked back toward the convent and schoolyard, gliding, as it were, with her feet wrapped in a cloud.

The following day, December 1, Germaine Degeimbre, the mother of Andree and little Gilberte, determined to go with her children and see for herself exactly who, or what, was frightening them from the bridge. She was convinced it was all some sort of practical joke, as was the group of neighbors who accompanied her. This time the children caught a glimpse of the lady as they made their way up the walk to the convent door. She stood before them briefly on the walkway, then suddenly disappeared. As the children continued on to collect Gilberte, Germaine and her crew fanned out over the schoolyard, searching for the perpetrator.

They soon heard a chorus of "oohs and aahs" coming from the children, for as they made their way from the convent door with Gilberte, the lady appeared to them again. This time, she was close to the ground, but still standing on her little cloud. She was poised between the front door and the Lourdes grotto near the entrance to the yard. She disappeared quickly again, after smiling at the children. That's right—there was a little replica of the Lourdes grotto in the schoolyard.

As the children hurried down the walkway toward the worried group of grown-ups, they saw her a third time. This time she seemed to be rising out of the shrubbery between the gate and the grotto. The five children were standing among a group of six adults, and while all the children could see the vision, the adults saw nothing. After briefly discussing the incident with some of the sisters, who offered little but skepticism, the group returned to the Degeimbre home. The children were in a state, particularly little Gilberte, who could not stop sobbing.

Later that same evening, shortly after eight o'clock, Mrs. Degeimbre and Mrs. Voisin returned to the schoolyard with the children, determined to get to the bottom of what was surely a hoax. They left the two Gilbertes at home to mind each other, bringing Albert, Fernande, and Andree. As the children entered the schoolyard, they suddenly cried, "There she is!" All three fell to their knees with an impressive thud. They began praying the Hail Mary together, over and over, in weird, high-pitched voices.

Germaine Degeimbre could see that the children's eyes were all intently focused on the same place, a hawthorn tree between the fence and the center walk, so she went over to investigate. As she neared the tree, Andree cried out, "Stop Mother! You will walk over her!"

The children all sighed with regret as the vision disappeared. Mr. Voisin, the father of Albert, Fernande, and big Gilberte, arrived just as the children were getting up. Together with the other adults, he staged a full search of the yard and surrounding areas, but came up empty-handed.

This particular vision set the pattern for most of the ones that followed. From that point on, the Lady always appeared to the five children standing over the branch of the hawthorn tree—the Beauraing—

or beautiful branch that we encountered earlier in the Lourdes story. As they came back to the convent yard, night after night, the children would fall to their knees in unison when she appeared, almost as if they had been forcefully thrown down. Their eyes locked on the same point, but on something that others could not see. They would pray together aloud, but in those unusually high-pitched voices; voices they never used beyond their trance state. While locked in this communion with their unseen visitor, they seemed oblivious to any other sensory stimuli, almost as if their senses had been withdrawn and redirected. The five children were exhibiting that bizarre, spontaneous, religious ecstasy that we've come to associate with these Marian apparitions.

By Saturday, December 3, the crowds were beginning to gather. Approximately 150 people were waiting outside the convent gates that evening. The Reverend Mother Theophile had begun locking them out and setting the dogs loose in the yard, in a futile attempt to discourage any further apparitions. Meanwhile, the children were subjected to intense questioning and growing scorn from all quarters, including their parents and families, Mother Theophile and her nuns, and an increasing number of curiosity seekers. Like the children at Fatima, they did not seem to enjoy the attention, but they stood by their story, despite the constant attempts to discredit them.

As the nightly visions continued, young Albert Voisin emerged as the spokesperson for the group. Not only had he been the first to see her, but, like Lucia at Fatima, he also seemed to have developed the initial rapport that allowed him to talk with the Lady and report on her actions and responses to the crowd.

THE INITIAL INTERROGATION

On December 5, the children were interrogated by Adrien Laurent, a local attorney. He was able to question them separately and to challenge their answers in cross-examination. He could not find any disagreement in their testimonies, but he was more impressed by what he had witnessed himself during the apparitions. That evening, Mr. Laurent saw the children fall to their knees in unison after they approached the schoolyard. They prayed the Hail Mary together, and then, as one, sighed with regret and said, "She's gone."

Just as the little group was getting back up and on their feet, they suddenly fell to their knees again with the same violent thud and began another Hail Mary. She had returned. This Lady of the Hawthorn seemed to come and go rather capriciously. Laurent thought that this sudden reversal argued against connivance among the children, and that their reactions, although united in some mysterious way, did appear entirely spontaneous.[1]

The children described the Lady as small, standing about four and a half feet tall, very young and beautiful, and wearing a white dress with blue reflections. She radiated light, especially about her head, where the children described seeing golden rays emanating like those of the sun. Her long, white dress seemed to fall in folds into a cloud, obscuring her feet.

In an interesting development, on December 6, the Lady appeared holding a rosary for the first time. When questioned by Attorney Laurent, the children had all said that she didn't have a rosary. However, the parish priest, Fr. Lambert, who was trying to maintain a dignified distance from the developments, had just that day suggested to the children that they pray the rosary during the apparitions. They had respectfully complied, and sure enough, that evening the Lady thought to bring her beads. From that point on, she always appeared bearing a rosary.

By this time, hundreds of people were gathering for the nightly vigils, pressing in upon the children in importunate crowds that made it difficult to get to their appointed place before the hawthorn. By December 7, the story had made all the papers. People were hounding the Voisins and Degeimbres around the clock, badgering them with questions and treating their private homes like public property. Mrs. Voisin and Mrs. Degeimbre were under tremendous pressure, and their children grew exhausted and weak.

THE DOCTORS AND THEIR EXAMINATIONS

A team of medical doctors had begun to attend the apparitions regularly, led by Dr. Fernand Maistriaux. He published the first brochure on the apparitions, entitled "What's Going On at Beauraing," which chronicled the events up to December 20. Dr. Maistriaux, who had practiced in Beauraing since 1927, had been hooked on the apparitions since December 5, when, on a routine trip to the post office, he had overheard the children's voices raised in prayer. He was immediately intrigued by their unusual tone and pitch. Their voices were perfectly normal until the Lady appeared, but then suddenly became much louder and piercingly high-pitched. They also spoke much faster once they went into their trance. Dr. Maistriaux called in several colleagues to join him in his investigations, so the children were under constant medical observation.

In response to a question from Albert, the Lady had specifically requested that the children seek her on the Feast of the Immaculate Conception, which falls on December 8, nine months before the Virgin's birthday on September 8. By this time, the apparitions in Beauraing had become famous throughout Belgium, and by 3:00 p.m. on the 8th, the town was overrun with visitors. Estimates are that ten to fifteen thousand came to Beauraing that day, seven thousand by railroad alone. Every one of them seemed to be expecting some kind of a sign or a miracle. Although none had been promised, hope springs eternal.

Around 6:00 p.m., escorted by a phalanx of local bodyguards, the children made their way through the massive throng to their place at the hawthorn, where they immediately fell to their knees, entranced at the appearance of the Lady. The team of doctors who accompanied them to the front were able to conduct a series of tests, the results of which are almost miraculous in their own right, even if they weren't exactly what the crowds were expecting.

Dr. Maistriaux was accompanied by another Beauraing doctor, Francois Questiaux, and by Dr. Raymond Lurquin of Houyet, and Dr. Goethals of Hastiere. Dr. Maistriaux stood near Albert, and as soon as Albert fell to his knees, the doctor checked the boy's pulse. Albert briefly turned to look at the doctor, but then focused again on the apparition. The children continued to pray the rosary. Little Gilberte Degeimbre was sobbing as she prayed, and Dr. Maistriaux asked her why she was crying. Gilberte replied, "She is so beautiful."

After a few minutes, Dr. Maistriaux asked her the same question, but this time he received no reply, for she had not heard him at all. Dr. Maistriaux then turned to check Albert's pulse again. This time, the boy did not respond to him and his eyes did not leave the vision. The doctors realized that as the vision progressed, the children were becoming increasingly insensible to external stimuli. They began to experiment.

Dr. Lurquin of Houyet took a lighted match and held it beneath the hand of Gilberte Voisin. The doctors and other witnesses watched the flame lick her hand until the match was almost consumed. The girl never responded, and later, when her hand was examined after the vision, there was no indication of any burns. With their curiosity fueled, Dr. Lurquin then performed the same experiment on Gilberte Degeimbre. Witnesses saw the flame moving along the edge of her hand, but again, she showed no reaction while in trance and showed no burns afterward.

For the sake of comparison, the doctors held a burning match to the hand of another little girl in attendance, who wasn't in trance, and she immediately moved her hand away from the flame. The experiments continued, as Dr. Goethals and Dr. Maistriaux began pinching the flesh of Gilberte and Fernande Voisin and Andree Degeimbre. The girls did not respond. Dr. Lurquin began prodding Gilberte Voisin with a penknife, poking her hands and cheeks. Again, she showed no response and there were no marks to show afterward.

As Dr. Lurquin remarked at the time, "I would not care to submit to this experiment, because I am convinced I would bear its traces." The doctors then shone bright flashlights into the eyes of Gilberte Voisin and Andree Degeimbre. While their pupils showed the normal responses to the light, their eyelids and heads remained motionless, fixed on the vision.

Soon enough, the apparition came to an end. The Virgin had said nothing this time, Albert reported, but she was more brilliantly beautiful than before. The children were taken away from the crowds and into the convent for further examination. They still showed no effects from all the burning and pinching; in fact, little Gilberte Voisin is said to have laughingly remarked to her father, "What do you think of that, Daddy? They tried to make me believe that they pinched and burned me!"

After briefly questioning the two youngest visionaries, the police commissioner, deeply impressed, gave his full consent to allow the apparitions to continue. The crowds had dispersed, somewhat disappointed, for most had been too far away to see the doctors' examinations. However, once the news of the doctors' findings spread throughout France and Belgium, people began to believe they had been given a sign after all.

A brief lull followed, between the eighth of December and the thirteenth, when the children did not see the Lady at all. The apparition on the Feast of the Immaculate Conception was definitely the high point of Beauraing. Afterward, the visions took on a somewhat different character. There was less focus and unity among the children, but they still continued to draw the crowds.

THE CHARTS

This series of visions in Beauraing continued through January 3, 1933, when the children saw the Virgin for the last time. In analyzing the prevailing astrological conditions, it is immediately apparent that this was no ordinary time. Unique planetary alignments had formed in the astrological signs Virgo and Cancer, generating that kind of psychological and spiritual "weather" that can precipitate mystical encounters of this nature.

First Vision at Beauraing
Nov. 29, 1932
6:26 p.m. UT +0:00
Beauraing, Belgium

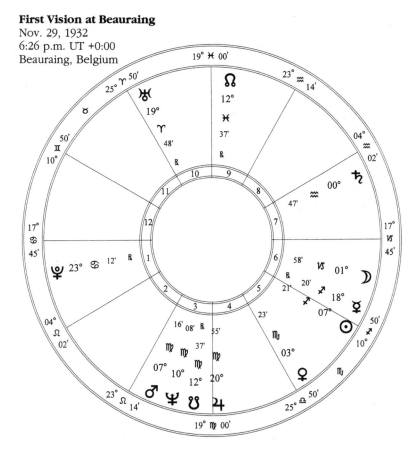

First vision at Beauraing. Concentration of planets in Virgo ♍.

In the chart for the initial apparition, the planet Pluto is rising in Cancer, near the Cancer Ascendant, while a cluster of angular planets in the sign Virgo are gathered about the IC. A particularly mystical stellium is forming in Virgo, involving Mars, Neptune, the Moon's South Node, and Jupiter, convening planetary forces in the sign of the Virgin. The astrological influence of the planet Neptune, which rules the kind of dream-like, mental states that are most receptive to visionary experiences, could be particularly significant, especially as Neptune approaches a conjunction with both Mars and the Moon's South Node.

Albert Voisin
Sept. 3, 1921
8:00 p.m. BST -1:00
Beauraing, Belgium

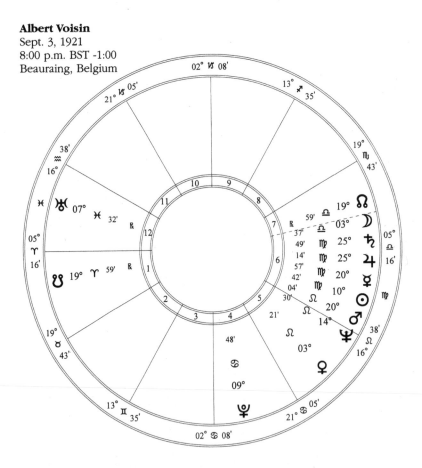

Albert Voisin. Concentration of planets in Virgo ♍.

In Virgo, Neptune can manifest its otherworldly nature in imagery or experiences consistent with the sign's archetypal symbolism. When Albert Voisin suddenly pointed out the Lady in white to the rest of the children, his consciousness was being directly stimulated with that symbolic Virgo imagery. Our next chart is cast for Albert's birth in 1921. I am deeply indebted to the late, lamented Ed Steinbrecher for the birth time, which he obtained from the Belgian birth record.

Albert was a Virgo, born shortly after the New Moon in Virgo. His Moon in Libra is angular and conjunct his Descendant. He was also born with a very close conjunction of Jupiter and Saturn in Virgo, for these two massive planets are well within 1 degree of zodiacal longitude of one another. Mercury, the planetary ruler of Virgo, is also present in its home sign, further highlighting the Virgo influence.

Let's examine the way that Albert's birth chart interacted with the chart for the initial vision. We can insert Albert into the moment, and diagram that with a bi-wheel. Our next chart consists of the map for the initial apparition in the inner wheel and on the angles, while Albert's birth chart is arrayed around it in the outer wheel. This type of display makes certain points immediately obvious. Not only was Albert born with a distinct planetary emphasis in the astrological sign Virgo, but at that very moment, his natal Virgo planets were being directly influenced by the transiting planets in Virgo. If you look down to the angle called the IC, opposite the Midheaven at the bottom of the chart, we see that the current, or transiting, Jupiter in Virgo is exactly conjunct Albert's natal, or birth, Mercury. Also, the transiting Neptune in Virgo is exactly conjunct Albert's natal Virgo Sun, while the transiting Mars in Virgo is opposing Albert's natal Uranus in the opposite sign, Pisces. Those are some very direct hits.

At that point in time, his consciousness was literally flooded with mystical and religious Virgo imagery, the source of which I can more

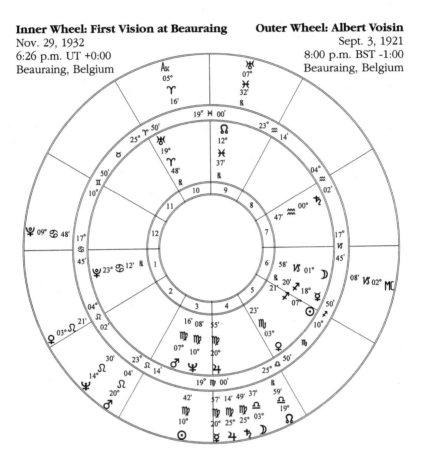

Inner Wheel: First Vision at Beauraing
Nov. 29, 1932
6:26 p.m. UT +0:00
Beauraing, Belgium

Outer Wheel: Albert Voisin
Sept. 3, 1921
8:00 p.m. BST -1:00
Beauraing, Belgium

*Inner wheel: first vision at Beauraing; outer wheel: Albert Voisin.
Close conjunctions between the chart of the first vision at
Beauraing and Albert's chart, clustered around the IC in Virgo ♍.*

clearly indicate than define. However, it manifested right then in the
vision of the beautiful Lady in white walking across the railroad
bridge; which is not to say that she wasn't there! On some level, I
think the charts confirm that his perception of the sudden appearance
of a feminine deity, one that we would generally recognize as the Virgin Mary, was in perfect accordance with the temper of the times.

Both transiting Mars and the transiting South Node were actually
heading toward a conjunction with transiting Neptune on Albert's

natal Virgo Sun, a once (if ever) in a lifetime occurrence. The boy
was standing right in the Virgo spotlight.

Mars joined together with Neptune on Albert's Sun (10 degrees
Virgo) on December 7 and December 8, culminating in the appearance on the Feast of the Immaculate Conception when the group's
ecstasies were the most unified and extreme. As these two planets
focused their influence through Albert's Virgo Sun, he played that central leadership role within the group. Afterward, as the planets moved
on and that conjunction separated, his ecstasies became less focused,
and both his leadership, and the unity of the group, diminished.

As the children at Beauraing continued to meet with the Virgin
regularly throughout December, Neptune and the Moon's South Node
moved ever closer together, forming their exact conjunction around
Christmas day, again at 10 degrees Virgo, and again on Albert's Virgo
Sun. This is a more defuse and confusing planetary combination.
While Albert was still the focus of public attention, and still experiencing visions of the mystical Virgin, his attention waned and he was
more easily distracted, like a normal boy.

If you will recall, at Fatima in 1917, the Moon's South Node was
regressing through the sign Cancer, crossing over Lucia's natal Moon
and Neptune in Cancer; and creating a similar kind of mystical, archetypal energy. During the Fatima series of apparitions, the Moon's
South Node was closing in on an exact conjunction with transiting
Pluto in Cancer. The conjunction of Pluto and the South Node per-
fected (became exact) at 5 degrees Cancer in October, just prior to the
famous Miracle of the Sun. At Beauraing, the Nodes, which define the
Moon's path, were again connecting with the position of a powerful
outer planet; this time, Neptune in Virgo.

THE OTHERS

While Albert was definitely the Virgo of the group, his sisters Fernande and Gilberte represented the Cancer contingent. Gilberte was

Gilberte Voisin
Natal Chart
June 20, 1919
7:00 a.m. -2:00
Beauraing, Belgium

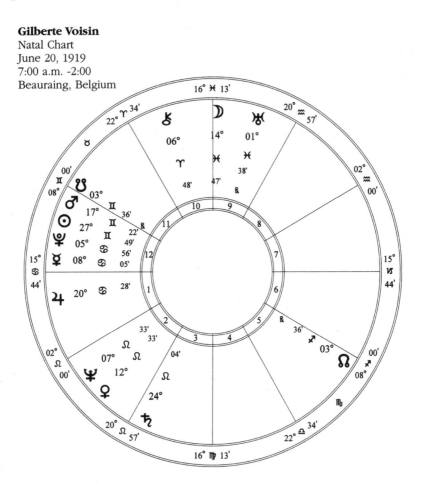

Gilberte Voisin.

born with Jupiter, Pluto, and Mercury rising in Cancer, forming a harmonious trine (120 degree) aspect to her Pisces Moon. Fernande has
the Moon, the South Node, Pluto, Venus, and Saturn in the Moon's
sign, while her Sun at 29 degrees Gemini, seems to be stretching
across the cusp to embrace Pluto in Cancer within its rays. Again, I'm
very grateful to Ed Steinbrecher for getting the seers' birth times from
the official birth certificates.

Fernande Voisin
Natal Chart
June 21, 1917
8:10 a.m. -2:00
Beauraing, Belgium

Fernande Voisin.

THE CRAB AND THE VIRGIN?

So what of this Crab, the lowly creature that so often accompanies the Virgin when she comes? And what binds Cancer and the Moon together as sign and ruler? The Greeks held that the great goddess Hera honored the Crab with his place in the sky. The feisty creature was so bold as to attack Heracles, pinching the toes of the mighty hero on Hera's behalf, as Heracles battled the Hydra in the marsh of Lerna as part of his legendary twelve labors. Heracles crushed the

Crab, and eventually defeated the Hydra, but Hera was eternally grateful for the little fellow's sacrifice.

The Greek tales of Heracles's labors are relatively recent additions to Cancer's lore, but they do place the Crab firmly in the great goddess's camp, especially in her epic campaign against the solar hero, Heracles, her adversary and namesake.

Cancer's designation as the house of the Moon is at least as old as Ptolemy, who was drawing upon ancient Egyptian and Babylonian sources within the Hellenistic mindset of Alexandria in the second century AD. However, the association of Cancer, this dark, indistinct, and rather uncrablike cluster of stars, with the sea and the source of life, stems from much deeper roots.

According to Richard Hinkley Allen, in his classic book *Star Names: Their Lore and Meaning*,[2] the constellation was widely identified as a crab by the ancient Persians, Chaldeans, Hindus, Hebrews, and Arabians. In De Finibus, Cicero uses *Nepa,* probably from the Latin *Nep,* meaning "a scorpion or crab." Other classical writers use both *Astacus* (lobster, crab, or crayfish) or *Cammarus* (lobster or sea crab). Manilius and Ovid referred to it as *Litoreus,* or shore-inhabiting. In other works, Ovid refers to the sign as *Octipes,* the octopus.

Even allowing for cultural variations, there would appear to be a fairly consistent identification of Cancer with the ocean, and with creatures that dwell on that inconstant border between the sea and dry land. Therein lies at least part of Cancer's connection with the Moon and maternity, with the rhythm of the tides and the mysterious depths of the very matrix of life.

In a variation on the same theme, the Egyptians (circa 2000 BC) pictured Cancer as their Scarabeus; the sacred (sacer) water beetle rolling its eggs in a nest-ball between its outstretched claws. The Chaldeans and the Platonist philosophers called Cancer the "Gate of Men," and taught that souls passed through this constellation as they descended from heaven into human bodies.

Additionally, the themes of comfort and nurture are spread throughout the stars of this ill-defined figure. The name Cancer itself, from the Latin for crab, like its Greek name, *Karkinos,* both imply holding, or encircling. The Arabic name, *Al Saratan,* like the Hebrew Sartan, signifies one who holds or binds. *Acubene,* the alpha star, marks the claw, which Pliny referred to as the Acetabula, or arm sockets of the Crab. The Copts designated this area by the name *Ermelia,* meaning nurturing. These terms all refer to the embracing, enfolding motion of the arms of the crab, which are portrayed symbolically within the encircling glyph for Cancer. This glyph communicates on many levels, but it strikes me as an apt depiction of the arms enfolded over the stomach and breasts, the parts of the human body traditionally attributed to Cancer's rulership.

However, there is another, interior constellation hidden within the warmth of that embrace. From time immemorial, sky watchers also identified the stars within this constellation as a stable, enfolding cattle, two asses, and a manger. Does that sound a bit familiar? Eratosthenes (276–195 BC) called this constellation the Crab, the Asses, and the Crib. In the zodiac of Denderah it is called *Klaria,* or the cattlefolds. The Arab name *Tegmine,* for the star marking the tail of the crab, means "in the covering," or "the sheltering or hiding place." Meanwhile, in the very midst of the body of the crab lie the two stars known as the Ascelli, the northern and southern asses.

The most famous body in the constellation, by far, is the striking nebula we now call the Beehive Cluster, but this name is a very recent attribution. It was known in the classical world as the *Praesaepe,* and depicted throughout as a stall, crib, or manger. The Arabians called it *Al Ma'laf,* the stall, while Aratos, writing in the third century BC, refers to it in the Prognostica as "A murky manger" flanked by the two hungry asses, using the same Greek word, *phatne* (manger), that Ptolemy later employs. Praesaepe is a direct Latin translation of *phatne* and signifies a crib, manger, or stall where cattle/horses feed. Additionally, praesaepe was also defined as a brothel, haunt, lodging, or home turf. Now we're getting a lot closer to not only the modern astrological association of the sign Cancer with the home and nourishment, but also to the origins of those fabulous tales of the birth of little Lord Jesus, away in a manger, tucked in somewhere between the friendly beasts.

The manger story only appears in the gospel of Luke. He emphatically states three separate times in chapter 2 that the newborn baby Jesus was laid in a manger, implying that because there was no room at the inn, Christ was born in a stable. However, the amount of popular lore that has sprung up around the nativity, considering the relative paucity of biblical sources, indicates to me that the author of Luke was tapping into a legendary theme that already had a strong hold on the public imagination. This theme continues in the work of Christian writers, like Caesius, in their later attempts to Christianize the zodiac, referring to the praesaepe and *ascelli* as Jesus' manger flanked by the ox and the ass.

In Italy today, the popular Christmas nativity scenes are still called *il presepe*. Even though the Italian language contains common words for both manger *(mangiatoia)* and for crèche, or crib *(greppia),* the Italians continue to use the traditional Latin *praesaepe*. The famous Roman Basilica of Santa Maria Maggiore, or Mary Major, the premier Marian shrine of Rome, was first known as Sancta Maria ad Prasepe and tradition holds that it originally included a chapel containing stones from the grotto of the nativity in Bethlehem. Incidentally, St. Mary Major was built, so the legend goes, in response to a Marian apparition. The Virgin appeared to a couple in a dream on August 4, AD 352 and requested a shrine. Her request was very generously granted.

This same internal constellation within a constellation, the stable within the crab, also appears in another Biblical context, in the various attempts to match the signs of the zodiac to the twelve tribes of

Israel. In what does sound like an apt description of the Ascelli and the Praesaepe in their proximity to Cancer, the patriarch Jacob/Israel delivers this blessing to two of his twelve sons in Genesis 49:13 (translation from the Masoretic text):

> Zebulon shall dwell at the shore of the sea, and he shall be a shore for ships, and his flank shall be upon Zidon.

And in Genesis 49:14:

> Issachar is a large-boned ass, couching down between the sheepfolds.

The King James Version translates this as "Issachar is a strong ass, couching down between two burdens.

In modern, Western, astrology, Cancer is a timid, sensitive creature, as deep and impressionable as the sea, the very source of life, relying on its hard shell to shield and protect it from a cruel world. The sign Cancer symbolizes the security and comfort of home, nourishment, and the protective warmth of a mother's love; the very things that support life when it is most vulnerable. Cancer, the Crab, has come to represent those tough but timid creatures emerging from the primordial matrix of life, creeping out of the sea to stand on the shore and face the sun.

Like Virgo, the sign Cancer has obviously undergone a thorough evolution through the ages right along with us, just as our idea of the Queen of Heaven and the Mother of God has continually evolved in response to ever-changing needs. At the same time, the stars of the constellation Cancer, which in the centuries surrounding the birth of Christ coincided with the fourth sign on the ecliptic, marking the Sun's position at the summer solstice, have, due to the precession of the equinoxes, moved along the ecliptic to the point where many of them are now in the sign Leo. But, notwithstanding the detailed and ongoing arguments about the proper boundaries of the constellations, by most accounts, the Praesaepe and the Ascelli were in the sign Cancer for the birth of Christ, and their lore has been firmly bound up in his legends, and those of his mother.

THE PARTING

The apparitions at Beauraing, which started on November 29 and reached their climax on December 8, the Immaculate Conception, slowly played themselves out until January 3 of the following year. Initially there was unity among the children, focused on Albert's leadership. They all saw the same thing at the same time, and their reports were consistent with each other. As the planetary alignments moved on, the nature of the group experience changed too. The children gradually lost their clarity and cohesion. They still saw the Virgin on the branch of the hawthorn tree, but sometimes one or more of the seers were left out of the experience. Toward the end of December, there were two occasions when only Fernande Voisin, the oldest of the group, could see her.

Just after New Year's Day, the Virgin told the children that she would soon see them for the last time. On January 3, she came to say goodbye. Almost thirty-five thousand people showed up on the appointed day. When the children arrived that evening, they all went into their trance at her appearance, except for Fernande. She couldn't see anything.

After the short visit had ended and the Lady had given each of the children a private message and a fond farewell, Fernande lingered in the courtyard, weeping for the Lady. She stubbornly refused to leave, praying the rosary as the others departed.

Suddenly, a crackling flash of light split the sky over the hawthorn tree, sending sparks flying, and a roaring thunderclap echoed through the schoolyard. Fernande was seen falling to her knees. The Lady had come back for her! She received her personal message and tearfully said goodbye to the Lady forever.

VIRGIN FEVER

This combination of Virgo and lunar elements seems to have precipitated an outbreak of Virgin fever during the early 1930s. There were copycat sightings throughout Belgium, including one at Banneux that was later approved by the church, and many more that weren't. Reports of apparitions surfaced in both the Flemish and Walloon areas, including Chaineux, Etikhove, Lokeren, Melen, Onkerzele, Rotselaer, and Tubise.[3] Several other visionaries even claimed subsequent sightings at Beauraing, but they were all dismissed by the church for various reasons as unworthy of approval.

Across Europe, there were at least fifteen different locations that reported sightings. The previous summer, in June of 1931, at the New Moon in Cancer, two children in a village in the Spanish Pyrenees were greeted by a luminous lady one afternoon, setting off years of apparitions and hysteria in Ezquioga and throughout the Basque provinces. The Ezquioga sightings will never be approved, but they do give unique insight into Spanish spirituality in general, and Basque sentiments in particular.[4] (The charts and story are included in chapter 8.)

The Roman Church does not encourage these apparitions, and does exhaustive investigations that most claims fail to withstand. The approval process has matured with experience; for instance, after the embarrassing decline of the visionaries of La Salette, it is now a given that any prospective visionaries must be of sterling character. Also, any messages revealed in the visions must conform to church teachings and, perhaps more to the point, support the local church authorities. The presiding bishop, and not Rome, is the deciding voice in the approval process. Nothing will prosper without his cooperation and support. We have already seen how this can result in serious repackaging of the facts, and indeed, even in the complete distortion of the truth, but it also helps to weed out the wackos.

Like young Albert Voisin, any child between the ages of ten and thirteen in 1932 would have been born with Pluto in Cancer and Jupiter, Saturn, or possibly both, somewhere in Virgo. The many children who reported visions may have been responding to the same archetypal stimulus that inspired Albert's visions. They may have even been responding to the advances of the same otherworldly being. In the midst of this impressive wave of sightings, there was one that followed close on the heels of Beauraing and did meet all the criteria for official approval. These were the visions of little Mariette Beco, in the tiny Belgian village of Banneux.

THE VIRGIN OF THE POOR

Mariette Beco was not a bad child, but she wasn't a particularly good one either. Her attention to her schoolwork left something to be desired, and her church attendance and devotion to the sacraments waned significantly with each passing year. Her family, precariously ensconced among the ranks of the working poor, was struggling to make ends meet in the midst of the worldwide depression.

On the evening of Sunday, January 15, 1933, around 7:00 p.m.,[5] Mariette was looking out of a second-story window, hoping to see her brother returning home. Instead, she was surprised by the figure of a luminous Lady in white, floating above the vegetable garden in the front yard. She called to her mother to come and have a look. Mrs. Beco always affirmed that she did indeed see a white form in the garden that night, but she refused to allow her daughter to go outside.

Mariette later described the Lady as dressed in white, with a white veil and a bright blue sash. No one believed the child when they heard the story, but they couldn't help but notice the immediate and drastic change in her behavior. While the Beco family was not actively religious in any way, Mariette began attending church each morning before school. She suddenly began taking great pains with her school lessons and resumed attendance at the religious education classes.

On the following Wednesday evening, just before 7:00 p.m., Mariette was mysteriously drawn outside to the garden. This time, her father followed and when he saw Mariette fall to her knees communicating with the unseen, he ran to fetch some witnesses.

They returned to find Mariette heading out the driveway and up the road, seemingly in a trance. She repeatedly fell crashing to her knees and prayed, enraptured with the object of her vision. Each time she would get up again unhurt, and continue until eventually she arrived at

Mariette Beco
March 25, 1921
5:00 a.m. BST -1:00
Louveign, Belgium

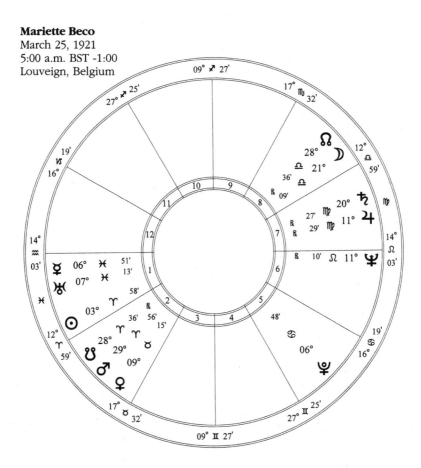

Mariette Beco. Mercury ☿ and Uranus ♅ are opposite
Jupiter ♃ and Saturn ♄ in Virgo ♍.

a small stream. Mariette later reported that the Lady led her to the stream and told her to plunge her hand into the icy water. When the child did this, the Lady told her, "This spring is reserved for me."

On eight separate occasions, the Lady appeared to Mariette in the vegetable garden at about 7:00 p.m., and led her to the spring. While there were no doctors around to examine her, due to the remote location of the village, Mariette reportedly exhibited the same types of ecstatic behavior as the children of Beauraing; especially, speaking her rosary prayers in a high-pitched, unnatural voice, falling to her knees with great force, even on the stoniest of surfaces, and failing to respond to external stimuli. She often appeared distraught at the Lady's parting, even falling into a faint on one occasion when the Lady left her.

Mariette reported that the Lady identified herself as the "Virgin of the Poor." She said the spring was for all nations, "to relieve the sick." Many subsequent cures were documented there. The Lady asked for a little chapel to be built by the stream, and the simple, modest structure was completed and dedicated on the Feast of the Assumption on August 15, 1933.

THE CHARTS

Like Albert Voisin, Mariette, age eleven, was born with both Jupiter and Saturn in the sign Virgo. In Mariette's chart, those Virgo planets are found in her natal 7th house, the house of partners and relationships. Again, I am eternally grateful to Ed Steinbrecher for providing me with Mariette's birth time, which he obtained from the official birth record.

Mariette, an Aries, was born at the Full Moon in Libra. Her natal Jupiter in Virgo is opposed by an interesting conjunction of Mercury and Uranus in Pisces, and is also in trine aspect (forming a 120-degree angle) to her Venus in Taurus, dignified in the sign of her rulership. Visionary Neptune is on Mariette's Descendant, the cusp of

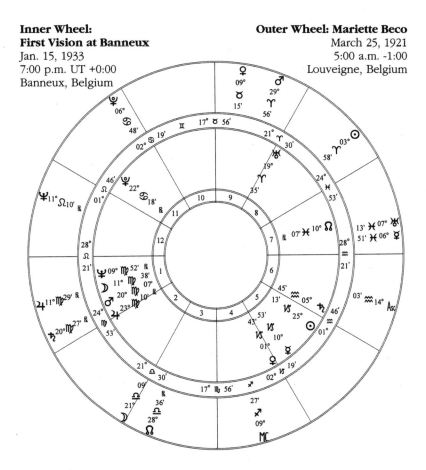

Inner wheel: first vision at Banneux; outer wheel: Mariette Beco.
Multiple opposition and conjunctions in Virgo ♍
and Pisces ♓, spanning the 1st and 7th houses.

her 7th house, indicating the mystical, otherworldly nature of her relationships.

Using the same real-time format, we can insert Mariette's chart into the apparition event, diagramming the astrological influences in effect when she first looked out the window into her vegetable garden. Our next chart is set up as a bi-wheel, with the event chart in the inner wheel and on the angles, while the birth chart for Mariette is displayed around it in the outer wheel. Like Albert Voisin at Beauraing, Mariette was experiencing exact hits to her natal Virgo planets. I doubt this was mere coincidence.

At the time of the initial apparition in Banneux, the Moon was in Virgo, joining with Jupiter, Mars, Neptune, and the South Node in the sign of the Virgin. The transiting Moon was exactly conjunct Mariette's natal Jupiter in Virgo, while transiting Mars in Virgo was exactly conjunct her natal Saturn. The transiting North Node in Pisces is conjunct her natal Mercury-Uranus conjunction, and this alignment spans the 1st through 7th house axis. Like Albert Voisin, Mariette's consciousness was being directly stimulated with archetypal images of the heavenly Virgin, so when she looked out her window, the Lady in white was there, waiting for her.

A WORLD OUT OF WORK

Everyone was being affected by the transit of so many planets through Virgo, but each in his or her own, unique way. The overall effect was a massive, worldwide depression that thrust more and more people back into Virgo's working class—except that there was less and less work for them to do.

Let us recall the Lady of La Salette and her distress over the common people working through the Sabbath, and the famine that would follow. The single worst year of the depression was 1932, bringing record unemployment and more breadlines, perhaps the most powerful symbol of those desperate times. There had been riots throughout Belgium during the year, as workers railed against the overwhelming scarcity. The Virgo emphasis on the common, working people and their struggle for their daily bread was very much to the fore.

Meanwhile, the Nazi sabre-rattling across the border in Germany would hardly go unnoticed. Banneux had been no stranger to fighting in World War I, as it was only about fifteen miles from Liege, the German Army's gateway into France. Banneux's recovery from the ravages of war had been curtailed by the depression. Only a few years later, Belgium would be overrun by Nazi forces, and Banneux, because of its proximity to the Ardennes region, witnessed some of the fiercest fighting of World War II in the Battle of the Bulge. In this light, the Virgin of the Poor, with her healing spring and her humble, little chapel, appears as a source of simple comfort to people in great need.

The messages of both apparitions were short and to the point. The Lady of Beauraing had only a very few, simple words to say for herself. She first spoke on December 2, when, evoking that Virgo sense of purity and perfectionism, she told the children, "Always be good." They all dutifully promised that they would. Later that same day, she asked them, "Is it true that you will always be good?" She also asked for a chapel so people could come there on pilgrimage. On December 22 she identified herself simply as the "Immaculate Virgin"; not the immaculate conception, but the Immaculate Virgin. She spoke very little in all. On December 30 she told the children to "Pray. Pray very much." On January 1 she said, "Pray always." She also identified herself to Andree during her final visit on January 3 as the Mother of God and the Queen of Heaven.

Beauraing detractors actually dismissed the vision as trite, claiming that they could hardly believe the blessed Virgin would come all the way to earth to be so prosaic. But this was a no-fuss, no-frills Virgin, and in this seemingly insignificant little town, only four miles from the French border, she was reaching out to the hard-pressed working people whose modern settlements dotted the ancient homelands of the Celtic tribes.

CAESAR'S BELGAE

Long before these lands were Christianized, they were inhabited by deeply religious people who relied on the priestly orders of the Druids for both spiritual and secular direction. The Romans made a point of destroying the Druid orders to uproot their influence, but the people never really changed. Many of their old ways were almost seamlessly caught up within the new Christian religion, their holy water and holy trees, as well as their reliance on priests to interpret the meaning of the mysteries and to intercede for them between this world and the next. While the Roman Church clearly perpetuated this dependence to their own ends, they can hardly be accused of inventing it. In the same way, many of the old Druid customs were incorporated into the rites and rituals of the Roman Catholic worship of the Virgin.

Caesar wrote that Chartres was the great center[6] of Druid influence in Gaul. The Druids held their principal convocations there and it was the seat of their supreme chief, or, pope, if you will. The area where the cathedral now stands was then a sacred grove, and within that wooded grove was a small cave, or grotto. Tradition has it that within that grotto was a shrine and statue dedicated to the worship of the Virgo partitura, the virgin who *will bring forth*.

She was an object of great devotion among the Celts of Gaul, who were no mean astrologers themselves, at least according to Caesar. Shrines dedicated to her worship can be found from England to Germany, but she also figures into the mythology and lore of the Latins, Chaldeans, Persians, and Egyptians, as well as in the inspired utterances of the Hebrew prophet Isaiah.

It is possible that the Celtic religion's anticipation of this virgin birth helped to accelerate their acceptance of Christianity upon the arrival of the first Christian missionaries in Gaul and the British Isles. The Christianity practiced by these earliest and most fervent converts was a far cry from our modern religion. It was more often a mixture of Egyptian and Middle Eastern practices, cultivated within the crucible of what remained of the old Druid schools. The extensive Druid educational system was quickly converted, and the youth of the aristocracy who would have been instructed by the Druids soon flocked to the monasteries for their education.

To use the term monasteries to describe these earliest communities is misleading, for long centuries stood between them and the impending rule of St. Benedict. These earliest monasteries were famously tolerant, often admitting both men and women, while transmitting a more truly catholic range of traditions. Their broad leanings eventually provoked the censure and discipline of the Roman Church, and in time, the Romans conquered the Druids again, imposing a much narrower creed and curriculum.

But returning to the grotto beneath the great cathedral of Our Lady at Chartres, it is still preserved within the crypt, and the ancient statue of the Virgo partitura remained enshrined there. It continued to be worshipped until the time of the Revolution, when it was carted off in a fit of republican fervor. An exact description remains, from which we learn that it was carved of wood, seemingly from the trunk of a tree, and was well blackened with age, but it represented the Virgin seated in a chair, holding the Holy Child on her knee.

The great enthusiasm the French have always felt for Chartres has its roots in the faith of their Celtic fathers. The beauty and genius of the architecture is but a by-product of that ancient ardor, not the cause of it. The love of the people for the place inspired them to labor so famously to build a temple of medieval perfection, fit to occupy the most sacred site in Gaul and to house its relics. The architects were very careful not to disturb the ancient grotto, and lovingly enshrined its image, so as not to "dry up a fount of grace."[7]

In his book *Celebrated Sanctuaries of the Madonna*, Rev. J. Spencer Northcote quotes from the twelfth-century author Guibert of Nugent,[8] who wrote that his monastery was erected on the site of one of the sacred woods of the Druid priests, where they had been used to sacrifice to the "Mother of the God who was to be born"— *Matri futura Dei nascituri.*

These tantalizing references to the absorption of their sites and beliefs into the young church offer stolen glimpses through the

Druids' curtain of literary silence, granting us some insight into their inscrutable ways and their influence on the development of Marian Christianity in the aftermath of their suppression.

THE BEAUTIFUL BRANCH

One aspect of the Celtic beliefs that has come down to us concerns their veneration of trees. Whether they actually worshipped trees is subject to debate, but they certainly worshipped among them, in the open-air temples of their sacred groves. They did develop an elaborate body of lore about the magical attributes of different trees, much of which has survived in folk beliefs and folk medicine.

The mighty oak was particularly sacred to them, as was the mistletoe that crowned it. The ash, the yew, the willow, the birch, and so on, all had their unique personalities and attributes. The Druids did possess an alphabet, even if they declined to use it to record their wisdom, and that alphabet was also rooted in their tree lore. Each letter was associated with a plant or tree whose name began with the same sound. The hawthorn tree had its own letter, which corresponded to the *h* sound.

I raised the point earlier, in the chapter on Lourdes, that Ruth Harris made about the association of the Virgin Mary with both the hawthorn and the wild rose (eglantine). In her book *Lourdes: Body and Spirit in the Secular Age,* Harris mentions twenty-eight shrines to the Virgin in the area surrounding Lourdes that involved either a hawthorn or a wild rose.[9] In the apparition at Lourdes, the Lady appeared among the branches of the eglantine growing over the grotto. The Virgin Mary is often described or depicted as a mystical rose among thorns, but why she should have such an affinity for the spiny boughs of the hawthorn is a little harder to pin down, even if the apparitions on the beautiful branch at Beauraing do seem to reinforce the point.

In what survives of the lore of the hawthorn, we do find intriguing connections to certain goddesses and the marriage or courtship traditions that would have been their special concern. There are at least fifty varieties of hawthorn, and almost as many names, but the whitethorn, the may, or the quickset, as it is also called, favors lovers and speeds the quest for a good match. In some parts of medieval Europe, a man proposed by leaving a branch of hawthorn at his beloved's door. In ancient Greece, the blossoms were woven into crowns for the wedding couple. The boughs were carried as torches in wedding processions, and decked the altars of Hymen, the god of marriage and the protector of young girls. The Roman virgin goddess Cardea had a special connection with the hawthorn, and its flowers and branches adorned her festivals in May.

The hawthorn has a unique and consistent role in the springtime rites of May, hence its common name, "May." This may have come about because it blooms early enough to decorate even the Beltane festivities with its flowery boughs. In a manuscript called *The State of Eton School,* AD 1560, from the British Museum, we read:

> If it be fair weather, and the master grants leave, those boys who choose it may rise at four o'clock, to gather May branches, if they can do it without wetting their feet; and on that day they adorn the windows of the bed-chamber with green leaves, and the houses are perfumed with fragrant herbs.

The sixteenth-century English poet Edmund Spenser also makes reference to the hawthorn:

> Youngthes folk now flocke in everywhere
> To gather May buskets and smelling Brere;
> And home they hasten the postes to dight,
> And all the kirk (church) pillours eare day-light
> With Hawthorne buds and sweet Eglantine.[10]

In Spenser's lines, we have a fascinating reference to the use of both the hawthorn and the eglantine to deck not only homes, but also church pillars in a May Day celebration. The Irish sometimes referred to the hawthorn as the fairy bush, and it was considered very bad luck to cut it and disturb the fairies. However, that geiss, or magical prohibition, was suspended during the May Day celebrations when the collecting of the sprigs and branches was encouraged.

The traditional May celebrations were often bawdy affairs, celebrating romance and sexuality. Such ribald pastimes, rooted deep in the pagan past, helped to erase the memory of winter's bitter cold and remained very popular, well into Christian times. Attempting to distance itself from these excesses, the Roman Church proclaimed May Mary's month, a time of special devotion to the ever-virgin Mother of God. The origins of this custom are unclear, but the Egyptian Copts and the Abyssinian Christians still celebrate the Virgin Mary's nativity on the first of May; further evidence of an ancient connection between May Day, the hawthorn, and the Queen of Heaven.

To this day, May is still celebrated as Mary's special month in parishes around the world. Central to the modern Marian May Day celebrations is the crowning of a statue of our Lady with a wreath woven of fresh flowers. It is also traditional for the faithful to honor her by presenting her statue with bouquets or baskets of flowers. Consider the lyrics to the chorus of this popular May hymn, Bring Flowers of the Fairest: "O Mary, we crown thee with flowers today. Queen of the Angels, and Queen of the May." These simple words, sung by adoring Catholics for generations, take on an even richer meaning when we remember Mary's longstanding but mysterious association with the hawthorn, or the "May."

THE LADY IN THE TREE

Whether they were aware of it or not, the children who worshipped the Virgin in the branches of the hawthorn tree at Beauraing were carrying forward an ancestral style of devotion. In keeping with their ancestors' passion for worshipping among trees, the Belgian people have an interesting habit of worshipping the Virgin in trees. For instance, in nearby Walcourt, there is a very popular Marian shrine that dates back to the fourth century. Tradition says it was built by St.

Maternus, an early Christian convert with a very maternal name. After converting the local warlord to the new religion and convincing him to cease his predations upon the people, Maternus constructed a small chapel to Our Lady on the former tyrant's lands, in the very shadow of his fortress. St. Maternus himself is credited with carving a statue of Our Lady and installing it in his new chapel. This popular shrine may well be one of the oldest of its kind in Christendom.

Devotion continued at this site for almost a thousand years, but in the thirteenth century, enemies set the chapel on fire, reducing it to ashes. In her book *Miraculous Images of Our Lady,* author Joan Carroll Cruz quotes the local records for this account of the fire:

> All the townsfolk witnessed the prodigy; they saw the holy image rise from the midst of the flames, lifted by a supernatural force and born to a nearby place called "Jardinet," where it was set on a tree. In spite of all their efforts, the people were unable to remove it and the miraculous statue dwelt on the tree until the day when they besought the intervention of Count Thierry de Rochefort, the Seigneur of Walcourt. The Count rode out to the tree, followed by his squire, but his horse recoiled before the statue of the Virgin Mary, which was surrounded by a host of angels.
>
> Thrice did the Count try to advance. Then, dismounting, he knelt at the foot of the tree, and vowed to found a monastery in the valley and to rebuild the burnt chapel. Then, to the amazement of the people, they saw the miraculous statue leave the tree and descend into the arms of the Count, who hastened to carry it back to Walcourt.[11]

To this day, a memorial procession is held annually on Trinity Sunday, traveling along the route taken by the statue from the shrine to Jardinet and back again. There are fifteen chapels along the processional route, and the people stop to pray at each one along the way. A replica statue is hung from the branches of the tree in Jardinet, and placed in the arms of the person representing the Count, who then carries it back to Walcourt.

Further to the north is the Belgian shrine of Montaigu, the "sharp hill." This distinct promontory rises abruptly from the surrounding countryside, and from time immemorial, was crowned by a solitary oak tree. It was well known as a site of Druid worship, long before the advent of Christianity. Legend has it that in the fourteenth century, the people decided to Christianize the site by placing a statue of the Virgin in a cavity of the oak; not exactly a giant leap in the Christian direction, but that's the story. It became a popular Marian shrine, or perhaps, more exactly, it continued to be a popular place to seek the help and guidance of the heavenly mother.

One day, a shepherd noticed that the statue had been blown out of its place in the oak tree. He tried to pick it up and carry it to his home, but he found he could not move it at all, except in the direction of the statue's home in the oak. He dutifully returned it to its place, and told the townspeople about what had happened. As that story spread, the shrine became more popular than ever.

The statue was attacked and destroyed by the Gueux, a radical group, in 1579, but people continued to flock to the oak tree to pray. In 1586 a replacement statue was found that looked so remarkably like the original that it was installed in the oak and the worship continued. Through the years, while the reputation of the shrine for wonders and cures grew, it was often attacked by rebels or heretics, and caught up in the turbulence of the times. The statue (or the replacement statue) miraculously escaped a number of attacks, so the people decided to build a hilltop fortress to defend the shrine. The old oak tree, or what little remained of it after being stripped by relic hunters for centuries, was finally cut down, and its wood used to make replica statues for the gentry. A high altar was put in its place. The fortress and basilica were completed in 1627.

The shrine of Our Lady of Foy dates to July 6, 1609 (Cancer), when a forester, felling an old oak, discovered the remains of a wayside shrine enclosed within the tree. There was a statue of Our Lady, some beads, a votive lock of hair, and the iron bars of a protective grill. The statue was cleaned up and eventually presented to the Lord of the Manor, the Baron of Celles, who undertook to build a new shrine for it near the old tree. In the meantime, the statue was adored in the Baron's private chapel, and its reputation for miraculous cures and other wonders began to spread.[12]

One of the most famous Marian shrines in Belgium is Our Lady of the Branch in Antwerp. Legend places the origins of this cult within the Norman invasions at the dawn of the tenth century. The Norman forces had finally been repelled at Gheule in AD 891, but before they retreated, they set fire to a nearby forest. All the trees burned save one, and upon investigation, a precious statue of Our Lady was found hanging upon it. This statue was enshrined in the Cathedral in Antwerp, where its long history of devotions and adventures could more than fill a book of its own.

Not far from Antwerp is the town of Duffel, and its beloved shrine of Our Lady of Good Will. According to legend, two small children were out minding the sheep on the vigil of the Assumption in 1637, when they found a small terra cotta statue of Our Lady nailed to a willow tree. People began to come out to pray to it, eventually hanging a lamp before it, which burned day and night. In time, a chapel was erected on the site. The statue was credited with saving Duffel during an outbreak of fever, and the shrine's popularity increased accordingly.[13]

What emerges here is a pattern of worshipping the Virgin, or images of the Virgin, in trees, often to miraculous effect. This practice seems fairly widespread in Belgium, but it is also encountered in other parts of Europe; for instance, the famous Oak of Viterbo, Italy, where a portrait of Our Lady has been enthusiastically worshipped in an oak tree since 1417, despite repeated attempts to remove it.[14] The appearance of Our Lady on the beautiful branch of the hawthorn in Beauraing, while a rare event in modern times, actually perpetuates an established pattern of worship rooted deeply within the pre-Christian practices of the ancestors of modern Europeans.

These patterns of devotion run so very deep that even the school-children unwittingly preserve them. In spite of every effort to tailor these apparition events to fit within a narrow, orthodox framework, the evidence overflows the boundaries set by the Roman Church and demands to be appreciated within a much broader, more universal context. The Holy Spring at Banneux and the hawthorn tree in Beau-raing show that, whether consciously or unconsciously, we continue to repeat these ancient patterns of worship, no matter how many times our religious leaders change the rules or change the names. This shared history, long suppressed, is our common heritage, our birthright—the true faith of our fathers.

The astrological charts reveal the consistency of the cosmic forces at work, and the interplay of our perceptions within the unfolding order of the universe, forcing us to think outside of the box of ortho-dox religion. When we are free to reset these Marian encounters within that larger, more universal framework, we don't lose any of the holiness or the miracle of the moment. What we lose is the need to selfishly claim it as ours alone, to exclude nonbelievers from sharing in it. We lose the fear and insecurity that makes us judge and con-demn those who think differently. On the other hand, we gain an expanded frame of reference that is considerably more loving and inclusive than the more limited paradigms of orthodox religion. Orthodoxy, by its very definition, spawns divisions, heresies, and per-secution—now more than ever. Christians are still fighting Muslims, and Muslims are still fighting Jews, each with a sense of urgent self-righteousness and a distinct separateness under the same God. We need those unifying, universal truths that bind us together and emphasize our common heritage.

The celestial Virgin, the Queen of Heaven, and the Mother of God were all worshipped and adored long before they were co-opted by Christianity and repackaged into the image of the Blessed Virgin Mary. Our human perception of the female aspects of divinity, of God's better half, is constantly evolving. Our images of her, exalted reflections of ourselves, have grown, changed, regressed, and exploded again in a new worldwide wave of Marian devotion.

In the act of worshipping her, we come to emulate the very virtues we have projected upon her image. That image is evolving constantly, just as we ourselves evolve through the art of worship; and yet she remains the same, as constant as the heavens to which we aspire in both our wildest dreams and most heartfelt prayers. We need to strive for the highest ideals; so high that we must constantly outdo ourselves to reach them. How marvelous then, when the very epitome and apotheosis of our aspirations, in an act of mercy and love, bends down and reaches out to us.

Endnotes

1. Don Sharkey and Joseph DeBergh, O. M. J., *Our Lady of Beauraing* (Garden City, NY: Hanover House, 1958), 72. My narrative of the events at Beauraing is drawn from this book and others, including: Bob Lord and Penny Lord, *The Many Faces of Mary: A Love Story* (Journeys of Faith, 1987); Catherine M. Odell, *Those Who Saw Her: The Apparitions of Mary* (Huntington, IN: Our Sunday Visitor Publishing Division, 1986); Rev. Paul Piron SJ, *Five Children* (New York: Benziger Bros., 1938).

2. Richard Hinkley Allen, *Star Names: Their Lore and Meaning* (New York: Dover Publications, 1963), 108–109.

3. David Blackbourn, *Marpingen: Apparitions of the Virgin Mary in a Nineteenth-Century German Village* (New York: Vintage Books/Random House, 1993), 328.

4. William A. Christian Jr., *Visionaries: The Spanish Republic and the Reign of Christ* (Berkeley: University of California Press, 1996).

5. The time for Mariette's visions can be found in: John Delaney, ed. *A Woman Clothed With the Sun* (New York: Doubleday, 1961), 243; Odell, *Those Who Saw Her.*

6. Julius Caesar, *Gallic Wars*, book 6.

7. Rev. J. Spencer Northcote, *Celebrated Sanctuaries of the Madonna* (London: Longmans, Green and Co., 1868), 170.

8. Ibid. Northcote quotes Guibert of Nugent, de Vita sua, Libr. II, c.I.

9. Ruth Harris, *Lourdes: Body and Spirit in the Secular Age* (New York: Viking/Penguin), 68.

10. The quotes in reference to the hawthorn, from Eton School and from Spenser, were both taken from this website: www.2020site.org/trees/hawthorn.html.

11. Joan Carroll Cruz, *Miraculous Images of Our Lady: 100 Famous Catholic Portraits and Statues* (Rockford, IL: Tan Books and Publishers, 1993), 19–20.

12. Ibid. The stories of the shrines at Montaigu and at Foy are also taken from this book.

13. E. W. Beck, "The City of the Mother of God: Antwerp, Belgium, Notre Dame, Indiana," *The Ave Maria,* vol. XXXV, no. 27 (Dec. 31, 1892). This article is the source for the stories of "Our Lady of the Branch and Duffel."

14. Cruz, *Miraculous Images of Our Lady,* 171–175.

Seven

APPARITIONS: THEN AND NOW

So numerous are the reports of visions and appearances of the Virgin throughout history that it would be very hard to present a truly definitive list. This chapter contains only a brief and cursory introduction to some of my favorites, ranging from the fully approved to the totally discredited. As hard as it is to pick and choose among apparitions, with so many stories begging to be told, I have had to limit myself to those for which I have reliable data, both for the dates and the circumstances.

ST. SIMON STOCK AND THE BROWN SCAPULAR

Although an ancient apparition, it is authoritatively dated to July 16, 1251. The Carmelite Order had recently come to England from the Holy Land, but they were not very popular with the established clergy. Simon Stock was the head of the order in England, and he was deeply discouraged by the antagonisms that had developed. He spent the night in prayer to the Virgin, and in the early morning of July 16, she appeared to him, holding the baby Jesus and accompanied by a host of angels. She presented him with the brown scapular, and identified herself as the Lady of Mount Carmel. (A Christianized goddess

Mary Appears to St. Simon Stock
July 16, 1251 OS
6:00 a.m. LMT -0:01:56
Aylesford, England

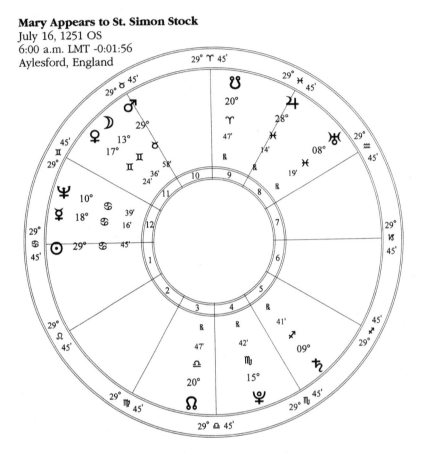

Mary appears to St. Simon Stock.

from the high places of the Holy Land?) She promised protection to
his order, and many blessings to those who spread devotion to the
scapular. The scapular has remained a very popular sacramental
down through the ages, and many still wear it today.

The chart reveals an emphasis on the sign Cancer. The Sun is in
Cancer, trine Jupiter in Pisces. There is a (separating) conjunction of
Mercury and Neptune in Cancer, while the Moon aligns with Venus in
a conjunction in Gemini.

THE VIRGIN OF KAZAN

The national icon of Russia, the ancient image of the Virgin of Kazan holding her child embodies the prayers and hopes of the Russian people. It is believed to date back to apostolic times, or perhaps even earlier. The image rose to prominence in the eleventh century, following the conversion of Russia, but was lost in the thirteenth century when Kazan was overrun by enemy armies.

Finding of the Statue at Kazan
July 8, 1859 OS
12:01 p.m. LMT -3:16:32
Kazan, Russia

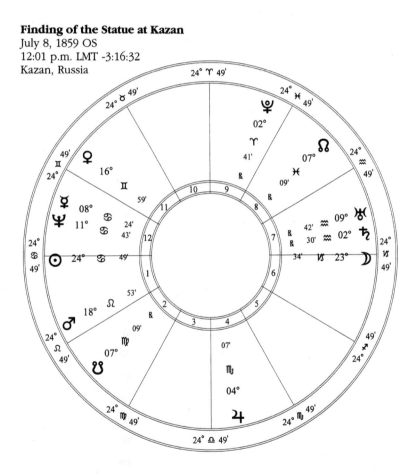

Finding the statue at Kazan.

In 1579, Kazan was under attack again and most of the town had been burned. A nine-year-old girl named Matrona Onuchkin experienced three visions of the Virgin in a dream. The Virgin told her to look for the missing icon underneath the rubble of the girl's burned-down home. On July 8, Matrona went to look for the icon, and she found it wrapped in a cloth beneath the ruins of the stove.

This miraculous story advanced the popularity of the image and its importance for the Russian people. It was eventually invoked as the Protectress of Russia and the czars built a great basilica for it in Moscow. The Bolsheviks destroyed this basilica and the icon was reportedly spirited away on October 13, 1917, the same day as the Miracle of the Sun in Fatima.

This chart is not timed, but is set for July 8, 1579, when Matrona unearthed the long-lost icon and reunited the mother with her people. It reveals the Sun, Mercury, and Neptune in Cancer, just like the chart for St. Simon Stock's vision. Additionally, the Cancer planets are opposed by the Full Moon in Capricorn. This Cancer-Capricorn emphasis communicates that sense of family and national identity, and the shared memories and history that bind a people together.

VILA BOAS, PORTUGAL

On September 4, 1673, the Virgin appeared to a twelve-year-old girl named Maria Trigo. The date comes from the book *Aparicoes Em Portugal Dos Sec. XIV a XX,* by Seomara Da Veiga Ferreira.

The chart, for which the time is unknown, reveals the Sun conjunct Mars in Virgo, along with Pluto and Venus in Cancer.

Vision at Vila Boas
Sept. 4, 1673 NS
12:01 p.m. LMT +0:36:32
Lisbon, Portugal

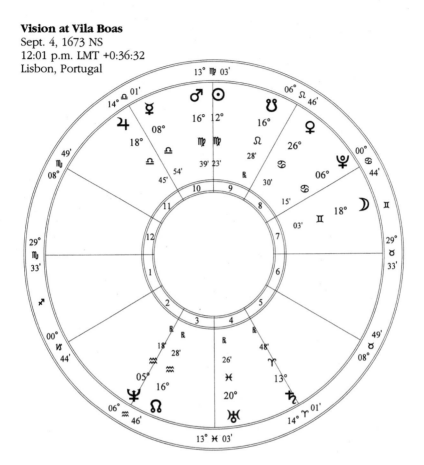

Vision at Vila Boas.

PONTMAIN

This apparition involves a touching story from the Franco-Prussian War. The tiny French town of Pontmain lay in the path of the advancing Prussian troops, who had already taken Paris. Prayers went up from the village that morning for their safety, and for the thirty-eight villagers who had been conscripted to fight in this now hopeless cause. Around 5:30 p.m., little Eugene Barbedette stepped outside of his father's barn and saw a beautiful Lady suspended in the sky. He

Vision at Pontmain
Jan. 17, 1871 NS
5:25 p.m. -0:12:28
Pontmain, France

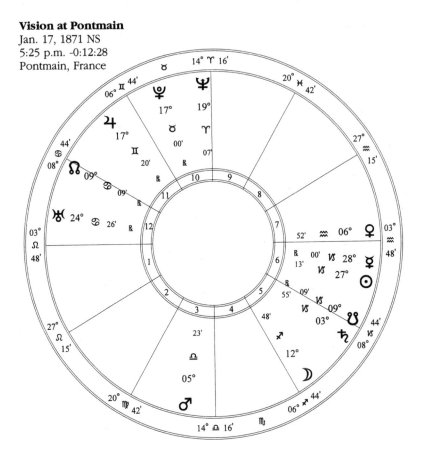

Vision at Pontmain.

called out the others, but only his younger brother Joseph could see
her. His parents and the other adults saw nothing. Two other children
came by, and they immediately saw the Lady. A little later, two other
children arrived and they saw her as well, but none of the adults
could. A crowd soon gathered, led together in prayer by a local nun.

The Lady appeared to be about eighteen years old, and wore a
blue robe covered with golden stars. On her head was a golden
crown surrounded by three stars, under which she wore a black veil.

Her blue shoes had gold ribbons. The apparition transformed as the crowd prayed to it. It was motionless for two hours, but then a blue frame formed around it, with four candles. A small, red cross formed over her heart, and there seemed to be more stars in her robe. A scroll appeared under her feet, with words in gold that said, "But pray, my children." Later, the scroll read, "God will soon grant your request," and then, "My Son allows Himself to be moved."

When the parish priest arrived and began leading the prayers, a white veil rose up from her feet and covered her until she disappeared!

Later, the villagers learned that the Prussian troops had halted their advance at 5:30 p.m. Some said that the soldiers had seen a Lady themselves. The war was soon over and all the village soldiers returned, unharmed.

The chart for the initial apparition reveals an angular Venus in Aquarius conjunct the Descendant, similar to Fatima and Lourdes. Mystical Neptune is conjunct the Midheaven. Also, like Lourdes and the apparition at the Rue de Bac in Paris, there is an opposition in the last third (decan) of Cancer-Capricorn, involving the Sun and Mercury in Capricorn opposing Uranus in Cancer. The North Node is in Cancer, and the South Node is close to Saturn in Capricorn.

MARPINGEN

On July 3, 1876, on the outskirts of this tiny village in the northern Saarland of Bismark's Germany, three little girls went out picking berries in the woods while the rest of their families were making hay. Margaretha Kunz, Katharina Hubertus, and Susanna Leist were all eight years old. They heard the evening Angelus bells ring and began to make their way home, across a broad meadow. Susanna suddenly cried out, drawing her friends' attention to what the girls later described as a "white figure" carrying a child in its arms. The next day, they returned to the spot, and after saying the Lord's Prayer

First Vision at Marpingen
July 3, 1876 NS
6:00 p.m. LMT -0:27:56
Marpingen, Germany

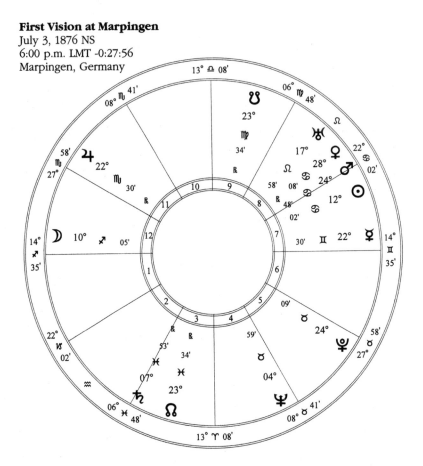

First vision at Marpingen.

three times, the woman appeared again. This time Susanna could not see her, but the other two did. They asked who she was and reported that she replied, "The Immaculately Conceived."

The girls continued to see her over the next several days, during which time the Lady made the usual requests for a chapel to be built, and encouraged the sick to come there and pray. She also asked that water be brought from a spring in the Hartelwald. Thousands of believers descended upon the area, reporting miraculous cures.

Marpingen quickly became both famous and controversial. The emerging German society was struggling against itself at this site, as modernists and nationalists clashed with the faithful, who felt vindicated in this visit from the Virgin Mary.

Whatever the original impetus, the visions dragged on for some fourteen months, and eventually became ridiculous. Charges of fraud and public disorder were even brought against some of the villagers, but they were acquitted in a sensational trial. The girls eventually recanted or retracted much of their testimony.

The apparitions at Marpingen will never be approved, but I have to wonder, when examining the chart for the initial encounter, if the girls didn't see something. The demands and expectations of the times may have eventually distorted the experience, but with the Sun, Mars, and Venus in Cancer, an angular Moon, and an emphasis on the 7th house in the apparition chart, it's not entirely inconceivable that the girls did see a glowing, white Lady in the meadow that day.

KNOCK

Far off the beaten track in the rocky hinterlands of Co. Mayo, Ireland, the people of the little town of Knock (Cnoc druma Calraigh—the hill/ridge of the Calraighs) were treated to a splendid vision of the Virgin, flanked by two attendants who were identified as St. Joseph and St. John. Legend has it that St. Patrick specially blessed this place and declared that one day it would be a great pilgrimage site. There is some evidence that it was a pilgrimage site in pre-Christian times, recognized by travelers for the welcoming fires on its hills. A holy well dedicated to a female St. Keelin, which is annually venerated at the end of July, indicates some history of devotion to the feminine aspects of divinity. Apparently, there was an outbreak of healings and visions at the old chapel during the 1820s as well, so even though the town seems mighty insignificant, it has a history.

Vision at Knock
August 21, 1879 NS
7:15 p.m. LMT +0:35:04
Knock, Ireland

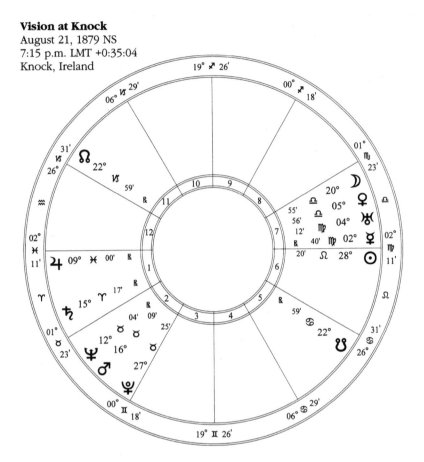

Vision at Knock.

The fateful evening of August 21, 1879 was wet and dreary, but there was nothing unusual about that. The parish priest, Archdeacon Cavanagh, had been out visiting, and was soaked through when he came in. After 7:00 p.m., his housekeeper, Mary McLaughlin, also went out visiting, and she thought she saw some statues standing out by the church in the rain. She returned shortly afterward with a neighbor, Mary Byrne, and the two women approached the chapel to lock it up. Both women realized that the church gable appeared to be lit with a great light, and that Mary McLaughlin's "statues" were now fully illuminated and looked like living beings.

The women called out their neighbors and relations. A crowd gathered in the rain, about fifteen in all, for everyone could see the vision. There were no reports of trances or ecstatic states. Portrayed against the gray stone gable wall was a holy tableau, emblazoned with light, of three figures gathered about an altar. The Virgin Mary was central, but she was flanked by two male figures, which the crowd assumed to be St. Joseph and St. John the Evangelist. Some of the witnesses thought they recognized them from statues they had seen in other churches. Beside the three was an altar, surmounted by a cross and a lamb. Some witnesses reported seeing stars or brilliant lights circulating about the lamb.

The figures appeared to be just in front of the gable wall, and suspended about a foot and a half above the ground. They did not get wet in the rain, and when one witness dared to go close enough to try to touch them, her hands grasped nothing but the empty air. The white figures never moved, nor said anything to the gathering crowd. The vision lasted until about half past nine, when the crowd decided to visit an old woman who lay in bed dying. When they returned, the figures were gone.

This uniquely Irish apparition does not seem to fit any category other than its own, and has had its share of detractors. The grouping of three is a distinctly Irish feature, and many of the pre-Christian practices that survive within Irish Catholicism involve the number three, particularly in the rituals at holy wells and turas stations.

The apparition at Knock was approved, and the site has grown into a huge pilgrimage center, with its own airport. Dignitaries like the pope and Mother Theresa have flown in to pay their respects at the old gable wall.

The chart reveals an emphasis, not only on the sign Virgo, but also on the number three. When Mary McLaughlin first noticed the three statues, shortly after 7:00 p.m., a stellium of three planets was setting on the Descendant. The Sun at the end of Leo was conjunct Mercury and Uranus in Virgo, opposing Jupiter rising in Pisces. As the crowds gathered through the evening, Venus and the Moon in Libra set on the Descendant.

LE PAILLY, FRANCE

On September 9, 1909, our Lady appeared to Fr. Pere Lamy, who was dedicated to praying the rosary. This priest claimed that she predicted the outbreak of World War I and World War II, healed his eczema, and straightened the disfigurations in his feet. She requested a shrine,

Apparition at Le Pailly
Sept. 9, 1909
12:01 p.m. -0.16 -0:09:20
Le Pailly, France

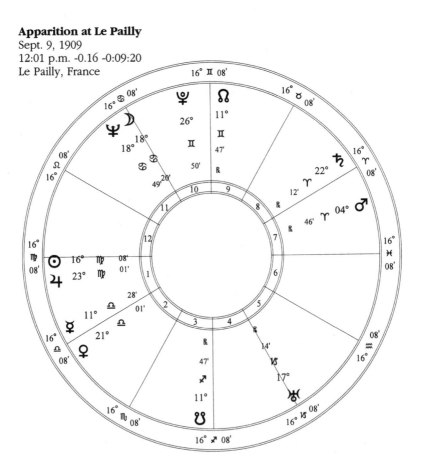

Apparition at Le Pailly.

which Fr. Lamy established, called the Lady of the Woodlands. Many other miraculous cures have been attributed to this Lady of the Woodlands, and to the holy water found at her shrine.

The chart for the apparition on September 9, 1909, for which the time is unknown, features the Sun conjunct Jupiter in Virgo, and the Moon near Neptune in Cancer.

EZKIOGA, SPAIN

I referred to this long series of visions in the chapter on Beauraing and Banneux. The Basque Catholics of the Pyrenees felt under attack in June of 1931. The previous month, over one hundred churches and convents had been torched by arsonists, and the new, anti-clerical government of the Second Republic was leaning evermore to the left. The changes looming large on the Spanish cultural horizon were particularly unsettling to the people of the rural Basque provinces. Deeply religious and equally mistrustful of anything either urban or Spanish, the national elections at the end of June had spawned deadly riots throughout the region.

On the day after the elections, in the remote Basque town of Ezkioga, two children reported they had seen a Lady. The crowds closed in quickly, and soon thousands were seeing her in large, out-door gatherings. Dozens of seers emerged, both children and adults, male and female, and experienced nightly visions and states of ecstasy to the delight of the growing crowds. During July, there were sometimes as many as eighty thousand people gathered on the hill-side outside Ezkioga, in what was possibly the largest gatherings ever held in the Basque Country.

The visions dragged on for years and people were seeing her everywhere. The movement generally ran afoul of the local church authorities, so it will never be approved. The chart for the initial vision (for which the time is unknown) reveals the Sun and Mercury in Can-cer opposed by the Full Moon in Capricorn, and Jupiter and Pluto in

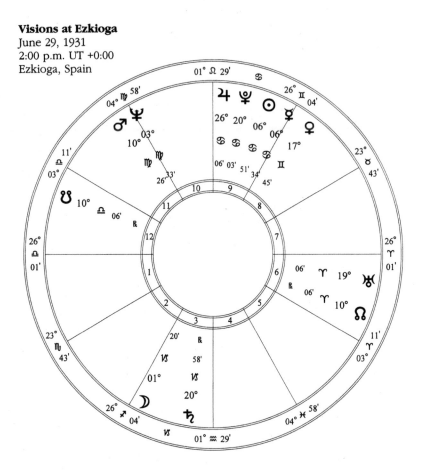

Visions at Ezkioga
June 29, 1931
2:00 p.m. UT +0:00
Ezkioga, Spain

Visions at Ezkioga.

Cancer, opposed by Saturn in Capricorn. Both Mars and Neptune are in Virgo.

AMSTERDAM

In the waning days of the second world war, Ida Peerdeman, a forty-year-old single woman, was at home with her sisters and a visiting priest, when she suddenly felt drawn into the next room. When she entered, she saw a light, and as she drew near it, she said the wall

Apparition to Ida in Amsterdam
March 25, 1945
12:01 p.m. CET -1:00
Amsterdam, Netherlands

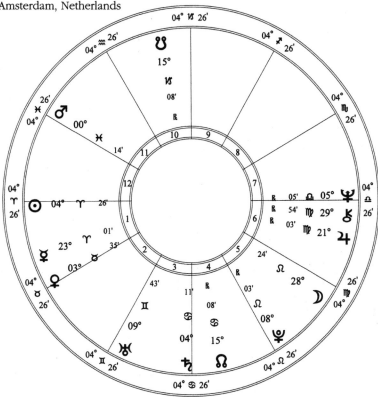

Apparition to Ida in Amsterdam.

disappeared and she felt she was standing in a sea of light and empty space. A female figure moved forward, robed in white with a sash, and reached out for her. Ida immediately assumed that it was the Virgin Mary, and began receiving messages from her. These visions and messages, of a fairly orthodox nature, continued until Ida's death in 1996. The local bishop has withheld full approval, but devotion still continues to this apparition, under the title of Our Lady of All Nations.

The date of the initial apparition, March 25, is the Feast of the Annunciation, which is celebrated annually in honor of the angel Gabriel's appearance to Mary to announce the upcoming birth of Jesus. That has become a very popular day for seeing the Virgin in recent years. Several of the visions of the 1980s have also occurred on the Feast of the Annunciation.

Ida's initial vision occurred on March 25, 1945, but the time is uncertain. The chart includes Jupiter and Chiron in Virgo, and Saturn and the Moon's North Node in Cancer.

JERUSALEM

In his book *The Great Apparitions of Mary,* Ingo Swann asserts that Mary appeared to a group of schoolchildren here on July 18, 1954. In the Coptic school of St. Anthony of Egypt, the children were just going on break when suddenly several students saw a vision of a Lady outside the window. They called her *El Adra,* "the virgin." None of the adults could see her. She then appeared inside the classroom, becoming most visible when she stood in contrast in front of a wall.

She appeared again on July 25 during a Coptic church service. She seemed to be floating above the heads of the congregation and moving about between the people for almost fifteen minutes. The Coptic bishop gave his approval, explaining that she came because the place was so holy, being near both Calvary and the Tomb of Christ.

The exact time of the initial apparition is unknown, but this chart is set for noon. It is full of Marian signatures, with the Sun, Uranus, the South Node, Mercury, and Jupiter in Cancer, and Venus in Virgo.

Apparition at Jerusalem
July 18, 1954
12:00 p.m. EEDT -3:00
Jerusalem, Israel

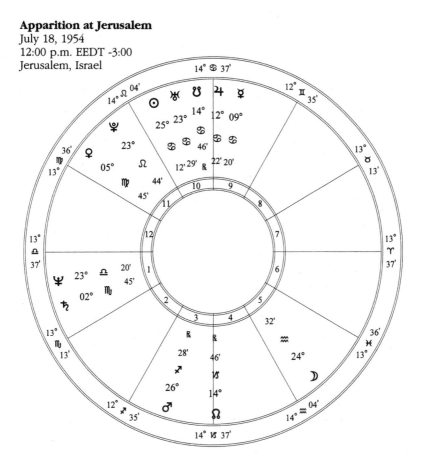

Apparition at Jerusalem.

GARABANDEL

This dramatic series of apparitions in a remote Spanish mountain village will never be approved, but it continues to be very influential and is certainly one of the most entertaining religious dramas of our time.

An angel greeted a group of schoolgirls one Sunday afternoon in June of 1961. This revelation provoked the usual skeptical reactions, but the visits continued. The angel identified himself as Michael, the Guardian Angel of Spain, like the angel at Fatima. He began appearing to them regularly, and the girls' ecstatic, trancelike behavior during the visits drew the attention of local doctors. The angel promised the girls a visit from our Lady on July 2, 1961.

Just after 6:00 p.m. she appeared to the girls as Our Lady of Mt. Carmel. The chart for the initial apparition is full of Marian signatures, including the Sun and Mercury in Cancer, a Mars-Pluto conjunction in Virgo opposing a Moon-Chiron conjunction in Pisces, Venus in Taurus, Saturn in Capricorn, and a grand trine in water signs linking the Pisces Moon, the Cancer Sun, and Neptune in Scorpio. There is also

Virgin Appears at Garabandel
July 2, 1961
6:06 p.m. CET -1:00
Garabandel, Spain

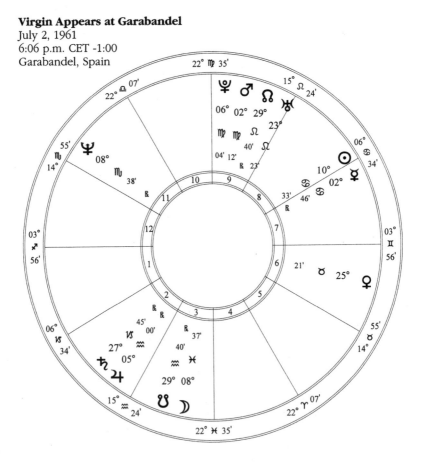

Virgin appears at Garabandel.

a bizarre stellium spanning the cusp of the signs Leo-Virgo, bunching up Uranus and the Moon's North Node in the last degrees of Leo with Mars and Pluto in the early degrees of Virgo.

The Lady continued to appear to the girls for years, making her final visit on November 13, 1965. The hysteria, ecstasies, paranormal phenomena, possession, and controversy surrounding the years of visions at Garabandel leave a confusing impression, and perhaps can best be compared to the events at Medjugorje in revealing how very modern, complex, and ongoing these Marian apparitions have become. Even St. Bernadette might have eventually turned into some kind of sideshow freak if she had continued to have public visits with her aquero for four solid years. Whatever the original impetus, it seems that the longer these things go on, the more opportunity there is for other influences to come to the fore.

The people of Garabandel, living in the mountainous Basque territory not so very far from Lourdes, have a unique tradition. At the end of their regular Catholic prayers, they add a few invocations in honor of Nuestra Señora bien aparecida en la montaña, which loosely translated means "Our Lady who has appeared well on the mountain." Presumably this devotion harkens back to a seventeenth-century apparition, indicating a history in Garabandel of Marian apparitions. Still, I wonder if we aren't hearing echoes of the Basque Mari in this name for a majestic Lady appearing on the mountains?

CONCHITA GONZALES

Conchita was the chief visionary at Garabandel; the first to see the angel and enter the trance state, and the one who served as the initial spokesperson for the group. To this day, she is revered by Marian Catholics around the world as a seer and a spiritual leader, even though the apparitions at Garabandel have fallen far short of official approval.

Conchita is an Aquarius, born on February 2, 1949, with the Sun, Mars, Mercury, and Venus in the sign of the Water Bearer. Her natal

Conchita Gonzalez
Feb. 7, 1949
12:01 p.m. CET -1:00
Garabandel, Spain

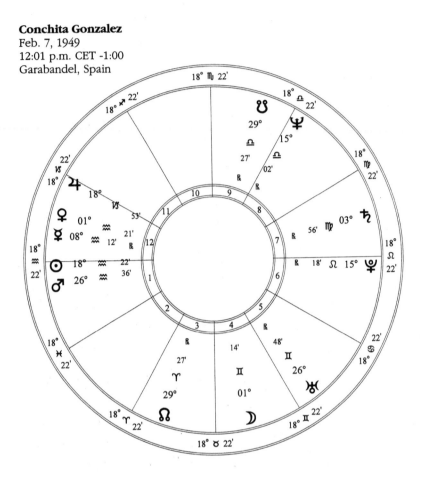

Conchita Gonzales.

Saturn in Virgo was tightly aspected by the planets in the chart for
the initial apparition of Our Lady, and conjunct the transiting Mars in
Virgo. All of the Garabandel visionaries were born with their natal
Saturn near Conchita's, so the transiting stellium of Uranus, Mars,
Pluto, and the Moon's North Node linked them together, through
their natal Saturns, in this bizarre and abortive venture.

SAN DAMIANO

A series of apparitions took place in this rural Italian town in the 1960s involving a seer named Rosa Quattrini. Rosa had lived a difficult life, full of hard work and ill health. The cesarean births of her children took a terrible toll on her body, and she suffered from a form of "perforated peritonitis." Her intestines were pushing through herniated holes in her abdominal muscles; the aftermath of sloppy caesareans.

Rosa is Healed by "Mary"
Sept. 29, 1961
12:05 p.m. CET -1:00
San Damiano d'Asti, Italy

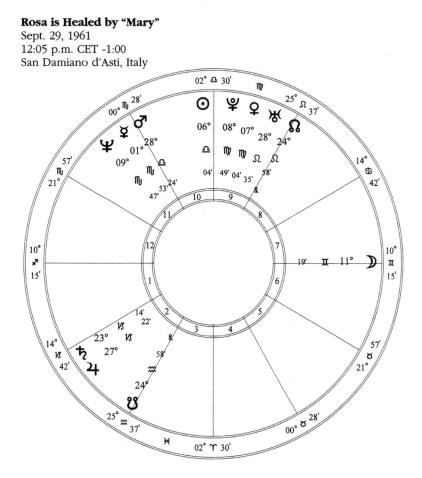

Rosa is healed by "Mary."

Even after numerous surgeries and treatments, she remained bedridden, unable to eat, and almost helpless.

She was laid up on the day of September 29, 1961, at the age of fifty-two. Rosa's aunt, who was tending her, answered the door to let in a lovely, young woman who said she was collecting alms for Padre Pio. The aunt explained they were very poor, and that her niece, Rosa, was bedridden. The young lady asked to see the invalid.

Inner Wheel: The Tree Miracles   **Outer Wheel: Rosa Quattrini**
Oct. 16, 1964   Jan. 26, 1909
12:05 p.m. CET -1:00   12:01 p.m. CET -1:00
San Damiano d'Asti, Italy   San Damiano d'Asti, Italy

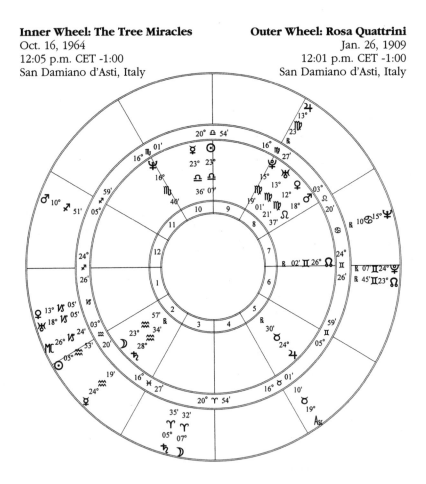

Inner wheel: the tree miracles; outer wheel: Rosa Quattrini.

She was taken into Rosa's chamber, just as the noon angelus bells rang out. The lady took Rosa's hands and told her to get up. Rosa said she felt a shock go through her, and from that day, she was healed and could resume a normal lifestyle. The young lady told Rosa that she must go and see the famous healing priest, Padre Pio. Rosa later came to believe that this young lady was her "Heavenly Mama," for she saw her again when she went to seek Padre Pio in San Giovanni Rotundo.

The chart for this healing reveals some interesting alignments. We can time it by the noon bells. The Moon in Gemini is angular, on the Descendant. There is an emphasis on the sign Virgo, where a "healing" conjunction of Venus and Pluto has formed. Coincidentally, Virgo rules the intestines in medical astrology.

This healing set Rosa off on her spiritual adventures through the Italy of Vatican II. It is not my intention to delve into the reactionary politics of that era, but suffice it to say that Rosa and the apparitions at San Damiano will never be approved.

Rosa's main claim to fame was a Marian apparition that occurred on October 16, 1964. Rosa was praying that day, after hearing the noon angelus bells ring. (Those angelus bells have proven, time and time again, to be a great blessing to astrology!) She heard a voice call her outside to the garden of her home, where the Virgin then appeared to her, descending in a cloud onto the branches of a plum tree. The Virgin wore a white robe over a blue gown with a white sash. A white rosary hung at her side. There were stars about her neck, and rays of light pouring from her hands.

The Virgin requested prayer, and asked Rosa to deliver a warning of chastisements to come. Rosa was afraid, and cried that no one would believe her. She begged for a sign to give her some kind of credibility. The Madonna replied that in leaving, she would cause the trees to flower.

And miraculously, she did. Even though it was October, as the Virgin departed, the nearby pear tree that had been almost bare burst into full bloom. The beautiful branch of the plum tree where she appeared was suddenly covered with delicate flowers! People gathered about immediately, shocked at how the pear tree, which still held the last of its summer fruit, was suddenly white with blossoms. Even in the heavy rains that followed, the flowers lasted almost twenty days.

The chart for this miracle is extraordinary. I have arranged it as a bi-wheel, with the chart for the event in the inner wheel and on the angles, and Rosa's birth chart, arranged about it in the outer wheel. Rosa's chart is set for noon, as her birth time is unknown.

Let me draw your attention to the mysterious 8th house, where a transiting stellium is forming in Virgo, uniting Venus, Uranus, and Pluto in the sign of the harvest maiden. Both Venus and Uranus are tightly conjunct Rosa's natal Jupiter in Virgo, and trine her natal Venus-Uranus conjunction in Capricorn.

The charts also contain a distinct emphasis on the Moon's Nodes. Rosa was born with an intriguing conjunction of Pluto and the Moon's North Node in Gemini. Her natal Gemini conjunction is right on the current Descendant. Further, the transiting North Node has returned to 25 degrees Gemini, conjunct Rosa's natal position.

ZEITUN, EGYPT

On the evening of April 2, 1968, in the Cairo suburb of Zeitun, the mechanics at the local transit station were leaving work around 8:30 p.m. On the roof of the Coptic Church across the street, they saw a lady dressed in a robe that looked as if it were made of white light. She was walking back and forth across the roof, and the workers initially thought she must have been a nun contemplating suicide. A crowd began to gather, and the lady kept them all enthralled until she slowly disappeared.

One week later, she was back, and began appearing regularly until May of 1971. Millions of people saw her; as many as 250,000 a night, in crowds composed of Muslims, Coptic Christians, and Jews, all praying together. There were other strange phenomena accompanying the apparitions, many of which have been photographed. These include doves and streaking balls of light flying about the Lady. She would often bow to the crowds, and bless them. *Zeitun* means "olive" in Arabic, and the Lady would sometimes hold out an olive branch to the crowds.

The Coptic Patriarch ordered a thorough investigation in April of 1968. The civil authorities ordered their own investigations as well. While the circumstances would certainly suggest the probability of a hoax, none was ever uncovered. The apparitions were given official approval by the Coptic Church and many miraculous healings were attributed to the Lady of Zeitun.

Christian roots run very deep in Egypt, where the apostle Mark founded the Coptic Church shortly after the crucifixion. The church at Zeitun has a distinctly Marian history. The ancient name of the site is Mataria, and according to legend, this is the place where Mary and Joseph stopped on their flight into Egypt. The church is believed to enshrine the spot where the Holy Family lived during their exile. Churches have been built, destroyed, and rebuilt here through the ages, reflecting the religious and political changes in the region, but in 1918, the site was derelict. It was owned by a Coptic family, and reportedly, the Virgin appeared to one of the members and requested that a church be built there, hinting that she had special plans for it. The family donated the property to the Coptic Church, which built the current St. Mary's Church on the property.

The chart for the initial apparition reveals an emphasis on the Uranus-Pluto conjunction in Virgo that dominated the skies during the 1960s. Mercury and Venus are conjunct at 22 degrees Pisces and oppose both Uranus and Pluto in Virgo, linking all four planets

First Appearance at Zeitun
April 2, 1968
8:30 p.m. EET -2:00
Cairo, Egypt

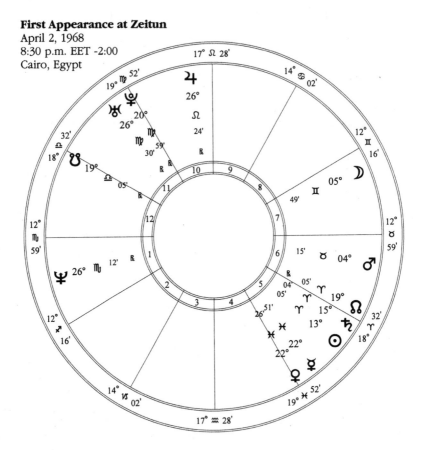

First apparition at Zeitun.

together in that Virgo-Pisces axis. Mystical Neptune also feeds its visionary influence into this axis by trine and sextile aspects to either end.

BETANIA

The Virgin first appeared here to forty-seven-year-old Maria Esperanza
Medrano de Bianchini on March 25, 1976. Maria was a housewife and
mother of seven, but she had been a Franciscan nun before her marriage. She was known to enjoy remarkable spiritual gifts, such as clair-
voyance, prophecy, levitation, and healing. The vision occurred on

Maria's farm, Betania, which is in the village of Cua, Venezuela. She had always wanted to build a spiritual community and felt led by the Virgin to purchase the farm and live out her dream there. Maria was praying on a hillside, beside both a spring and a grotto, when she had the first vision.

The apparitions continued, and crowds began to come regularly. One distinct feature of Betania is that other people began to see the Virgin too. On March 25, 1984, the Virgin appeared to the crowd seven different times throughout the afternoon. Of the many who

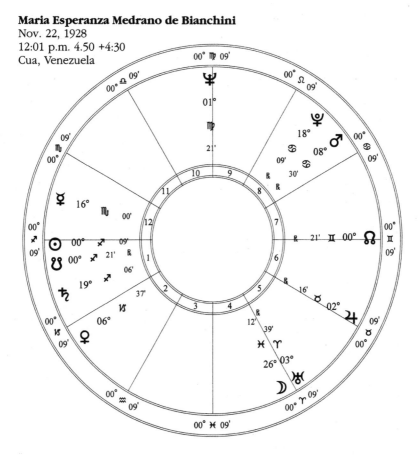

Maria Esperanza Medrano de Bianchini
Nov. 22, 1928
12:01 p.m. 4.50 +4:30
Cua, Venezuela

Maria Esperanza Medrano de Bianchini.

First Apparition at Betania
March 25, 1976
12:01 p.m. 4.50 +4:30
Cua, Venezuela

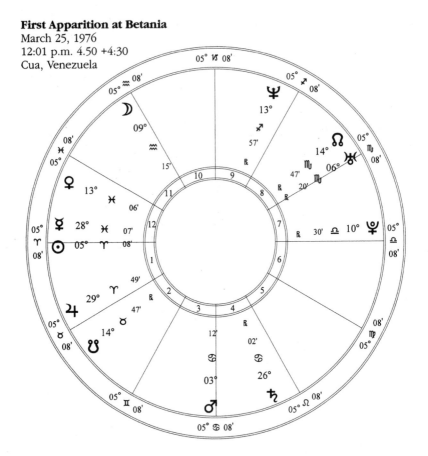

First apparition at Betania.

have seen her, the descriptions vary. Sometimes she looks like Our Lady of Lourdes (which is odd, because even Our Lady of Lourdes didn't look like Our Lady of Lourdes), whereas others describe her as similar to the Miraculous Medal, or Our Lady of Mt. Carmel.

The local bishop has done a remarkable job of cultivating and spiritually directing the devotions at the site, building a charismatic but scrupulously orthodox movement that has consistently borne good fruit and won approval at every level. The water from the spring and the nearby waterfall are much sought-after for their healing properties.

Maria Medrano de Bianchini was born with an exact conjunction of the Sun and the Moon's South Node in Sagittarius, in a tight square, or 90-degree angle to, mystical Neptune in Virgo. She has Mars in Cancer opposite Venus in Capricorn, and Pluto in Cancer as well. The original apparition occurred on the Feast of the Annunciation, which seems to be a popular day for seeing the Virgin now. The apparition chart reveals both Mars and Saturn in Cancer. Both charts are untimed.

CUAPA, NICARAGUA

Bernardo Martinez, a humble peasant, began seeing the Virgin here in May of 1980. There is an interesting connection in the names, for the name of this town, Cuapa, contains the same root as Cua, the name of the town in the previous apparition. In the Nahautl Indian language, *cua* means "serpent," and *pa* means "on." The name "Cuapa" has been translated as meaning "crushing the serpent's head with a blow" by supporters of the site, which would link the Virgin seen here to Eve in Genesis, whose seed was prophesied to bruise the serpent's head. I respectfully submit that perhaps Cuapa means "on the serpent," or even "serpent on," a simpler translation, but just as replete with symbolism.

The root word *cua* also appears in the name of the most famous apparition of the New World, Guadalupe. The apparition at Guadalupe is not included in this work simply because it is very difficult to verify the dates with any certainty and much more research is needed before I can produce accurate charts. Guadalupe was the "latinized" version of the name by which the Lady identified herself to the seer, Juan Diego. She actually said she and her image should be called Santa Maria de Tecoalaxopueh. Between the more traditional Catholics, who prefer to picture their Lady stomping on a serpent, and the promoters of the native culture who see her in a more simpatico relationship with the reptile, there is some disagreement about

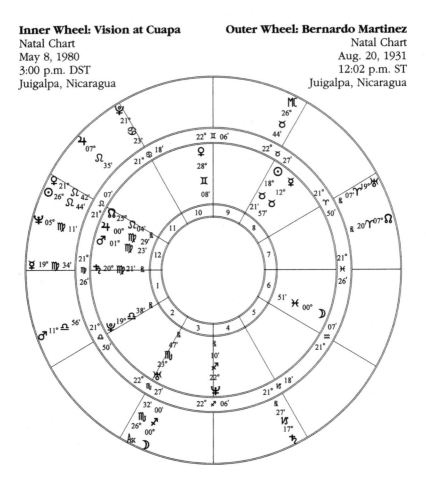

Inner Wheel: Vision at Cuapa
Natal Chart
May 8, 1980
3:00 p.m. DST
Juigalpa, Nicaragua

Outer Wheel: Bernardo Martinez
Natal Chart
Aug. 20, 1931
12:02 p.m. ST
Juigalpa, Nicaragua

Inner wheel: vision at Cuapa; outer wheel: Bernardo Martinez.

what that name actually means. I prefer to do more research before choosing a side in that fray, but there are some profound implications there.

Returning to our narrative, Bernardo Martinez, born August 20, 1931 (time unknown), was the volunteer assistant to the priest at the local church in Cuapa. He had always wanted to be a priest himself, but circumstances had intervened, keeping him poor, uneducated, and laboring away in manual trades. He maintained an active prayer

life and gave what service he could to the community. In April of
1980 he began having some mystical experiences. It seemed to him
that the statue of the Virgin in the chapel was lighting up on its own.

He was struggling in his depths, out of money and out of work,
when on the eighth of May, after a sleepless night, he spent the day
fishing and relaxing on the river. As he headed back into town, at
three o'clock, he was surprised by the appearance of a luminous lady
atop a pile of stones. On top of the stones was a little tree, and on
top of the little tree was a cloud, and her bare feet were resting on
that cloud. She wore a long, white dress with a cord about her waist,
and was covered in a creamy white veil, edged in gold.

Bernardo continued to see her throughout 1980, and on numerous
occasions since. Crowds began to gather regularly at the pile of
stones, and devotions spread quickly throughout the area. The
apparition has received a partial approval from the local bishop. Perhaps of greater importance, in keeping with his fondest wish, after
much personal struggle, Bernardo was accepted into a seminary, and
on August 20, 1995, he was ordained a priest.

The time for the initial apparition comes from Bernardo himself,
and I obtained it from Rene Laurentin's book *The Apparitions of the
Blessed Virgin Mary Today,* and in *God Sent: A History of the Accredited Apparitions of Mary,* by Roy Abraham Varghese.

The chart is displayed as a bi-wheel, with the timed apparition
chart in the inner wheel and on the angles, and Bernardo's untimed
birth chart displayed around it in the outer wheel. Using this type of
display, we can quickly see that transiting Saturn was rising on the
Ascendant in Virgo, tightly conjunct Bernardo's natal Mercury in
Virgo. That would go a long way toward explaining the depressive
thoughts he had been entertaining, and the restrictions and limita-
tions that had so recently occupied his mind.

There is a strong emphasis on the Virgo-Pisces axis in the apparition chart, with transiting Jupiter conjunct Mars in Virgo, in opposition

to the transiting Moon in Pisces. Both Jupiter and Mars are applying to a conjunction with Bernardo's natal Neptune in Virgo, while the transiting North Node is conjunct Bernardo's natal Sun in Leo.

MEDUGORJE

Perhaps no other apparitions have generated such a worldwide, popular appeal as these, set in a small mountain village southwest of Sarajevo. Still, in light of the tragic civil war that followed, too many of the locals failed to heed the messages of peace and reconciliation spread by the young visionaries.

In the late afternoon of June 24, 1981, Ivanka Ivankovic, fifteen, and Mirjana Dragicevic, sixteen, were walking in the mountains near their village of Bijakovici, trying to sneak a smoke. They thought they saw what looked like the Virgin suspended in the air over the top of nearby Podbrdo Hill. They initially fled, and went to recruit some of their friends to come and have a look. First they found thirteen-year-old Milka Pavlovic, who was on her way to gather in the family's sheep. Milka saw something on the hill too, so the girls continued on to the home of sixteen-year-old Vicka Ivankovic. Vicka was taking a nap, so they left a message asking her to join them later. Then they went to the home of ten-year-old Jacov Colo, whose house commanded a good view of the hill.

Vicka followed them a little later to Jacov's home, where she was told that the group was already up on the hill. She found her friends soon enough, but after taking one look at the mysterious figure in white, Vicka ran away. On her way down the hill, she literally ran into Ivan Dragicevic, sixteen, and Ivan Ivankovic, twenty-one. They offered to escort her back to her friends, assuring her that there was nothing to fear. Once they came within viewing distance, Ivan Dragecevic also saw the white form and immediately fled. The rest of the group stayed a little while before returning to Milka's home by about 6:30 p.m.

The following evening, Ivanka, Mirjana, Vicka, and Ivan Dragicevic went out to check the hilltop again. When they saw the same white figure, they ran to get Jacov and Milka. Milka's mother wanted her to stay home and do some chores, so her sister, Marija, went with them instead. The group of six young people gathered at the bottom of the hill at about 6:15 p.m. Several adults came with them to see what would happen. They were not disappointed.

The group of six later reported that the Madonna seemed to call them and pull them up the hill. The witnesses said that the group suddenly ran up the difficult terrain at what seemed like a miraculous pace and then abruptly dropped to their knees, as one, on the rocky surface. While it normally takes about fifteen minutes to climb Podbrdo, the witnesses reported it seemed to take the children only a few minutes to scramble to the top. The visionaries were already displaying the signs of the ecstatic trance state.

These six young people began having daily contact with the Lady in public apparitions that lasted for years, and some of them continue to see her. While Ivan Ivankovic and Milka Pavlovic had seen the Lady on the first day, neither of them saw her again. Responding to pressure from the communist authorities, the group was soon forced to abandon the hilltop and meet their visitor daily in a side room of the local church. These daily apparitions became major events, attended by thousands, with masses and confessions led by the local Franciscans. Under the Franciscan's guidance, the apparitions at Medjugorje quickly mushroomed into an international phenomenon, attracting pilgrims by the millions from all around the globe to hear the Lady's messages of peace and reconciliation.

The area surrounding Medjugorje is dominated by a singular landmark, Krizevac Hill, or the Hill of the Cross. It is surmounted by a giant cross, erected in 1933 on the orders of Pope Pius XI. He dreamed one night, so the story goes, of a cross, mounted on the highest hill in Hercegovina, an area that has historically marked the

First Appearance at Medjugorje
June 24, 1981
5:30 p.m. CET -1:00
Medjugorje, Yugoslavia

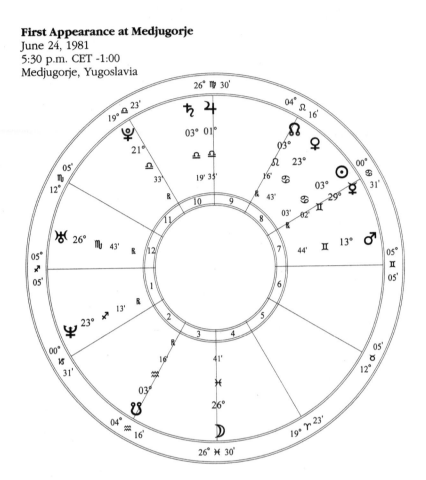

First appearance at Medjugorje.

bitter boundary between the Eastern and Western churches. The locals, who labored to realize the pope's dream, believe that the cross was responsible for breaking up the fierce storms and lightning that threatened their agriculture throughout the depression years of the 1920s and '30s.

It does make the chart for the initial sighting rather ironic, for it actually depicts a cross; specifically, an angular Grand Cross straddling the solstice and equinox points. The configuration involves the

Sun in Cancer conjunct a (retrograde) Mercury in Gemini, the Moon at the end of Pisces, Jupiter and Saturn in the first degrees of Libra, and visionary Neptune rising in Sagittarius. The chart is set for 5:30 p.m., based upon the witnesses' accounts. That is an approximate time. The girls may have seen her thirty or forty minutes earlier, whereas the group of seers probably gathered a bit later.

The charts for the visionaries, while all different, do reveal a distinct emphasis on the signs Virgo and Pisces. During the 1960s, both Uranus and Pluto were transiting through Virgo, and for a time, Saturn was moving through Pisces in opposition to them. These revolutionary influences in the sign of the Virgin coincided with the apparitions at Garabandel, San Damiano, and ultimately, Zeitun. However, five of the six visionaries at Medjugorje were born during this time. Their charts all feature that Virgo-Pisces opposition, particularly between 12 degrees and 16 degrees, in the very middle of both signs. None of the birth charts for the visionaries are timed. They are all set for noon on their birth dates.

Ivanka, who was the first to see the Lady, along with Mirjana, was born at the New Moon. Ivanka's Venus in Pisces is in a tight opposition to her Uranus and Pluto, which are in a very close conjunction in Virgo. Her friend, Mirjana, was born at the Full Moon. Mirjana's chart reveals Mars, Pluto, and Uranus in Virgo, in opposition to Saturn, the planetoid Chiron, and Venus in Pisces.

These two girls, whose afternoon outing in the hills ignited a worldwide Marian cult, share a unique intermeshing of planets in the middle of the signs Virgo and Pisces between their two charts. The chart of Ivan Dragecevic locks into their charts as well, again through planets in the very middle of Virgo and Pisces. Ivan was born with Saturn at 16 degrees Pisces, opposite Mars at 15 degrees Virgo.

Marija was born at the New Moon, and has Mars conjunct Uranus and Pluto in Virgo, in tight opposition to Saturn in Pisces. Marija, like Ivan, was born with the Moon's Nodes at 15 degrees Gemini-Sagittarius, forming an exact square to the group's Virgo-Pisces planets.

Ivanka Ivankovic
April 21, 1966
12:01 p.m. CET -1:00
Sarajevo, Yugoslavia

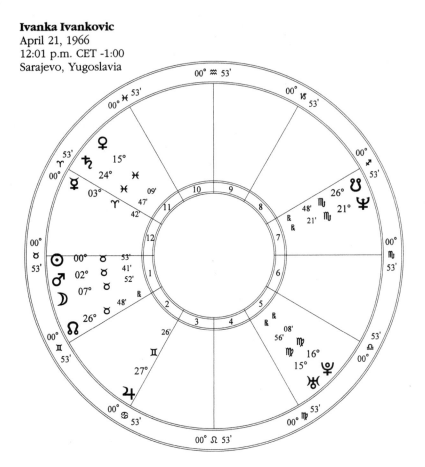

Ivanka Ivankovic.

Vicka, the Cancer of the group, was born with the Sun and Mercury in the Moon's sign. She also has Uranus and Pluto in Virgo
opposing Saturn and Chiron in Pisces. The sixth visionary, Jacov Colo,
was much younger than the other five, and was born on June 3, 1971.

There are a number of complications that have stalled the approval
process at Medjugorje. Bosnia is a place of deep divisions and longstanding ethnic feuds between the Orthodox Serbs, the Catholic
Croats, the Muslims, and the Communists. They are all strangers to
peace. Even within the Catholic Croatian community, there is a bitter

Mirjana Dragecevic
March 18, 1965
12:01 p.m. CET -1:00
Sarajevo, Yugoslavia

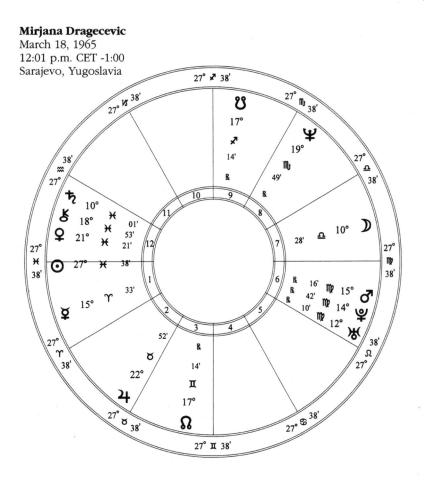

Mirjana Dragicevic.

and ongoing territorial dispute between the diocesan authorities under
the Bishop of Mostar and the members of the local Franciscan Order.

The Franciscans have been in the region for centuries, suffering
alongside the people throughout the endless conflicts. The lay people
have a great love and loyalty for them, an affection bolstered by the
fact that the Franciscans built and continue to run many of the
parishes. On the other hand, the Franciscans are perhaps a little too
close to the people, playing their own subversive role in the ongoing
ethnic warfare.

Ivan Ivankovic
May 25, 1965
12:01 p.m. CET -1:00
Sarajevo, Yugoslavia

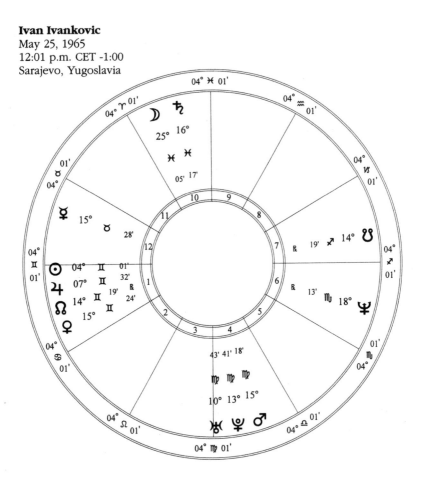

Ivan Ivankovic.

In the week before the apparitions began, the Bishop of Mostar decided to annex a number of Franciscan parishes to the diocese in a hostile takeover. The two sides had only just begun to fight over that decision when the Gospa intervened.

Medjugorje is a Franciscan parish, and the parish priest quickly aligned with the visionaries. That left the Bishop on the other side, and to this day, he has denied approval in a long and acrimonious battle of arguments and insinuations. While there have been faults and irregularities on both sides, in the meantime, Medjugorje has pro-

Marija Pavlovic
April 1, 1965
12:01 p.m. CET -1:00
Sarajevo, Yugoslavia

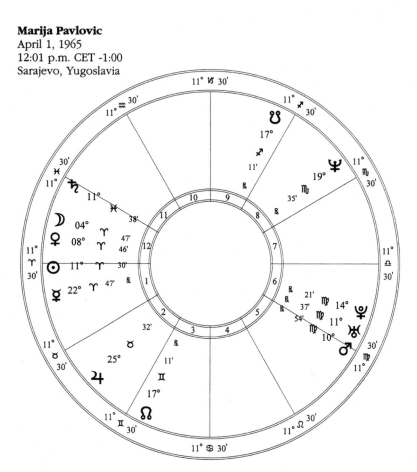

Marija Pavlovic.

duced prodigious spiritual fruits, and spawned a thriving pilgrimage industry, all without official approval. The Vatican, which is conducting its own investigations after expressing some dissatisfaction with the Bishop's decisions, has yet to decide on any other position. This could take a while.

Meanwhile, there are other complaints against Medjugorje that come from outside the diocese. The financial success of the pilgrimage industry has attracted skeptical attention from many quarters, but particularly from Protestant fundamentalists and Catholic conservatives.

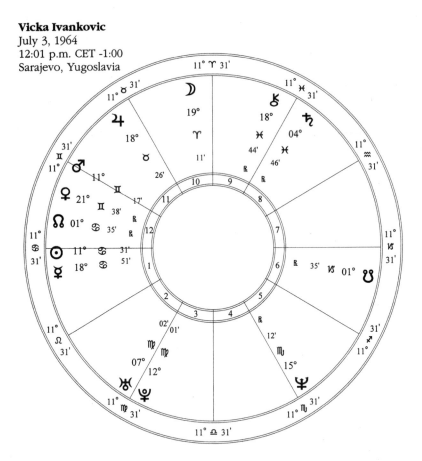

Vicka Ivankovic
July 3, 1964
12:01 p.m. CET -1:00
Sarajevo, Yugoslavia

Vicka Ivankovic.

They are particularly annoyed because it seems the Gospa, as they call the Virgin in Bosnia, is even more ecumenical than the current pope. The visionaries have reported many messages from her over the years that urge the faithful to respect other religions and to focus on our unity in God rather than our manmade differences. On June 29, 1981, just days after the visions began, she was reported by the visionaries to have said, "In God there are no religions; there are no divisions. But you men have made divisions."

That kind of talk in this particular region is radical in the extreme, and obviously long overdue. However, the very messages of peace and reconciliation that have endeared the Virgin of Medjugorje to the citizens of the world as they watched the Bosnian people stumble toward their inevitable and appalling civil war have the fundamentalists fuming that those crazy kids must have been entertaining the very author of evil himself.

In short, despite an abundance of good fruits, the supporters of Medjugorje have a real mess on their hands. It's the kind of mess that underscores the failure of modern religion to inspire us to love anybody but ourselves. The conversions, confessions, and healings have been undermined by the medieval power struggles that continue to dominate the agenda of the Roman Church. The very Christian calls for peace and tolerance among these perpetually warring people (who all claim to worship the same God) are being used to spread even more hatred and division. Sadly, these are the modern fruits of orthodoxy.

One of the many blessings to come from Medjugorje has been the opportunity it afforded modern researchers to study the condition of religious ecstasy. All the standard ecstatic behaviors have been very much in evidence since that second day on the hill. Since 1981, the visionaries have been observed, photographed, videotaped, monitored with electroencephalographs, hypnotized, and subjected to intense investigative scrutiny by a steady stream of international doctors and experts.

In some of the more famous experiments in 1984, Dr. Henri Joyeaux of France observed and recorded the seers during the daily apparitions and measured their reactions using a range of modern medical equipment. After analyzing the data from their neural and optical responses, he was able to demonstrate the perfect synchronization of the visionaries' involuntary reactions to their perceived visitor.

An Italian team measured their brain wave activity during the apparitions and demonstrated that the seers were neither asleep, dreaming, nor hallucinating, but rather in a continuous alpha state, similar to the state experienced by yogi adepts, contemplatives, and mystics. Experiments using an algometer demonstrated that the visionaries were indeed impervious to pain during their trance, and further experiments with an electrooculograph on the entranced seers failed to produce any reactions in their eyes to external stimuli.

In recent years, the number of worldwide Marian sightings has increased dramatically and it is rumored that more people are seeing her than ever. At the same time, the social implications of the visions have become increasingly complicated, separating them, in my mind, from much of what has gone before. I like to draw the line here, at Medjugorje, as good a stopping place as any.

Eight

DRAWING THE VEIL

The modern Roman Catholic image of the Virgin Mary is a far cry from the young girl who once gave birth to Jesus Christ, and in unravelling the mystery of how she got from there to here we do learn a lot about ourselves, and the religious archetypes that motivate us most deeply. The current Blessed Virgin represents a modern amalgam, a conflated collation of the attributes and qualities of the great goddesses of the ancient world, the very ones worshipped by the ancestors of the modern-day devotees of the Mother of God.

While the Roman Church generally denies this history of borrowing, masking the very basic, human needs that are met in her worship with increasingly complex Marian theology, the facts remain. I don't think I'm adding anything new to that argument. The case for accretion and syncretism throughout the development of her cults has been made many times over by better writers and researchers, and I'm not at all interested in denouncing the church over it.

Rather than invalidating her worship, the facts that emerge regarding the true origin of her cults demonstrate, somewhat ironically, that whatever the intentions of the Roman Church, the Virgin Mary has been the vehicle for the continuation of goddess worship within

Christianity. Instead of replacing or uprooting pagan practices, through popular devotion she has evolved into the Christian Mother goddess; another variation on the same old theme. Again, I'm not trying to bash the Roman Church over this, because the same sort of accretion occurred throughout the development of the cults and imagery of the older goddesses too. Inanna, Ishtar, Isis, Demeter, Cybele—they all, throughout the course of thousands of years of worship and legend, conquest and conversion, evolved and transformed, one into another, from one culture to another. It's a perfectly natural, ongoing, and very human process that permeates culture at every level.

Given a choice, the Roman Church, like the Protestants who rose against it, might have preferred to bypass Mary altogether, but she addresses such fundamental needs within the human heart that if she didn't exist, they would have had to invent her. Our first instinct as a child, when threatened in any way, is to cry for our mother, but the Virgin Mother of God is more than a mere spiritual pacifier for our endless infantilism.

Mary Craig, in her excellent book *Spark From Heaven,* puts it so eloquently:

> . . . any such archetype must be the Eternal Feminine, always evoked at time of crisis. In its early stages, this will be projected as a mother figure, but with greater maturity, it becomes what Jung called the anima, the source of humanity's deepest insights, the key to its capacity to transcend itself, to its self-knowledge and wholeness. Its arousal can only be good.

Craig goes on to quote Geoffrey Ashe:

> On Jung's showing, devotion to Mary should activate the archetype and help to unlock the treasury of the psychical depths, with results which no rational or dogmatic system can keep under control.

If I am contributing anything new to these old arguments, it is merely in pointing out the astrological dimension, which I hope I have done to some satisfaction. The goddesses enfolded within the modern Virgin Mother of God have always had their place in the sky, and she appears to have inherited their astrological attributes, along with everything else. If we look out at the stars and see her, it is because she has been in us from the beginning.

The graph on the following page demonstrates that within the forty-four charts of the visions and the visionaries included in this work, there is a marked preponderance of planets within the signs Cancer and Virgo. The chart points used in the calculation are the Moon, the Sun, Mercury, Venus, Mars, Jupiter, Saturn, Uranus, Neptune, Pluto, and the Moon's North Node. I haven't included the Ascendants or Midheavens because I don't have accurate times for all the charts. However, in sorting those ten points by sign, Cancer scores the highest, with sixty-six, while Virgo is right behind, with sixty-two.

While this group of charts does contain the data for all of the most important modern apparitions, it is still a relatively small sample. I have also compiled a larger database of 130 charts of visions and visionaries, spanning the years from AD 1233 to AD 1982, and it appears to demonstrate the same planetary emphasis in the signs Cancer and Virgo. While I do thoroughly intend to continue that research and publish more on it in the future, it remains beyond the scope of this current work. We need to be very cautious in any attempts to quantify the quality of mystical experience, and I have only introduced those figures to further emphasize what I perceive as a persistent astrological element in Marian apparitions. This astrological element is not at all limited to signs of the zodiac. It also seems to manifest through particular types of planetary alignments and through the diurnal motion of the planets as they pass through the rising, setting, and culmination points. I also don't doubt for one minute that there are other profound implications within this data that I have completely failed to notice. I'm sure they will be brought to my attention!

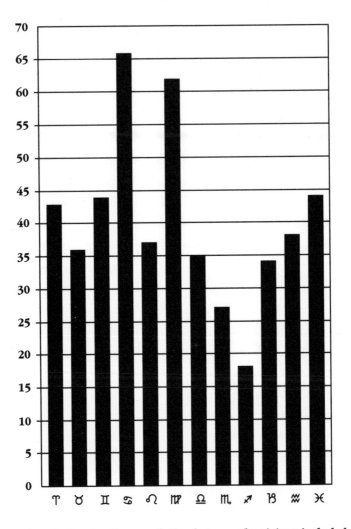

***Graph showing the correlation between the visions included
in this book and the preponderance of planets within
the signs Cancer ♋ and Virgo ♍.***

We are quick to attribute a fatalistic causality to astrological influences, but that is obviously too simplistic. Neither the constellation
nor the sign Virgo is making anyone see a Lady in White, but there is
some kind of a coincidence factor. Perhaps our consciousness is
formed as much from star-stuff as our bodies, and evolves along the

same lines as the rest of the cosmos, so that we are archetypically hard-wired for certain types of religious experience, to the extent that we can trace an astrological concomitant for it. But what does that really mean? Astrologers themselves are only just beginning to address the larger philosophical issues that a serious study of the cosmos raises, and can become surprisingly inarticulate when trying to describe the astrological model of consciousness.

We astrologers are very quick to fall back on archetypal psychology, on our own neo-Jungian collective unconscious, and that ineradicable Platonism underlying all our idealism, but we're still talking about planetary gods living in people's heads, and seemingly deifying our personalities. I would think this must be terribly off-putting to outsiders. I desperately want to communicate the astrological paradigm more clearly, but the paradigm itself is in dire need of clarification. I'm afraid the best I can do at this point is present the evidence and raise the questions. I'm sure that in time, the answers will come.

THE SUBJECT IS THE OBJECT

But is she real? Is this Lady who visits the seers a mere psychological construct, the burgeoning imagery of an overstimulated religious imagination? Does she exist outside of the seers' perceptions? Are we missing something important by casting her as a great, overriding, archetypal template? Can we explain her without explaining her away?

She is confusingly inconsistent in her manifestations. In the typical Roman Catholic vision, some can see her, but most can't. As the experiments at Medjugorje have demonstrated, the visionaries do respond simultaneously to the same external "something." Their senses are often overwhelmed to the extent that they don't respond to anything else, almost as if she had momentarily drawn the seers into her world. Meanwhile, others, even those standing close by, can't see anything at all.

In contrast, at Knock, or even better, Zeitun, hundreds of thousands all saw her without the need of trances or ecstasies. Were all these people, in their different and varying states, responding to the same visitor? Is there more than one of "her"?

Where do these encounters fit along the subject-object scale? Does the archetypal Great Mother embody existence in an objective sense, well beyond our need to believe in her? Is she a separate and distinct being, apart from all the projections we cast upon her manifold imagery? Maybe we are so programmed to perceive her because she is so hard to miss. Above and beyond her role as a human social construct, as a political construct, as an emotional and mythical construct, is she some sort of living being who comes down and visits when the time is right?

Then again, consider those dynamic Marian personalities like St. Bernadette, or Sr. Lucia. Both girls were born with angular alignments involving oppositions to the Moon along their natal MC/IC axis. They both served as lightning rods for Marian devotion, drawing people by the thousands to witness their ecstasies, and continued to function as a centralizing force within Marian Christianity even after they had been locked away in convents for decades. Are these girls the unwitting operators in some form of mass hypnosis, or channels of the divine?

WHOSE VIRGIN IS SHE?

At Zeitun, the Virgin appeared to huge crowds of Jews, Muslims, and Coptic, Protestant, and Orthodox Christians. Everyone could see her and people of all faiths responded passionately to her appearances, praying and crying out loud. The apparition was thoroughly investigated, not only by the Coptic Church, but also by the Egyptian government, and no fraud was ever uncovered. I think the last thing the Egyptian government would have wanted in Cairo was the Virgin Mary on the roof, so I'm presuming they did their best to try to knock her off.

This particular apparition demonstrates the universality of her appeal, and the way she naturally transcends the bounds of orthodoxy. Whoever she is, she belongs to everyone, and she appeals to everyone. No one religion can claim her for its own, and it is only by severely managing and editing the stories of its prize apparitions that the Roman Church has staked its proprietary claim.

The Virgin provides an underlying link, a common ground among nations, and we need that now more than ever. How is it, in the new millennium, that Christians and Jews are still fighting the Muslims over the Holy Land? The blind are still leading the blind into the ditch. That primitive, reactionary need to claim God as our own, to the exclusion of outsiders, is as strong as ever.

How ironic that among Christians, the Blessed Virgin Mary is so controversial that the very mention of her name causes Protestant fundamentalists to start spewing invective. They have a very clear sense of exactly how her cults developed and rightly identify her as a means of continuing the goddess worship of older religions—but they insist this was inspired by the devil to lead good Christians away from worshipping their exclusively masculine God. This need to judge, to condemn, to hate, and to exclude is expressly forbidden by Christ many times over in the Gospels. Still, these people really believe they are doing the right thing, just like the Roman clergy who repackaged the apparitions really believed they were doing the right thing. This is how many of us have been raised.

It's so easy to blame, to think in terms of "us" and "them," but "they" are "we." We're all the same. Whatever evil has taken place within the church, things were often much worse outside of it. The church didn't invent ambition, cruelty, injustice, or hypocrisy. Those very human traits were all alive and well long before the birth of Christ and will no doubt outlive us all.

Any religion is made up of human beings and must function within human society. Even if you don't buy into the whole doctrine of original sin, you would have to admit that we humans have at least one or two significant shortcomings. We bring all of that into the church, into any church, along with our faith, hopes, and aspirations. So maybe it's better to stop casting stones at "them" and let he who is without sin live in that glass house.

If even Pope John Paul II, who was deeply influenced by Our Lady of Fatima in the aftermath of his assassination attempt, can become a passionate and progressive advocate for ecumenism, then there's hope for us all. He hasn't had to abandon his own religion to do it. Perhaps meditating upon the mysteries of Jung's divine anima during his convalescence opened him up to an expanded perspective where he could better appreciate our unity in God. Maybe not. Still, in obscure but crucial places like Medjugorje and Zeitun, the Virgin invites us to do just that.

Astrology provides a valuable insight in this direction, in showing how different types of people respond to different types of devotion. Individuals with a strong Virgo or Lunar emphasis in their charts may feel more affinity with the Virgin Mary, or with a feminine concept of the divine. Others, with more masculine charts, perhaps a strong Solar or Mars influence, may be more comfortable worshipping God as Father.

Similarly, some individuals have very fundamental personalities. They need simple, absolute beliefs and want to act on them. Other personalities can handle more ambivalence and duality, and often enjoy discussing and debating ideas. One size does not fit all, and many of our religious differences might actually be rooted in personality differences. In respecting the unique character and beauty of different beliefs, including astrology, we can better honor the source of life who created us all. Whatever you may take from this work, please don't leave that thought behind.

GLOSSARY OF ASTROLOGICAL TERMS

Air

One of the four astrological elements, along with fire, earth, and water. The air element is mental and abstract, operating through thought and communication. The air signs are Gemini, Libra, and Aquarius; unlike the other signs of the zodiac, the air signs are either human or inanimate, not animals.

Aquarius

The Water Bearer. The eleventh sign of the tropical zodiac and the opposite sign of Leo. The Sun is in Aquarius from approximately January 21 through February 22. Aquarius is a fixed sign and an air sign. (Not a water sign!) It is traditionally ruled by Saturn, but since the discovery of Uranus in 1781, Uranus is considered a co-ruler. Sociable and ingenious, Aquarius prefers lots of company while remaining stubbornly aloof and individualistic. Idealistic and humanitarian but with a marked detachment.

Aries

The Ram. The first sign of the tropical zodiac and the opposite sign of Libra. The Sun is in Aries from approximately March 21 through April

21. Aries is a cardinal sign and a fire sign. It is ruled by the planet Mars and is the sign of the Sun's exaltation. High energy, impulsive, competitive, creative, but easily distracted.

Ascendant

The angle of the chart that marks the point of rising in the east, also the cusp of the first house and the rising sign. The Ascendant rules that which the chart describes, whether a person, place, or thing.

Aspects

A series of angular relationships that form between the planets in their orbits. Some aspects facilitate the flow of energy between planets, for instance, the sextile and the trine, while others obstruct the flow of energy, like the square and the opposition. (See the individual aspects for more information.)

Benefic

Good, positive, fortunate, of benefit. Usually refers to the planet Jupiter, the greater benefic, or to the planet Venus, the lesser benefic.

Cancer

The Crab. The fourth sign of the tropical zodiac and the opposite sign of Capricorn. The Sun is in Cancer from approximately June 21 through July 22. Cancer is a cardinal sign and a water sign. It is ruled by the Moon and is the sign of Jupiter's exaltation. Sensitive, highly emotional, devoted to home and family. Deeply influenced by the mother. Nourishment (eating and drinking) can be an issue. Close to the sea; retentive memory with a great sense of history and lore.

Capricorn

The Sea Goat. The tenth sign of the tropical zodiac and the opposite sign of Cancer. The Sun is in Capricorn from approximately December 21 through January 22. Capricorn is a cardinal sign and an earth sign. It is ruled by Saturn and is the sign of Mars's exaltation. Practical and ambitious, deep insecurity fuels a tremendous need to achieve. Responsible with good organizational abilities; businesslike with natural leadership abilities but tends to be negative or depressive.

Cardinal

One of the three qualities, or modes, of the signs, along with fixed and mutable. Cardinal signs are always first: Aries, Cancer, Libra, and Capricorn are the signs that mark the beginning of the seasons, and correspond with the solstices and equinoxes. Cardinal signs are impulsive and initiating. They like to start things up but are not the best finishers, preferring to move on to something new.

Conjunction

An aspect that brings two planets together, usually in the same sign and usually within only a few degrees of each other. For example, if Mars is at 5 degrees Virgo and Saturn is at 6 degrees Virgo, the Mars is conjunct Saturn. A conjunction unites planets in zodiacal longitude. They are still very far away from each other in space. However, it does have the effect of blending the planetary energies together and creating a point of focus within the chart.

Degree

Each sign of the zodiac is divided into 30 degrees. The ecliptic, or the apparent path of the sun, is described as a circle of 360 degrees. It is further divided into twelve, equal sections of 30 degrees each. That is how we obtain the twelve signs of the zodiac. Each sign occupies 30 degrees of the ecliptic, numbered from 0 degrees at the beginning of the sign to 30 degrees at the end. The degrees make it easy to describe the location of a planet along the ecliptic by sign and degree. For instance, if Mercury is in the middle of the sign Gemini, it would be at 15 degrees Gemini. If it is at the very end of the sign Gemini, and about to enter the sign Cancer, it would be at

29 degrees or 30 degrees Gemini. We also use degrees to measure aspects.

Descendant

The angle of the chart that marks the point of setting in the west. It also marks the cusp of the 7th house. The Descendant symbolizes the point where the being described by the Ascendant, or rising sign, comes into contact with significant others. The Descendant and the 7th house rule relationships: marriage and important partnerships, contracts, and open enemies.

Earth

One of the four astrological elements, along with fire, air, and water. The earth element is practical, materialistic, and down to earth, operating through money, possessions, and values. The earth signs are Taurus, Virgo, and Capricorn.

Ecliptic

The great circle that depicts the apparent path of the Sun, from our perspective on Earth. The zodiac derives from the constellations that line the ecliptic.

Elements

The signs of the zodiac are classified by the four elements of classical science: fire, earth, air, and water. Each element has distinct characteristics and qualities. For further description, see the individual elements.

Equinox

From the Latin for "equal night." There are two equinoxes every year, on approximately March 21 and September 21, corresponding with the first day of spring and the first day of fall. The spring, or vernal equinox, marks the Sun's entrance into the astrological sign Aries, while the fall, or autumnal equinox, marks the Sun's entrance into the opposite astrological sign, Libra. At the equinox, day and night are of equal length, as opposed to the solstices, which mark the longest day and the longest night.

Fire

One of the four astrological elements, along with earth, air, and water. The fire element is energetic, creative, enthusiastic, and spiritual, operating through inspirations, visions, courage, and enterprise. The fire signs are Aries, Leo, and Sagittarius.

Fixed

One of the three qualities, or modes, of the signs of the zodiac, along with cardinal and mutable. The fixed signs are stable, enduring, and constant. They can also be stubborn, inflexible, and resistant to change. The fixed signs are Taurus, Leo, Scorpio, and Aquarius.

Gemini

The Twins. The third sign of the tropical zodiac and the opposite sign of Sagittarius. The Sun is in Gemini from approximately May 21 through June 22. Gemini is a mutable sign and an air sign. It is ruled by the planet Mercury. Talkative and lively, versatile with an emphasis on manual and verbal dexterity. Variable and not fond of making decisions, there are at least two twins within each Gemini. Constant travel and communication are necessary to engage the finely-tuned nervous system.

Geocentric

Measured from the Earth, or having the Earth as the center. Astronomy was geocentric until the Copernican revolution, which introduced the heliocentric, or sun-centered perspective. Astrology maintains the geocentric perspective to interpret how planetary influences affect life on earth.

Heliocentric

Measured from the sun, or using the sun as the center.

House

Any one of the twelve divisions of an astrological chart. The houses further divide the four sectors defined by the angles of the chart. Each house describes different activities, or areas of life. Planets placed within a particular house would tend to manifest their influences through, or emphasize, the areas or activities ruled by that house.

IC

The common abbreviation for Imum Coeli, one of the four angles of the astrological chart. The IC corresponds to the cusp of the 4th house, and marks the approximate position of the Sun at midnight.

Imum Coeli

From the Latin for the "bottom of the sky," one of the four angles of the astrological chart, marking the approximate position of the Sun at midnight. The Imum Coeli also marks the cusp of the 4th house in most house systems. It describes roots, foundations, history, family, origins, real estate, and so on, serving as an anchoring point or home base for the entity symbolized by the chart.

Jupiter

The largest planet in the solar system, second only to the Sun itself. A gas giant with no solid center, Jupiter expands into a massive retinue of fourteen moons. In mythology, Zeus (Jupiter) was the king of the gods, instituting a new order on Olympus after overthrowing his father Chronus (Saturn). In astrology, Jupiter is the great benefic. Its influence tends to be fortunate and expansive. Jupiter rules philosophy and religion, higher education and foreign travel. It brings luck in sports and adventure. It rules publishing, law, and morality. The type of people described by a strong Jupiter influence are clergy, lawyers, professors, diplomats, explorers, intellectuals, coaches, and civic or moral leaders. Jupiter rules the signs Sagittarius and Pisces. It is exalted in the sign Cancer.

Leo

The Lion. The fifth sign of the zodiac and the opposite sign of Aquarius. The Sun is in Leo from approximately July 22 through August 22. Leo is a fixed sign and a fire sign. Leo is ruled by the Sun. Positive, open, energetic, and creative, with a strong sense of identity and leadership, Leos attract attention and draw other beings into orbit around them. Both childlike and childish, strong-willed and stubborn, their warm-hearted romanticism and dynamic personalities make them hard to ignore.

Libra

The Scales. The seventh sign of the zodiac and the opposite sign of Aries. The Sun is in Libra from approximately September 22 until October 22. Libra is a cardinal sign and an air sign. Libra is ruled by the planet Venus and is the sign of Saturn's exaltation. Charming and attractive, with a strong sense of justice and fair play, they are popular and sociable, as long as the balance holds. When unbalanced, anything goes. Often artistically gifted or blessed with a talent for diplomacy, they strive to be pleasing to others because they value their relationships so highly.

Malefic

From the Latin *mal,* meaning "bad." A term used to describe astrological influences that are less than favorable, as opposed to benefic influences, which tend to be good. Saturn and Mars are the traditional malefic planets; the classical troublemakers.

Mars

The red planet, and the fourth planet from the Sun. In mythology, Mars was the God of War, feared for his destructiveness, but invoked for his courage and daring. In astrology, Mars conveys initiative and impulse. It is a point of masculine energy within the chart, and can be quarrelsome and violent when under stress, or constructive and industrious when well placed. The type of people indicated by a prominent Mars influence are soldiers, athletes, pioneers or leaders of men, police or firemen, violent criminals, butchers, surgeons, barbers, or engineers. Mars rules the signs Aries and Scorpio, and is exalted in Capricorn.

MC

A common abbreviation for the Latin *Medium Coeli,* or "the middle of the sky." One of the four angles of the chart, marking the point of the Sun's culmination at midday.

Mercury

The closest planet to the Sun. In mythology, Mercury was the messenger of the Gods, flying to and fro, with wings on his feet and his helmet. In astrology, Mercury rules thought and speech, writing, the habits of the mind, communication skills, and daily errands. Mercury's position in the chart indicates mental abilities and common sense. It can be brilliant and versatile when well placed, or dull and indecisive when under stress. The type of people indicated by a prominent Mercury influence are writers, journalists, teachers, salespeople, secretaries and receptionists, students, neighbors and kin, delivery men and drivers, gossips, con artists, pickpockets and thieves, repair technicians. Mercury rules the signs Gemini and Virgo, and is exalted in its own sign, Virgo.

Midheaven

One of the four angles of the chart, marking the point of the sun's culmination at midday. The Midheaven also marks the cusp of the 10th house, in most house systems. As the highest, most visible point of the chart, it rules the public life, status, honor, profession, and position.

Moon

The Earth's satellite. In astrology, the Moon rules the emotions, feelings, and unconscious habit patterns learned early in life from the mother. The Moon can indicate important women in the life, home and family, food and nutrition, security, dreams, instinct and intuition. The Moon can give great depth, compassion, and memory when well placed, or be overly sensitive and shy when under stress. The type of people indicated by a prominent Moon are women, mothers and grandmothers, infants and those needing care, nurses or caregivers, close family and trusted counselors, cooks and bakers, mariners and fishermen, homebodies. The Moon rules the sign Cancer and is exalted in Taurus.

Moon's Nodes

The points where the Moon crosses the ecliptic in its monthly orbit. The North Node marks the point in the zodiac where the Moon crosses the ecliptic heading North, and the South Node marks the point where the Moon crosses the ecliptic when heading back South. In astrology, the North Node indicates direction, focus, new patterns, and growth, while the South Node indicates diffusion, loss, old patterns, and repetition.

Mutable

One of the three qualities, or modes, of the signs of the zodiac, along with cardinal and fixed. The mutable signs are changeable, flexible, and versatile. They can also be indecisive, fickle, and neurotic. They tend to mediate between the enterprising but impulsive cardinal signs, and the stable but stubborn fixed signs, filling in the gaps and doing whatever it takes to make things work. The mutable signs are Gemini, Virgo, Sagittarius, and Pisces.

Neptune

The eighth planet from the Sun. A gas giant like Jupiter. In mythology, Neptune was the god of the sea, ruling beneath the waves with his trident. In astrology, Neptune rules beneath the surface of consciousness, dissolving the boundaries between the rational mind and the soul, ruling subliminal or mystical processes, including psychic or paranormal abilities, prayer and meditation, artistic inspiration, and faith. Neptune also rules deception and self-undoing, particularly through drug abuse or alcoholism, mental illness, delusion, institutionalization, or victimization. The type of people indicated by a prominent Neptune influence include mystics, mediums, seers, the faithful, religious leaders and healers, psychologists, psychiatrists and their patients, musicians, artists and dancers, drug addicts and alcoholics, photographers, glamorous film stars, pop idols, and demagogues. Neptune is the co-ruler of the sign Pisces, along with Jupiter.

North Node

A point that marks the place where the Moon, in its monthly orbit, crosses over the ecliptic as it is heading north. In astrology, the North Node signifies direction and growth.

Opposition

An aspect of 180 degrees, wherein two planets oppose each other from opposite sides of the zodiac, and usually from opposite signs. For example, if Mars is at 5 degrees Virgo and Saturn is at 6 degrees Pisces, then Mars is in opposition to Saturn. An opposition creates an axis of influence, but also pits the planetary forces against each other, pulling in two different directions while trying to meet in the middle. It demands balance and accommodation, and tends to objectify the issue by manifesting through close relationships.

Pisces

The Fishes. The twelfth sign of the zodiac and the opposite sign of Virgo. The Sun is in Pisces from approximately February 22 until March 22. Pisces is a mutable sign and a water sign. Pisces is traditionally ruled by the planet Jupiter, but since the discovery of Neptune in 1846, Neptune is considered the co-ruler. Pisces is the sign of Venus's exaltation. Intuitive and impressionable, with an aching sense of both the beauty and pain of life, Pisces can be pretty slippery if you try to pin them down. Great dreamers who sometimes dream true and seem to have it all, they are often born with a highly developed gift or talent that serves as both their salvation and their undoing. Their need to lie down and play the doormat for the most unworthy feet is frustrating, but it's also the source of their ineffable grace.

Pluto

The ninth planet from the Sun, tiny Pluto shares its eccentric orbit with a relatively large satellite, Charon, in what almost amounts to a double-planet system. In mythology, Pluto was the god of the dead and the underworld. In astrology, Pluto rules our deepest and most powerful drives, controlling obsessions and compulsions that well up from secret places beneath the surface. Pluto rules sexuality and the process of birth, death, and rebirth. Its power can be ultimately destructive or infinitely healing. The types of people indicated by a prominent Pluto influence are healers, doctors, researchers, investment bankers, occultists and magicians, detectives, undertakers, gangsters, murderers, the power behind the throne, wealthy plutocrats. Pluto is the co-ruler of the sign Scorpio, along with Mars.

Precession

Due to certain forces acting on the Earth's rotation, its axis wobbles a bit. From our geocentric perspective, this causes the point of the vernal equinox to move backward through the zodiac at a rate of approximately 1 degree every seventy-two years. Currently, the vernal equinox occurs when the Sun is in the early degrees of the constellation Pisces, but the equinox will eventually precess back into the constellation Aquarius.

Sagittarius

The Archer/Centaur. The ninth sign of the zodiac and the opposite sign of Gemini. The Sun is in Sagittarius from approximately November 22 until the December 22. Sagittarius is a mutable sign and a fire sign. Sagittarius is ruled by the planet Jupiter. Outgoing and optimistic, with a commitment to truth and freedom, the archer sends his arrows far and wide. Great travelers and communicators, their expansive energy needs both physical and intellectual expression. Details bore them but nobody sees the big picture on a wider screen. Born philosophers, but even with all the education in the world, still as dumb as a post. Commitments are tenuous; subject to change without notice, but their infallible luck gets them off the hook every time.

Saturn

The ringed planet, and the sixth planet from the Sun. In mythology, Saturn was a Roman god of agriculture, often represented holding a sickle. Saturn was overthrown by his son, Jupiter. Saturn is a planet of limits and responsibilities, of material realities and the hard, cold facts of life. It often represents lessons that must be mastered, or difficult situations that either breed maturity or break you. Saturn is cold, old, crystallized, confined, and hard at its worst. At its best, it is measured, moderate, just, lawful, and constructive. The type of people indicated by a prominent Saturn influence include builders, senior citizens, father figures, the boss, managers, politicians and civil servants, the poor and destitute. Saturn rules the signs Capricorn and Aquarius, and is exalted in Libra.

Scorpio

The Scorpion. The eighth sign of the zodiac and the opposite sign of Taurus. The Sun is in Scorpio from approximately October 22 until November 22. Scorpio is a fixed sign and a water sign. Scorpio is traditionally ruled by the planet Mars, but since the discovery of Pluto in 1930, Pluto is considered the co-ruler. Deep, intense, and resourceful, with a keen sense of the bottom line and who owns what, Scorpios are passionate and fixed in their feelings. The least superficial of the signs, an underlying, compulsive strength drives them to healing and regeneration through life-or-death or crisis experiences.

Sextile

An aspect of 60 degrees linking planets that are two signs apart; usually from fire to air signs or from water to earth signs. For example, if Mars is at 5 degrees Virgo and Saturn is at 6 degrees Scorpio, then Mars is sextile Saturn. A sextile is a comfortable, natural link that creates an easy, friendly flow of energy between the two planets.

South Node

A point that marks the place where the Moon, in its monthly orbit, crosses over the ecliptic as it is heading south. In astrology, the South Node signifies dispersion and old patterns of behavior.

Square

An aspect of 90 degrees that puts two planets at right angles to each other. Squares are usually formed between planets in signs of the same mode or quality, like fixed to fixed, or mutable to mutable. For example, if Mars is at 5 degrees Virgo and Saturn is at 6 degrees Sagittarius, then Mars is square Saturn. A square manifests as cross-purposes, in obstacles or difficulties that demand resolution, even when there is no resolution in sight. Tension results, which can either spur growth and development or harden into frustration and anger.

Sun

The center of our solar system, the Sun is the source of energy and light within the solar system and within the personality. In astrology, the Sun is possibly the most important point in the chart, to the extent that people often identify themselves by their sun sign. It symbolizes the ego as the organizing principle of the personality. Ideally, the Sun is a source of pride, warmth, and strength, but under stress, it can be self-centered, weak, and demanding. The Sun rules the sign Leo, and is exalted in Aries.

Taurus

The Bull. The second sign of the zodiac and the opposite sign of Scorpio. The Sun is in Taurus from approximately April 22 until May 22. Taurus is a fixed sign and an earth sign. Taurus is ruled by the planet Venus, and is the sign of the Moon's exaltation. Solid as a rock, Taurus is as down to earth as they come. Romantic and tender, with fixed affections, Taurus also possesses a keen sense of artistry, color, and sound. Money and values matter and Taurus keeps it real, never straying too far away from the bottom line. Stable, dependable, reliable, they just keep plugging away, day after day, doing what needs to be done. Almost allergic to change, but if you are looking for a rut to get stuck in, Taurus will be happy to dig it for you and keep you supplied there indefinitely.

Trine

An aspect of 120 degrees that usually links planets in signs of the same element, like earth to earth, or fire to fire. For example, if Mars is at 5 degrees Virgo and Saturn is at 6 degrees Capricorn, then Mars is trine Saturn. A trine creates a lucky, harmonious flow of energy between signs of compatible nature.

Uranus

The seventh planet from the sun, Uranus has a unique spin on its rotation. In mythology, Uranus was the god of the heavens, and the ruler of the gods until he was overthrown by his son, Saturn/Chronos. Uranus has a unique, revolutionary influence that strikes unexpectedly, like a bolt out of the blue. It is a force of genius, high-tech inventiveness, and futuristic insight, or, on the downside, it can be cranky, eccentric, and unpredictable. This communicative planet loves to ride the airwaves, whether in radio, video, or the Internet. Uranus is the co-ruler of the sign Aquarius, along with Saturn. The type of people indicated by a prominent Uranus influence include inventors, radicals, geniuses, astrologers, astronomers and astronauts, radio, video, or computer techs, green-haired punks and other counter-cultural iconoclasts.

Virgo

The Virgin. The sixth sign of the zodiac and the opposite sign of Pisces. The Sun is in Virgo from approximately September 22 until October 22. Virgo is a mutable sign and an earth sign. It is ruled by the planet Mercury, and is also the sign of Mercury's exaltation. Hard working, clean, and helpful, Virgo is a perfectionist and notorious for nitpicking. Analytical and detail-oriented, the sign is driven to make constant improvements. Interested in diet and nutrition. Shy, and avoids the limelight, preferring to criticize behind the scenes. Their attentive minds are easy to teach and train. Possessing great manual dexterity and versatility, with a peculiar nervousness all their own, Virgos can be socially awkward, feeling more comfortable in a work environment.

Water

One of the four astrological elements, along with fire, earth, and air. The water element is feminine, reflective, emotional, and impressionable, operating through feelings and intuitions. The water signs are Cancer, Scorpio, and Pisces.

BIBLIOGRAPHY

Albright, Judith M. *Our Lady at Garabandel*. Milford, OH: Faith Publishing Co., 1992.

Allen, Richard Hinkley. *Star Names: Their Lore and Meaning*. New York: Dover Publications, 1963.

Ashe, Geoffrey. *Dawn Behind the Dawn: A Search for the Earthly Paradise*. New York: Henry Holt and Co., 1992.

———. *The Virgin*. London: Paladin Books, 1977.

Ashton, Joan. *The People's Madonna: An Account of the Visions of Mary at Medjugorje*. London: Fount/Harper Collins, 1991.

at-Tabrisi, Abu Ali al-Fadl ibn al-Hasan ibnal-Fadl. "Fatimah: The Radiant, Daughter of the Apostle of Allah, Her Birth, Names, and Epithets" (I'lamu 'l-Wara vi A'lami 'I-Huda). Dar al-Ma'rifah, Beirut, 1979.

Baring, Anne, and Jules Cashford. *The Myth of the Goddess: Evolution of an Image*. London: Penguin Books/Viking Arkana, 1991.

Berger, Pamela. *The Goddess Obscured: Transformation of the Grain Protectress from Goddess to Saint*. Boston: Beacon Press, 1985.

Blackbourn, David. *Marpingen: Apparitions of the Virgin Mary in Nineteenth-Century Germany*. New York: Alfred A. Knopf, 1994.

Blanton, Margaret Gray. *The Miracle of Bernadette*. Englewood Cliffs, NJ: Prentice-Hall, 1958.

Brown, Michael H. *The Final Hour*. Milford, OH: Faith Publishing Co., 1992.

Bullfinch, Thomas. *The Age of Fable, or Beauties of Mythology*. New York: Mentor, New American Library, 1962.

Calvat, Melanie. *Apparition of the Blessed Virgin on the Mountain of La Salette*. The Internet Modern History Sourcebook, 1879.

Carpenter, Edward. *Pagan and Christian Creeds: Their Origin and Meaning*. New York: Harcourt, Brace, and Howe, 1920.

Christian, Jr., William A. *Visionaries: The Spanish Republic and the Reign of Christ*. Berkeley: University of California Press, 1996.

Connell, Janice T. *Meetings with Mary: Visions of the Blessed Mother*. New York: Ballantine Books, 1995.

Craig, Mary. *Spark From Heaven: The Mystery of the Madonna at Medjugorje*. Notre Dame, IN: Ave Maria Press, 1988.

Cruz, Joan Carroll. *Miraculous Images of Our Lady: 100 Famous Catholic Portraits and Statues*. Rockford, IL: Tan Books and Publishers, 1993.

———. *The Incorruptibles*. Rockford, IL: Tan Books and Publishers, 1977.

Cumont, Franz. *Astrology and Religion Among the Greeks and Romans*. New York: Dover Publications, Inc., 1960.

Cuneen, Sally. *In Search of Mary: The Woman and the Symbol*. New York: Ballantine Books, 1996.

Delaney, John J., ed. *A Woman Clothed With the Sun*. New York: Image Books, Doubleday, 1990.

Dennis, Mary Alice. *Melanie and the Story of Our Lady of La Salette*. Rockford, IL: Tan Books and Publishers, 1995.

Dirvin, Fr. Joseph. *St. Catherine Laboure of the Miraculous Medal.* Rockford, IL: Tan Books and Publishers, 1984.

Durham, Michael S. *Miracles of Mary: Apparitions, Legends, and Miraculous Works of the Blessed Virgin Mary.* New York: Blackberry Press, 1995.

Greeley, Andrew M. *The Mary Myth: On the Femininity of God.* New York: A Crossroad Book, The Seabury Press, 1977.

Hamilton, Edith. *Mythology: Timeless Tales of Gods and Heroes.* New York: Mentor, New American Library, 1940.

Laffineur, Fr. Materne, and M. T. le Pelletier. *Star on the Mountain.* Lindenhurst, NY: Our Lady of Mount Carmel de Garabandel, 1966.

Lane Fox, Robin. *Pagans and Christians.* New York: Alfred A. Knopf, 1986.

Laurentin, Fr. Rene. *Bernadette of Lourdes.* Minneapolis: Winston Press, 1979.

———. *The Apparitions of the Blessed Virgin Mary Today.* Dublin: Veritas Publications, 1990.

Lochet, Louis. *Apparitions of Our Lady.* Edinburgh and London: Nelson, 1960.

———. *The Lost Books of the Bible and The Forgotten Books of Eden.* World Bible Publishers, Alpha House, 1926 and 1927.

Motz, Lotte. *The Faces of the Goddess.* New York and Oxford: Oxford University Press, 1997.

Neary, Tom. *I Saw Our Lady.* Mayo, Ireland: The Custodians of the Knock Shrine, 1995.

Nolan, Mary Lee, and Sydney Nolan. *Christian Pilgrimage in Modern Western Europe.* Chapel Hill, NC: The University of North Carolina Press, 1989.

Northcote, Rev. J. Spencer. *Celebrated Sanctuaries of the Madonna.* London: Longmans, Green and Co., 1868.

O'Connor, Fr. Edward D. *Marian Apparitions Today: Why So Many?* Santa Barbara, CA: Queenship Publishing Co.,1996.

O'Dell, Catherine M. *Those Who Saw Her: The Apparitions of Mary.* Huntington, IN: Our Sunday Visitor Publishing Division, 1986.

Ordoui, Abu Muhammed. *Fatima, the Gracious.* Qum, Iran: Ansariyan Publications.

Parafita, Alexander. *O Maravilhoso Popular: Lendas, Contos, Mitos.* Lisbon: Platano Publishing Company, 2000.

Pickthall, Mohammed Marmaduke, trans. *The Meaning of the Glorious Koran.* New York: Mentor, New American Library, 1963.

Piron S. J., Rev. Paul. *Five Children.* New York: Benziger Bros., 1938.

Ravier, Andre. *Bernadette.* London: Collins, 1979.

Shariati, Dr. Ali. *Fatima is Fatima.* Tehran: Shariati Foundation and Hamdami Publishers, 1980.

Sharkey, Don, and Joseph DeBergh, O. M. J. *Our Lady of Beauraing: The Complete Story of Our Lady's Appearances at Beauraing.* Garden City, NY: Hanover House, 1958.

Sjoo, Monica, and Barbara Mor. *The Great Cosmic Mother: Rediscovering the Religion of the Earth.* San Francisco: Harper & Row, 1987.

Stone, Merlin. *When God Was a Woman.* New York: Harcourt, Brace, and Co., 1976.

Varghese, Roy Abraham. *God-Sent, A History of the Accredited Apparitions of Mary.* New York: The Crossroads Publishing Co., 2000.

Warner, Marina. *Alone of All Her Sex: The Myth and the Cult of the Virgin Mary.* New York: Alfred A. Knopf, 1976.

Yogananda, Paramahansa. *Autobiography of a Yogi.* Los Angeles: Self Realization Fellowship, 1973.

Zimdars-Swartz, Sandra L. *Encountering Mary: From La Salette to Medjugorje.* Princeton, NJ: Princeton University Press, 1991.

☽ ORDER LLEWELLYN BOOKS TODAY!

Llewellyn publishes hundreds of books on your favorite subjects! To get these exciting books, including the ones on the following pages, check your local bookstore or order them directly from Llewellyn.

Order Online:

Visit our website at www.llewellyn.com, select your books, and order them on our secure server.

Order by Phone:

- Call toll-free within the U.S. at 1-877-NEW-WRLD (1-877-639-9753)
  Call toll-free within Canada at 1-866-NEW-WRLD (1-866-639-9753)
- We accept VISA, MasterCard, and American Express

Order by Mail:

Send the full price of your order (MN residents add 7% sales tax) in U.S. funds, plus postage & handling to:

> **Llewellyn Worldwide**
> **P.O. Box 64383, Dept. 0-7387-0503-9**
> **St. Paul, MN 55164-0383, U.S.A.**

Postage & Handling:

> **Standard** (U.S., Mexico, & Canada). If your order is:
> > Up to $25.00, add $3.50
> > $25.01 - $48.99, add $4.00
> > $49.00 and over, FREE STANDARD SHIPPING
>
> (Continental U.S. orders ship UPS. AK, HI, PR, & P.O. Boxes ship USPS 1st class. Mex. & Can. ship PMB.)

> **International Orders:**
> > **Surface Mail:** For orders of $20.00 or less, add $5 plus $1 per item ordered. For orders of $20.01 and over, add $6 plus $1 per item ordered.
>
> > **Air Mail:**
> > *Books:* Postage & Handling is equal to the total retail price of all books in the order.
> > *Non-book items:* Add $5 for each item.

Orders are processed within 2 business days. Please allow for normal shipping time.
Postage and handling rates subject to change.

Buddhist Astrology

Chart Interpretation from a Buddhist Perspective

JHAMPA SHANEMAN AND JAN V. ANGEL

Use Buddhist wisdom and compassion to clarify your astrological readings.

Become your own astrological guru with the first book to apply Buddhist practice to Western astrology. *Buddhist Astrology* bridges familiar astrological thinking with the ideas of karma, interdependence, and impermanence. What if we consciously choose the compassionate way as we traverse those high peaks of a Pluto transit or climb to the summit of a Saturn cycle? Does such a response set up an array of rippling effects?

While Buddhism is theologically and metaphysically compelling, it is also very practical. Within its tenets every psychological state is embraced, integrated, and brought to light. It is spirit-medicine for modern astrology.

0-7387-0315-X
384 pp., 6 x 9 $19.95

Mapping Your Birthchart

Understanding Your Needs and Potential

STEPHANIE JEAN CLEMENT, PH.D.

You know your "sign," but that's just the tip of the astrological iceberg. You've got a moon sign, a rising sign, and loads of other factors in your astrological makeup. Together they form the complete picture of you as an individual: your desires, talents, emotions . . . and your public persona and your private needs.

Mapping Your Birthchart removes the mystery from astrology so you can look at any chart and get a basic understanding of the person behind it. Learn the importance of the planets, the different signs of the zodiac, and how they relate to your everyday life. Stephanie Jean Clement introduces the basics of the astrology chart, devotes a chapter to each planet—with information about signs, houses, and aspects—provides simple explanations of astrological and psychological factors, and includes examples from the charts of well-known people, including Tiger Woods, Celine Dion, and George W. Bush.

The free CD-ROM included with this book allows you to calculate and interpret your birthchart, and print out astrological reports and charts for yourself, your family, and friends.

0-7387-0202-1
240 pp., 7½ x 9⅛
Includes CD-ROM   **$19.95**